THE

MUSEUM AGE

*First American Edition published in the United States of America
in 1967 by*

UNIVERSE BOOKS Inc.
381 Park Avenue South
New York, N.Y. 10016

Library of Congress Catalog Card Number: 67-26914

© *Desoer S. A. Editions, Brussels 1967*

Printed in Belgium

THE MUSEUM AGE

by Germain Bazin

Translated from the French by Jane van Nuis Cahill

UNIVERSE BOOKS Inc., **PUBLISHERS - NEW YORK**

Foreword

To write a history of the museum is to give account of the evolution of two concepts: that of the Museum and that of Time. Regarding the nature of Time, our age has accumulated all kinds of studies: metaphysical, psychological, sociological, and ethnological and scientific; excepting the two last mentioned, which treat another aspect of the problem, all arrive at more or less the same conclusion, at the presence in the human consciousness of two notions of time: that of a time which passes and that of a time which endures. Archaic civilizations, with their denial of history, know only the second, which ethnologists have termed "absolute time" and in which primitive peoples, who by recourse to ritual and myth seek to abolish temporality, believe. Individual human existence becomes, then, so intimately integrated with that of the group that it is seen as part of a natural, universal continuum. One can rediscover this notion of absolute time within oneself by trying to recapture one's childhood where the role of games is comparable to the role of myth among primitives.

The burden of time increased when humanity became conscious of individual destiny—of secular destiny—holding itself responsible for its own actions, when the individual, disengaged from the group, thought of himself as cause and no longer just as effect.

The historical sense was engendered by a sequence of great political events which shook that masterpiece of the human conscience—the Greek city, of which Athens, at a given moment, had been the most accomplished example. If the Medic Wars confirmed the city's existence, the Peloponnesian Wars compromised it and the Philippic Wars ruined it. Chaeronea ended the life of a State established by the mutual consent of its citizens and replaced it with a monarchic State founded on personal power acquired by trickery and violence. Alexander's conquests brought to the concept of temporality the dimension of space, requisite for its evolution.

Cyclic time, by definition always returning upon itself, was a profound conception of the Greeks; it was valid, however, only within the confines of the city-state, where even conflicts—of a fraternal nature—could not project the citizen beyond the perception of the tutelary group into the perspectives of history.

Deprived suddenly of the history of their city, estranged from the familial life on a grand scale that it had meant, men felt like atoms lost in vast empires, no longer citizens but subjects. When the present becomes unbearable, there are two means of escaping it: the past and the future. Plato chose the second, assigning happiness a place in his utopia, and thereby gave to an immediate problem of the State an ideal Solution. During the Hellenistic period, one sought refuge in intemporal spheres which simultaneously abolished both novelty and the anguish it caused; religions of salvation prospered in this world thirsting for hope, as did the utopias of Plotinus who conceived of two beings in man: one in time, the other beyond time. But humanity equally indulged in the *"espérance à rebours"* [1] which is nostalgia. Established as an absolute, the past also becomes a refuge. Only when men sense the waning of a civilization do they suddenly become interested in its history and, probing, become aware of the force and uniqueness of the ideas it has fostered. Hegel said that the owl of Wisdom appears only at twilight. Hellenism, become conscious of its historical reality, turned to introspection and self-analysis; archives were consulted, documents compiled, writings collected in colossal libraries that were the bitter rivals, like Alexandria toward Pergamum, of each other. Museums coveted the artistic products of this classicism, judged inimitable, and even its earliest expressions generated interest. Man consoles himself for what he is by what he was.

Rome inherited from Greece museums and libraries; the historian and Hellenist, Polybius, viewed the achievements of the Greek civilization as a prelude to the historical climax wrought by Rome—the rationalization of Empire. If, as our contemporary historical philosophers Spengler, Toynbee and Mumford claim, the tendency toward the universality and hypertrophy of cities announces the decline of a civilization, Rome, at the moment when her empire reached the farthest, nurtured that instinctive feeling of recoil before the future which throws man back on his past. Museums and libraries sprang up all over Rome until the City of Cities was filled with them. The libraries have perished with their treasures but our museums are stocked with art recovered from the ruins of Rome's museums.

Perhaps we have been too insistent upon a rectilinear conception of time, inherited from the Hebraic religion, which makes each man responsible for realizing his destiny within the brief course of a lifetime. Adoring one God who is an historical personage, does not the Church live entirely in expectation of the Parousia to occur in a transcendent moment which will abolish at once both time and history? But Christianity has buried an historical past and the one it proposes as an antecedent, the span between Genesis and the Gospels, strays somewhat from the main artery of time. This past is set forth in the Holy Books which, because they are such, impart to this evolution a mythical character. Elsewere, too, is Christianity weighed down by the Hebraic notion that history is an act of God which man assumes the responsibility to work out.

Medieval men lived in the shelter and moral comfort of a cyclic time—for the agricultural population, the cycle of the seasons and for the ecclesiastical world, the cycle of the liturgical year. Museums had no part in their lives, except those which held vestiges of the only past to which they ascribed, that is, the treasuries with their relics of saints.

The Renaissance cut through ten centuries to exhume the past denied by Christianity. Involution was necessary to any evolution. Following a new route of responsibility to oneself rather than to God, Renaissance man turned to antiquity for confirmation of the destiny he proposed for himself. The Past again became a refuge, this time not from a discredited present but from a recent past one sought to break with. Museums, sanctuaries of forgotten classicism, experienced a rebirth. The intense curiosity to know tormented the human conscience to advance its once limited horizon to the ends of the earth. Study of the antique led to the study of nature. From the Mannerist period on, museums developed in two directions: science museums with collections that included authentic discoveries as well as more or less fabulous "curiosities" believed to contain the secret of nature; and art and history museums, more limited in their scope, with no other objective than to affirm this longed-for identity with the classical world despite the immense difference in time.

There were few changes of principle in the

history of this prosperous institution, the museum, until the French Revolution, with the exception of the slow metamorphosis during the course of the eighteenth century of princely or royal collections into public museums, open to all for the advancement of knowledge and the artistic education of the people.

The nineteenth century was the Century of History. Museums were flooded to the point of overflowing with products created by all kinds of human endeavor, by all peoples of all periods. Thus was initiated a great idolatry of the past, a counterbalance to a certain complaisance toward the present, a present that passed like a moment in the accelerated race toward the future, the perspectives of which were nightmarish.

The appetite for museums, still unabated in the twentieth century, is a complex phenomenon to analyze. A temple where Time seems suspended, the museum procures for today's man those momentary cultural epiphanies in which, since Gide, he has delighted. An entire literature for half a century has celebrated the supreme detachment from all appurtenances which makes of the instant a transcendent moment, lived in the innocence of a sensuality restored to its place as a virtue anterior to Original Sin. To detach from Time one of these contiguous fibers that is an instant, to make it vibrate like the string of a violin, is to give the being the illusion of knowing intuitively his essence and his strengths. The contemplation of the masterpieces of art or nature, listening to musical or theatrical works and reading great literature can induce in our contemporaries, educated by the Immoralist, this trance which can develop into a neurosis, as in the spectacle of the "happening." Since Taine, who considered the work of art a product of its time, the philosophies of art, which in the twentieth century have defined it as having its own existence, favor this tendency which in the museological situation manifests itself as the taste for ascetic presentation. All modern art is, moreover, founded on the supreme value placed on shock, the discharge of which assumes the value of a revelation.

This is a means through which the museum offers escape from time and even from absolute time. But very often today's visitors to museums seek a way to elude the relative time of the present. If the nineteenth century was the century of history, the twentieth devoted itself to prehistory. The enormous success of the latter after the Second World War is one of the most unexpected phenomena of contemporary psychology. This attraction of the prehistoric man, is it not indicative of a certain weariness with historical time and a profound aspiration for resurgence?

This taste for prehistory, for the period before recorded time, does it not derive from confused desire for a reunion with absolute time, the time of the myths? On the part of modern men, little by little cast out from all private groups—religious, familial, national, social—which served as frameworks for human life for millennia, to see themselves massed together like atoms, this call to the farthest reaches of space—does it not indicate at the same time a need to escape from the vertigo caused by the acceleration of time, some secret nostalgia for that past when man lived protected from history by the communal bonds of private groups? The evolution of the historical sense itself reveals a similar orientation. Does the prodigious success of popularized historical novels toll the knell for the real history of battles and heroes in order to affirm the contemporary interest in and concentration on the *uomo qualunque* through the centuries, whose "happy life" we seek to evoke in our antique-filled interiors? Museums, barometers of current taste, have yielded to this desire by installing "Period" rooms, which have enjoyed such success in the United States. But the museum has penetrated into private life. Nothing is better proof of the need to flee the present, to seek refuge in the warmth of an ancestral *ambiance* than this denial of modern furniture and the concomitant vogue for "period" interiors—quick money for antique dealers and copyists. Thus in his appeal for precedents, modern man seeks to regain his humanity even as it tries to escape him.

Each year, when the sun bathes the beaches,

humanity, as if bewitched, flees the city with its gradually more and more intolerable framework of life and races to vacation places, to temporary paradises. Lacunae in the inevitable procession of days when time seems suspended, vacations, which tend to become "real life," are united from one year to the next in the memory and constitute in the time which passes an oasis of everlasting time which man—uprooted, deprived of myth and religion, cut off little by little from all his traditions—neither can nor will renounce. In these temporal oases, museums number among the enchanted places; they are besieged by crowds of vacationers and thus the paradox arises that the museums of a country are often visited more by foreigners than by its own citizens (who cultivate their artistic tastes in other countries during their annual vacations).

However, while masterpieces of art and nature have become the object of a growing fervor, they appear to be more and more endangered. Two worlds are at odds today, the one slowly devouring the other; technology threatens to engulf art and nature, both allied in defense against a common peril. Oddly, poverty preserves and wealth destroys; peace, more than war, is a consumer of "cultural goods." A commission established in Italy to study the means of preserving the cultural patrimony of the country has disclosed that it is in the process of rapid destruction; in 1962, two hundred university professors sent an urgent letter to the Minister of Public Instruction, entreating him to act with haste. Half of Italy's 5,000 miles of shoreline had become such an eyesore that even the tourists were fleeing; in three years 100,000 trees were cut down along the highways; from 1957 to 1964 about fifty museums and seventy churches sustained robberies and some 900 pieces had disappeared from museums, galleries and private collections; in 1963 alone 3,000 antique tombs were destroyed by clandestine excavators. Until a few years ago, the Church was the bulwark of beauty and tradition; now, devitalized by recent innovations in the liturgy and by the vertigo of "progressism," a once inviolable patrimony is collapsing. All over Europe priests are liquidating the artistic treasures of their churches; in Italy, where this negotiation is particularly fruitful, the police recently discovered storehouses where monasteries had been accumulating works of art—building up stock for an eventual auction house. In France, one can foresee the disaffection of 18,000 churches. It is not always the hope of profit which motivates the ecclesiastics but an iconoclastic spirit which recalls that of the Huguenots; in a village in the Landes district in France, a curate, in a move to "modernize" his church, dismantled a baroque retable and, leaving to nature the task of destroying a once sacred object, interred it in a field.

The progress of erosion, accelerated in an industrial society, is threatening the most prestigious monuments and sites of the past. The Ravenna mosaics and the buildings on the Acropolis are shaken by the roar of airplanes; the needle-thin heels on women's shoes have damaged the parquetry in the Grande Galerie of the Louvre and the marble pavements of the Parthenon; the cave paintings of Lascaux and of Tarquinia are suffering effacement at the hands of their admirers; in Italy, acres of frescoes are about to break away from their walls; the cities of unbaked brick in the Middle East piously exhumed by archeologists, are disintegrating; Mohenjo-Daro is menaced by the inundations of the Indus; the *pietra serena* of Tuscan edifices is dissociating; sand dunes are building up and in time will re-bury Leptis Magna and Sabrata; the enchanting Renaissance gardens of the Château de Villandry are in danger of dying because a neighboring factory has deflected their source of water; Venice is sinking into the sea, the waves churned up by motor boats having weakened the pilings on which she rests—besides the fact that the water level in the lagoon has changed considerably; fine old cities—even those which are protected—are encumbered with dismal apartment buildings whose tenants are quick to flee them for houses in the country or resorts; 400 French cities have been designated as sites for preservation but thus far only twenty-one have instituted protective measures; Rome's pine trees are being asphyxiated by the fumes from automobiles. Can one imagine Rome without her pines? Rome, the city of seven hills, become the city of seven bald promontories, occupied only by the white bones of its ruins? If the men to whom the preservation of art works has been entrusted are worried, those who guard the riches of nature are at wit's end; they foresee a rapid sterilization of flora and fauna, the very same flora and fauna sought so eagerly by men on their vacations or even on brief weekends.

The danger is graver than is yet realized, especially by the political mind; in 1962 the German architectural magazine *Bauwelt* criticized a foreign government "for failing to express a feeling of tragedy at the destruction of one of the most beautiful countries in the world." The international solidarity behind the movement to save, through Herculean efforts, the temple of Abu Simbel from the waters backed up by the Aswan Dam is heartening. But which Head of State interpreted the proclamation as a call to safeguard the beauty of his own country? There was one. But was it the leader of one of the nations which boasts of being a "cradle of art"? It was President Johnson.

If he does not take heed, man will one day live in a world demolished by six billion insects, with the only remaining "culture" confined to a few geographical reserves and a scattering of museums where the imprisoned remains of the world's beauty will slowly perish.

Frontispiece, page 4.

1. **The Cloister of Saint-Michel de Cuxa at** *The Cloisters, Fort Tryon Park, New York. Opened in 1938, this museum was constructed to present and regroup the medieval architectural elements—chiefly from cloisters in France and Spain—which had been·acquired originally by George Grey Barnard and were later purchased by John D. Rockefeller Jr. as a gift for the Metropolitan Museum.*

Chapter 1
Prelude

Coccale: Ah, what beautiful statues, my dear Cynno! What sculptor could have carved this stone and who is the donor?

Cynno: These are the sons of Praxiteles. Do you not see the inscription on the base? And the donor is Euthies, son of Prexon.

Coccale: The blessings of the gods on them and on Euthies for such beautiful works. Look, my dear, at this child with her eyes focused on the apple. Were you not just going to say that if she cannot have the apple she will die? And this old man, Cynno! By the fates! Look at that child strangling the goose! Were it not for the stone, one would say the boy seems on the point of talking. Ah, in time men will end up giving life to stone.

270 B.C. Two courtesans have come to make an offering to Aesculapius in his temple at Cos. In order to be the first, they have arrived at dawn, before the crowds. To make the waiting pass more agreeably they chatter as they look at the statues surrounding the sanctuary. The sacristan arrives to open the temple. Our two gossips enter, Coccale marveling at the splendors she sees and Cynno, who already knows them, comments on them to her friend. This time they talk about paintings.

Coccale: Look, Cynno, what works of art! Athena herself must have fashioned these beautiful things! My respects to the goddess! The child there, the nude one—if I pinch him, it will leave a mark, won't it Cynno? His flesh looks warm, palpitating... The ox and the man leading him, the woman walking at the side, that man with the hooked nose and that curly-headed boy... do they not seem to see the light of life? If I did not think it would have been unbecoming for a lady, I would have uttered loud cries lest the ox—what an oblique stare in his eyes, Cynno!—hurt me.

Cynno: Yes, my dear, the hand of the painter from Ephesus, the hand of Apelles, revealed truth at every stroke of the brush and one cannot say of him, "There is an artist who favored only certain subjects and shied away from others." Whatever came into his fancy seemed to inspire him. One who is not in ecstasy, as is only right before such an artist or his works, I would like to see hanged by the feet at a carpet beater's.

2. **Statue of Eros, signed by Boethus,** *a second-century B.C. Greek sculptor from Bithynie. Musée du Bardo, Tunis. This bronze, along with other priceless works, was salvaged in 1907 from the wreck of a ship buried in waters about 130 feet deep off the coast of Madhia, between Sousse and Sfax. The vessel was possibly part of a convoy loaded with plunder taken from Greece by Sulla in 86 B.C. or, perhaps, part of a shipment of works of art to some Numidian prince.*

This idle talk and these proposals, which echo the art criticism of the time, animate a mime of Herodas, Greek author of the third century B.C. One could hear analogous conversations today while following visitors through the Louvre or the Metropolitan Museum or, as a more exact comparison perhaps, through the Museo dell'Opera del Duomo at Siena. Formed by a slow accumulation of ex-votos brought by the faithful, the treasuries of the temples were the first repositories of works of art in Greece. Visitors were welcomed if they were willing to pay an obolus to the sacristan and to offer obeisance to the local divinity. The *hieropoei,* committed to the guarding of the temples, were also responsible for the treasuries; their task was not a sinecure. Intact records—on marble—from many of the temples, especially those from the Temple of Apollo at Delos, inform us about the administration of the sanctuaries and, in particular, about the management of the collections. The latter included objects of *luxe* in gold, silver or bronze or some other precious material—depending on the wealth of the donor—and even paintings on pynakès. These works were often signed with the names of the greatest artists of Greece. The *hieropoei* took charge of the inventories; upon arrival the ex-votos were entered in a register; the works were then included in the next general inventory. Statues were placed in the parvis, statuettes and other objects in the *prodomos* or in the *naos* where they accumulated on shelves; the most precious or the most fragile were put in cases. Periodically, there were attempts at some kind of general arrangement and a consequent review of the inventory. This re-examination always occurred at the time of a change of magistracy. A contradictory inventory was a credit to an entering *hieropei,* a discredit to the retiring one. The inventories, like those of our museums today, were very detailed, listing the name of the object, its material, its weight, any specific markings, the name of the god to whom the offering was made, the occasion of its consecration, the date, the name and nationality of the donor.

Sometimes it was around the temple itself that the citizens of a particular city constructed a small monument or votive chapel *(thesaurus),* destined to receive their donations. Many such treasuries were preserved at Delphi and one of them, that of the Athenians, has been reconstructed.

Problems of conservation were already worrying the art lovers of the time. In the Stoa Poikile at Athens, the votive shields, Pausanias tells us, were coated with pitch to prevent corrosion from rust; in the Parthenon vats of oil were placed at the feet of the *Athena Parthenos* of Phidias as a protective measure against the excessive dryness of the atmosphere which was dissociating the complex structure of this chryselephantine statue. Periodically, in order to make room, the *hieropoei* elaborated the lists of surplus objects submitted to the council of the temple. As nothing was allowed to be destroyed, objects of little worth were buried in offertory reservoirs or favissae; those of the Temple of Hera Argiva at the source of the Sele in the Campania yielded to contemporary archeologists more than thirty thousand votive offerings for which a special museum was built at Paestum. Objects of precious metal but with little aesthetic value were sent to the foundry to be converted into ingots which contributed to the fortune of the god. Pieces of artistic quality were guarded with care; the *hieropoei* attended to the repair of those damaged accidentally, by the weather or, as in the case of ritual objects, by use.

3. **Treasury of the Athenians at Delphi.** *Fifth century B.C. The first museological collections in Greece were the treasuries of the temples, formed by the slow accumulation of votive offerings of the worshippers who paid tribute to the local deity. Near the Panhellenic sanctuaries at Olympia and Delphi small monuments were built to protect the treasures. The treasury of the Athenians at Delphi has been reconstructed.*

4. **Model of the Sanctuary of Athena at Pergamum.** *As is befitting, the library was situated in the Sanctuary of Athena, the goddess of wisdom. Above the great theatre is the ancient temple of Athena Polias Nikephoros, its oblique position being explained by the fact that it was built earlier than the terrace of Athena by Eumenie II. On one side of the courtyard a two-story portico gave access to the library. A replica of the Athena Promachos of Athens decorated the library, which was a kind of temple of learning, while a collection of statues and busts of great men made it an historical museum. The museum of Greek sculpture assembled by the Attalids was found divided up among their palaces.*

At the end of the antique world these treasuries of the sanctuaries were visited frequently, not only by devout pilgrims but also by tourists. One went there to admire the chefs d'œuvre of the great masters of Greek sculpture—at least those which had not been carried away by the Romans. It is these which Pausanias, in the second century A.D., was to see on a circum-Mediterranean voyage, describing for us countless paintings and statues, the pedestals of which have sometimes been found *in situ* but, alas, never the originals[1].

The classical Greeks also grouped the most celebrated works of their glorious schools of painting in pinakothekai, a word deriving from *pinas,* meaning plank; the paintings called *pinakès* were executed on wood. It is in the Acropolis of Athens that one finds the oldest mention of a pinakotheke; in the Propylaea, built by Mnesicles in the fifth century B.C., the northwest wing had been specially laid out to receive paintings; it was lighted by two windows opening on the south. There is some doubt about the nature of these paintings—they may have been executed on the wall; it seems however that it was a question of separate pictures which constituted a veritable museum because Pausanias, who described them, cites the works of different artists, among them the great Polygnotos. A strip of Eleusinian marble, comparable to the dado rail of our museums, blocked out the upper section of wall where the works were exhibited. Like medieval retables, the *pinakès* were provided with protective shutters; the interior walls of the Temple of Athena at Lindus still bear marks left by the encasements around paintings displayed there. These empty rectangles are haunting, poignant reminders of the loss of a whole art, that of antique painting.

As it was during the Middle Ages, the accumulating of art treasures in sanctuaries preceded the forming of collections by the powerful of the secular world. Not until the Hellenistic epoch did Greek princes in the Near East begin to collect statues, *objets d'art* and precious books. The excavations at Pergamum, corroborating the rare written testimonies, have brought to light some vestiges of the taste of those Greco-Asian tyrants, the Attalids

14

who, although rulers of only a small principality, were at that time the bulwark of the Hellenic civilization against the invasions of the barbarous Galatians. In the city plan they had evolved for their capital, which called for public buildings to be terraced up a hillside facing the sea, they had reserved an important place for the library, near the Temple of Athena. Excavations have revealed that this library which, according to certain investigations, numbered almost six hundred thousand volumes, was surrounded by a stoa, a colonnaded, sheltered walk. An architectural motif extremely popular in antiquity, it was frequently used to enclose the sides of libraries because it was believed that walking stimulated thought. When Leo von Klenze, many centuries later, built open-air loggias along the sides of the Alte Pinakothek in Munich, he returned to an old Hellenic tradition.

In addition to the areas devoted to the storage of books, the library of Pergamum had a reception hall which must have been used for academic conferences; pedestals unearthed there bear inscriptions which prove they served as supports for statues of poets, historians, philosophers; it was a kind of small historical museum, a tradition that Renaissance Italy was to revive. Those honored included Homer, Sappho, Alcaeus and Herodotus. A colossal statue of Athena, a replica of the *Athena Parthenos* of Phidias, was also found near the library along with a second representation of the same divinity. Henceforth the Goddess of Wisdom was to have her appointed place in that pinnacle of culture, the library. Rather than setting aside a special building for that purpose, the Attalids disposed throughout the palace a whole collection of sculptures and paintings that gave an insight into the evolution of Greek art; it comprised many originals, notably a bronze by the naturalistic portraitist, Silanion, and a masterpiece by Cephisodotus, father of Praxiteles, which was greatly admired by Pausanias. If original sculptures were lacking, the kings of Pergamum had copies made, some of which have been recovered in excavations. As for painting, archeologists at Delphi have exhumed an inscription which mentions two Pergamenians who were sent to copy the celebrated pictures of Polygnotos in the Cnidian Lesche at Delphi.

At this epoch, with the birth of the historical sense, when man began to examine his past, to plumb archives for aid in the reconstruction of its course, when catalogs, compilations and inventories were made, the collector-princes were not only interested in works of art of the classical era but also in archaic works, evidences of the first steps of Greek art. We know that they had a picture painted by one of the "primitives" of Greek painting: Pythagoras of Paros. As for statuary, we find references to a work by the Aeginetan sculptor, Onatas, to another by Bupālus, a sixth-century master from Chios, and to statues resembling the famous *Korai* of the Acropolis of Athens. Out of this ambiance of culture, with the resources of the library and the examples of the museum easily accessible, came the first researches on the history of Greek art. Scholars wrote critical studies on the works of different masters; these were bound together in a collection, lost today, that was called the *Canon* of Pergamum. It constituted authority at Rome where it served as a manual of taste of amateurs of art.

Courtiers scouted the entire cultivated world for rare books of art for the Attalids. The Ptolemies of Alexandria, proud of their own library, grew restless over the vigorous progress of the one at Pergamum; attempting to paralyze it, Ptolemy Philopator forbade the exportation of papyrus which scribes used for copying books. Eumenes II responded

15

to this cultural embargo with an invention which was to add to the luxury and longevity of books—that of parchment, a word deriving from Pergamum. Made from prepared animal skins, it is a process which was to be employed throughout the Middle Ages until the invention of printing. We know that at Rome the Attalid king made an offer of 600,000 sesterces for a painting by Aristides which was part of the spoils from Corinth, put up for sale in lots by the consul Mummius, conqueror of Greece. The Romans were still parvenus in the art of amateurism; the enormous sum offered for the work awakened Mummius to its possible value. Proclaiming it the most precious piece in the booty, he withdrew it from the sale and dedicated it to the Temple of Ceres. Thus it was the first foreign picture on public display in Rome. Soon, with the downfall of their kings, the Pergamenians were also to fear Rome's pillaging; they fought ferociously to prevent the exodus of their masterpieces.

Even if the Greco-Roman civilization had bona fide public collections, it had no special institution to manage them. The very word *museum* (*mouseion* in Greek, *museum* in Latin) designates something entirely different—it applies to sanctuaries dedicated to the muses, to philosophical academies or to institutions of advanced learning or of scientific research, over which the muses quite naturally presided. Such is the case with the famous *Mouseion* of Alexandria, founded by Ptolemy Soter or Ptolemy Philadelphus. It was a college of scholars, analogous to the modern Institute for Advanced Study at Princeton or to the Collège de France in Paris. It did not contain collections of art but there was a scientific museum comprising a botanical and zoological park, rooms devoted to the study of anatomy and installations for astronomical observation. Scholars lived there at the expense of the state. As for the artistic collections of the Ptolemies, they were housed in their palace. Since the modern city of Alexandria lies atop the ancient one, it has not been possible to excavate there—one of the reasons for the great lacunae in our knowledge of the Hellenistic era.

With the Romans the word *museum* was applied to specific villas, doubtlessly to designate a place reserved for philosophical discussion. The word was never applied to a collection of works of art—the Italian Renaissance was to give it that meaning.

Works of art were so precious that there was great concern about protecting them from the ravages of war. Some time after the year 174 A.D. Pausanias could see in Alexandria a vast repository of statues from all periods which had been amassed there in haste in order to protect them from pillaging when the city was menaced.

The position of the Romans regarding works of art can be compared to that of contemporary Americans in relation to masterpieces produced by Western civilization. To assemble them at great expense constituted an element of prestige associated with power and wealth. Further, sheer market value became, as in our time, one of the essential factors behind the search for works of art. Announced by posters, preceded by exhibitions, the public sales of Rome, a city with abundant, idle wealth, attracted crowds of the curious who intermingled with the amateurs. Antique literature is filled with anecdotes on this subject, like that, for instance, of the former usurer who fell asleep at his seat during a sale and whose noddings of the head were taken for approvals of the bids, so that by the end of the auction he found himself with 1,800,000 sesterces' worth of unwanted acquisitions. More piquant is the story Pliny tells of a courtesan who, having acquired in a single lot a bronze candelabrum and a hideous, hunchbacked slave whom the owner had paired with the masterpiece in a desperate move to be rid of him, took the hunchback as a lover who, having become the courtesan's heir, made a god of the candelabrum and founded a new cult.

The art dealers were clustered along the Via Sacra and in the Saepta Julia where under the colonnades all kinds of shops could be found which, in contrast to those of the Greeks, were luxuriously appointed. The Roman satirists Martial, Statius, Suetonius, Juvenal and Seneca have caricatured the types of collectors, from the disdainful patrician to the careful amateur who spends hours every day scouring the Saepta and finishes by carrying off two porringers for a bronze as.

It was through contact with Greece, conquered in the second century B.C., that the Romans acquired a taste for works of art. The spoils brought back from Greece and the East were displayed in triumphal processions and were afterwards divided among the temples, with the victor keeping his share. Such a transaction was regarded as a business venture, as was the selling of the captured slaves. Occasionally it happened that the provincial governors would fleece their administrators and strip the temples, as did the famous Verres, governor of Sicily, whose rapacity for art was condemned by Cicero in his celebrated *Verrine Orations*. We can get some idea of his character by considering another "amateur" of this type: Hermann Goering; he was so enamored of beautiful intaglios that when he saw one which particularly pleased him, he would wrest it from the owner on the pretext of looking at it more closely and would not return it. The underwater excavations of Madhia on the coast of Tunisia, of the Phocian port of Anticythera and off the cape of Artemision have yielded us magnificent antique bronzes lost when ships that were transporting works of art either pillaged or bought by the Romans were sunk. Repair work on a street in Piraeus in 1959, necessitated by a disastrous fire in a warehouse, brought to light a whole series of beautiful fourth-century statues, wrapped as if ready for shipment; the buried site had once been the shop of an exporter. One tends to ascribe these maritime transports to Sulla, the conqueror of Athens, who seems to have been particularly greedy for such riches. Epidaurus, Delphi and Olympia lost their treasures to him; at Piraeus he confiscated a rich library housing all the works of Aristotle. Their aesthetic sensibilities refined on the art they pillaged, the Romans became impassioned collectors without ceasing however to manifest the greatest scorn for artists. Singled out by destiny to dominate men and govern nations, they considered artists to be simple entertainers on a par with ballerinas and flutists. The remarks of Virgil, Horace and Cicero on this subject are well known. Cicero, who out of snobbishness amassed collections for his palaces and villas, in order to excuse himself for this "decadent" taste, attacked the amateurs who let themselves be taken in by such child's play; it is true that Verres considered him a Philistine (*idiota*) in that sphere.

Originals or copies of Greek statues, objects of gold or silver, ivory or tortoise shell, furniture of bronze, cedar, cypress, arborvitae or maple, Oriental carpets woven of gold thread, and intaglios accumulated in the palaces and, still more, in the luxurious villas of the Romans. Infatuated with intaglios, cameos and vases of precious stone, they constructed dactyliothecas for which objects in rock crystal and in amber from the Baltic

17

were particularly sought; an amber figurine was worth more than a slave. Caesar had six collections of precious stones which he gave to the Temple of Venus Genetrix, Pompey possessed the collection of Mithridates, whom he had conquered; it numbered two thousand pieces. Figurines of Corinthian bronze were worth their weight in gold, so esteemed was the art of the bronze workers in that city. They constructed special galleries—pinakothekai—to receive paintings. A contemporary of Augustus, the architect Vitruvius, assigned great importance to the orientation of the divers rooms of a dwelling and recommended facing the galleries to the north, "because the light is the same at every hour and therefore the colors always remain constant." In contrast, he prescribed opening libraries to the east "because their usage demands the light of the morning" and, further, "because the west and the south are subject to the humidity of the winds" which encourages worms and hastens the growth of mold. The presentation of such fragile books of antiquity required special precautions—for example, virtually indestructible shelves were made out of cedar or ivory. Adorned with a statue of Minerva and busts or terms of great men, libraries were also historical museums.

In their suburban villas, places of leisure in the country, the ancients loved the companionship of works of art, especially of statues which they scattered in their gardens. The most splendid and today the best preserved of these villas is the one Emperor Hadrian built some twenty miles to the northeast of Rome near the town of Tibur, now Tivoli, where it was protected from cold north winds but was open to the refreshing breezes from the sea. During the course of his different sojourns in Italy this conscientious emperor, who had toured the entire antique world, had a sizable complex of buildings erected in a general area that earlier had attracted Sulla, Caesar and Augustus. The royal traveler wanted to establish a sort of microcosm of the empire, reproducing those places that had most impressed him on his visits: the Lyceum, the Academy, the Prytaneum and the Stoa Poikile of Athens, the Vale of Tempe in Thessaly, the Canopus of the Egyptian delta; he had not even forgotten a representation of the Gates of Hell. In the mass of buildings whose ruins have come down to us, only the Canopus and the Serapeum can be identified with certainty; recent excavations have enabled us to reconstruct the latter and have further yielded intact four copies of caryatids from the Erechtheum, provided with arms, thus ending the long-lasting polemic about the position of the arms on these celebrated figures. The *Villa Adriana* was, in a sense, an open-air museum of the classical world which the emperor wished spread before his eyes. This attempt of the Roman world to rival the Greeks in the sphere of art manifests itself again in the innumerable copies Hadrian had made of famous statues. Excavated since the sixteenth century, the ruins of Hadrian's Villa at Tivoli have yielded a mine of antiquities that has enriched all the museums of the world, particularly those of Rome. These same ruins reserve still further surprises for archeologists.

This craze for copies should not be surprising; they were accepted as, if not equals, at least equivalents of originals in a period which attached especial significance to the Platonic notion of the "Idea" participating in the form invented by the artist. Copies were sold at high prices which, however, did not prevent forgers from providing them with spurious signatures and passing them off as originals. Specialists—as many for sculpture as for painting—restored damaged pieces. The masterpieces of classical Greek painting were overcome with decay by the time the Romans evinced an interest in them.

18

Then, as now, restorations were often worse than the evils they sought to remedy and paintings were irretrievably lost through the intervention of unskillful restorers.

As it is today with primitives, archaic Greek works met with favor among collectors; in fact certain ones owned only pre-Phidian art. Quintilian mocked the preference for "these almost crude works and what I call the infancy of future art over the productions of the more illustrious artists who followed, but in my opinion this is mere pretension." However, as early as the Augustan period this passion for "primitives," inherited from the Hellenistic princes, raged as a mania and Horace tells us of a certain Damasippus infected with it: "If a marble were awkwardly sculpted or a bronze worked in a dry, hard fashion, he would quickly offer 100,000 sesterces for it." All aging civilizations are haunted by a wish to return to their infancy; Claudius had Etruscan antiquities researched. Others preferred sketches to finished works because "these barely indicated strokes are the thoughts of the Master," as Pliny said. Fastidious amateurs sought *bozzetti*—those first attempts at creation—in paint, wax and terra cotta. Natural curiosities already had a certain place among works of art; they were found in temples, consecrated to the gods. Suetonius tells a story about how Augustus wanted to keep in his villa at Capri the gigantic bones from primordial animals and the unidentified stone weapons that legendary or mythological heroes might have used which were found during the digging of foundations for his villa.

Not all the marvels, however, were hidden in the palaces or villas of the emperors and the rich; the Quirites also had a rather large share. It happened several times that the *vox populi* condemned the monopolizing of works of art. Nero was blamed for hoarding so many wonders of art in his *Domus Aureus* out of the sight of all. When Emperor Tiberius transferred to his sleeping quarters the celebrated *Apoxyoménos* of Lysippus which Agrippa had placed before his baths, the populace grumbled so loudly that, emperor though he was, he had to return it to its original place. Agrippa, the minister and son-in-law of Augustus, delivered a magnificent speech, the substance of which Pliny has preserved for us, about the advisability of "rendering public all paintings and statues which would be of more value than exiling them to country houses." Imperial authority was seated upon a demagogic concept which had to take into account public opinion. Consecrated to the gods and given to the people by the emperors and the illustrious, works of art encumbered the public ways, principally the forums, the public gardens, the sanctuaries, the theatres, the basilicas and the baths. Filled with objects, the temples were transformed into veritable curio shops. The idols of Hellenic divinities, ravaged from temples in Greece or Asia, naturally found places in the temples of the Roman divinities with which they became identified. Situated at the extreme northwest of the Roman forum, at the foot of the Capitol, the Temple of Concord was rebuilt by Augustus on a vaster scale in celebration of the end of civil strife and the return of internal peace. "In his thoughts," states Leon Homo, "it was destined to become one of the principal museums of Imperial Rome." The collection deposited there included statues, paintings, precious stones and jewels, several of which were owed to the munificence of the Empress Livia. Exhibited objects were distributed around or even within the cella; one could see masterpieces by Zeuxis, Nikias, Euphranor, Sthennis of Olynthus, Nikeratos of Pergamum but the simpletons admired the four black obsidian elephants commended by the guide.

Life in antiquity was lived under porticoes where one could stroll along, sheltered from the sun and inclement weather. To construct a portico was an excellent way to win the gratitude of one's fellow citizens. It was an ideal place for displaying works of art—not surprising in a country where people lived out of doors—and certain porticoes, which can be considered veritable museums were constructed for that purpose. A case in point is the Portico of Octavia. Originally the colonnade had been built by Metellus to receive the collections of art which had figured in his triumphal procession, thereby avoiding their dispersal. In 32 B.C. Augustus ordered the loggia rebuilt and called it the *Porticus Octaviae.* A quadrangular enclosure surrounded by four open galleries, the interior housed two temples dedicated to Jupiter and Juno and a schola which served as an auditorium for certain Senate meetings, as a library and an art gallery. The collection of this most extensive museum of Imperial Rome was exhibited under the portico, in the two temples and in the schola. Flanking the central esplanade before the temple were twenty-six bronze equestrian statues, the warriors known as *The Companious of Alexander,* which the conqueror commissioned from Lysippus to commemorate the cavalry of hetaeria who fell at the Battle of Granicus; twenty-five of the statues represented the heroes and the twenty-sixth was of Alexander himself. Previously the group had been exhibited in the portico of Metellus who had it brought from Dion, a city in southern Macedonia.

Greatly admired in the Portico of Pompey was the entire gallery of paintings by Antiphilus, Nikias, Pausias, Polygnotos and statues dedicated to the glory of Pompey. Let us cite in passing the Portico of Marcius Philippus, the Saepta Julia, the Portico of the Argonauts and the Portico Vipsania, a sort of geographical museum where one went to contemplate a great map of the world erected under Agrippa'a supervision. The Portico of Apollo was decorated with fifty statues of the Danaïdes, to which corresponded, on the esplanade, fifty statues of their ill-fated husnands and four bronze oxen, originals by Myron, celebrated for his skill in the representation of animals. Early Romans would find astonishing the great admiration we accord the debris of what was once the wonder of the dying antique world.

Among the varied pleasures offered at the baths, which served as social clubs to which one was admitted for a small sum, there were conversation lounges, rooms for literary or musical recitals, libraries and collections of works of art; the spirit was the object of as much care as the body. The Baths of Titus yielded to excavators in 1506 the famous *Laocoön* group which may have come originally from Nero's *Domus Aureus.* In the Baths of Caracalla, rich in divers collections, the colossal Rhodian group known as the *Farnese Bull* was found which Gaius Asinius Pollio, the benefactor of Rome's first public library, had placed in the museum he had annexed to his city of books.

There were also public picture galleries, if we can believe Petronius who recounts for us a visit he made to one of them. He met there an old gentleman, a fine connoisseur who explained to him that the decadence in painting was attributable to the passion for money. "In former times when the rewards of poverty were still appreciated, the fine arts flourished... To speak only of sculptors, Lysippus died of hunger at the base of a statue he was passionately striving to perfect; Myron, that marvelous artist who made men as well as animals live in bronze, was so poor that he could find no one to accept his estate... Do you think 'they' go to the temple to ask for health?... One promises an

6. **Pavilion under the Trees, by Ts'ao Chih-po** *(hao, or studio name, Yün-hsi) (1272-1355). Musée Guimet, Paris. This painting, ink on paper, is a leaf from an album which had been mounted on a scroll. There are nine red stamps: one is the artist's seal, six are the seals of the Emperor Ch'ien Lung (reigned 1736-1796) and two are those of the Emperor Siuan-tong. Great importance was attached to the pedigree of works of art because of the veneration which the Chinese felt for everything which touched the past or one's ancestors. Thus the paintings, which more than any other objects were sought after by amateurs, bore the seals of the owners to whom they had belonged. The number of seals of famous collectors elevated the value of the works even though they were sometimes forgeries.*

offering if he buries a rich relative; another, if hale and hearty, gets his third million... And you are astonished that painting dies when, to the eyes of all, men and gods, an ingot of gold is another masterpiece than that which Apelles and Phidias, those little hare-brained Greeks, could have fashioned!" This could as well have been a present-day critic speaking about the starving impressionists, about the artists who followed them, wholesale merchants in painting, and about these sanctuaries of Mammon that are the armored, ingot-filled vaults of our banks.

In short, Rome had no museum per se but all Rome was a museum. The museum never was, in Rome, an institution with a structure and rules as were the public libraries which, since the times of Claudius, were all under the direction of one literate procurator or administrator; their surveillance and maintenance were entrusted to the individual guardians, the *aeditimui*. Recruitment of custodial personnel varied greatly. For the richest museums, like the Temple of Concord, there could only be Roman citizens; in general, however, they were freedmen, sometimes even simple slaves. These guardians were responsible for the collections; they saw to their upkeep, aided by subordinate personnel, and served as guides for the public, which guaranteed them an appreciable source of revenue. Then, as now, thefts were frequent and the *aeditimui* were forced to put up security; sometimes they were even directly answerable for collections, as in the case of the Temple of Jupiter Capitolinus or that of the Portico of the Saepta Julia.

The frequent fires which devastated Rome destroyed many collections of art; little by little the Greek paintings disintegrated. However, on the eve of the disaster to which she would succumb and despite the appropriations profiting Byzantium, the Eternal City abounded with works of art, precious and delicate masterpieces which in a century would become incomprehensible and, even worse, would be regarded as repulsive idols inspired by the demon, worthy of sending to the lime kiln or to the forge.

The museological situation in Rome can be considered the historical parallel of that of today by reason of the great public interest in works of art. Not until the eighteenth century would this *esprit public,* as far as concerns works of art, be slowly reborn. It can be said, moreover, that Roman museums stand out in history as those most nearly comparable to contemporary American museums; like the latter they were not dependent on institutional jurisdiction nor on civil administration but relied on private initiative. The collectors, too, as we have seen, resembled those of the United States. The more subtle art patrons in China and Japan bring to mind the princes and cardinals of the seventeenth and eighteenth centuries.

The taste for collecting goes back to the very origins of the Chinese empire, corresponding to that veneration of the past peculiar to the Heavenly Beings for whom what has been is proof of what is and what shall be. They had a cult for the great men of the past, the legendary emperors who had established the foundations of civilization and who had known how to charm the forces of universal energy by mastering the elements through the invention of astronomy, divination, the calendar, irrigation, silk weaving, agriculture, music, dance and the arts and by formulating the eternal principles which govern relations between sky and earth on the one hand and men on the other. In contrast to the West, perpetually moved by an internal force toward the future, successive generations in the East looked for direction to the past, which was considered the model to follow.

At a very early time the Chinese had a feeling for history. They inscribed their edicts on stone, and to assure their greatest diffusion, transferred them to paper by the method of estampage, analogous to the process of engraving which served the same purpose in the West. Later the invention of the paint brush permitted scholars and painters to copy and recopy them in beautiful calligraphy. Thus movable paintings were born, the work of scholars and poets as much as of artists.

At a time when the Western world was succumbing to barbarism, the Chinese were practicing, as they had for centuries, the art of amateurism. The first collectors were undoubtedly the emperors, some of whom were calligraphers who encouraged that art which was appreciated fully as much as painting in China. It is altogether possible that the great Ch'in imperialist, Shih Huang Ti (259-210 B.C.), founder of the Chinese Empire and administrator of genius, commissioned calligraphies and paintings for the splendid palace he had built at Hsien-Yang. The Han Dynasty (206 B.C.-220 A.D.) raised still higher the scepter of the arts, practicing painting and calligraphy as philosophical pursuits. Emperor Wu founded an imperial academy where he amassed from all the provinces of China the most renowned paintings and calligraphies. The last emperor of the Han Dynasty, Hien-ti (190-220) formed a sort of national gallery, grouping portraits of his ministers in a room called the Salon of the Unicorn (the fantastic animal of good omen), a forerunner of the portrait galleries established in Europe during the sixteenth and seventeenth centuries. A successor to the Han throne commissioned from the painter Yen-Chou, a master at portraiture, a series of likenesses of the ladies at court—an early parallel to the *cabinet des dames* of the seventeenth century.

In one of his palaces, that known as "The Two Mysterious Terraces," Emperor Wen Ti of the Sui Dynasty (589-604) installed two galleries; one, "Mysterious Calligraphy," housed countless masterpieces of that art; the other, "Precious Vestiges," was devoted to painting. Calligraphy and painting were held in equal esteem.

The T'ang emperors were patrons of the arts as well as conquerors and were sometimes artists themselves like the Emperor Hsuän-tsung who was both painter and calligrapher. During the Sung Dynasty (960-1260) the emperors often were more interested in arts and letters than in politics and many devoted themselves to painting. This excess of refinement was to cost them their empire.

This was the great era of art criticism in China; collectors fought for masterpieces by artists of the past or present. On these paintings, delicate and evanescent though they were, they imposed their stamps and sometimes even their expressions of satisfaction and approval. This custom, followed through successive dynasties, resulted in the disfigurement of Chinese paintings; overburdened with stamps, they aroused monetary rather than aesthetic interest because value was attached to pedigree and, as today, a celebrated provenance increased the worth of a piece.

It was during the Sung era that Japan, having been in contact with China for several centuries, began to imitate her example. Until then the only storehouses for works of art in Japan were the temples. Japanese amateurs acquired, at great expense, masterpieces by renowned artists of the Sung period and, more respectful than the Chinese collectors, they refrained from affixing their stamps which, in our eyes, gives these works, preserved in private collections in the Land of the Rising Sun, an especially precious character.

8. **Portrait of the Poet Li Tai Po** *(circa 700-762) by Liang K'ai (circa 1140-1210). Ink on paper. National Museum, Tokyo. After the prehistoric and primitive periods which show an independent art, Japan was to a large extent under Chinese influence. After the rule of the T'ang Dynasty, Chinese works of art abounded in Japan. Japanese art lovers became art collectors, especially of paintings. The famous portrait of the poet Li Tai Po by the Sung Dynasty painter Liang K'ai shows the signature of the artist on the left and on the right, above, the seal of the Ashikaga, a shogun family in power during the XIVth and XVth centuries, to whom the painting belonged. Such seals or stamps of the collectors are found less frequently on paintings in Japanese collections than in those in China where they reflected to a high degree the value attributed to the works.*

Chapter 2

Interlude

The museum foundered and sank with other institutions of the antique world. This gratuity of the work of art, to escape mortality, was incompatible with the new era in which all in human life was subject to a supreme finality in an afterlife. Moreover, medieval man had a notion of time like that of primitive civilizations; he lived deprived of one of its three dimensions: the past. History began with him, that is to say, with the Christian era, preceded by a prehistory that was the world of the Bible. All which was not of that order lacked reality, was cast again into the "outlying darkness," a sort of world in reverse image dominated by evil forces. However, of the Christian past there remained tokens which had to be preserved at all costs; these were the relics, remains from the instruments of the Passion, from the life of the Virgin, from the lives both of the apostles and of those men struck by divine illumination, the saints. The early Christians were already infusing linen or plaster with the blood of martyrs. In the Middle Ages such relics were vied for passionately and one stopped at neither theft nor murder in pursuit of them. They constituted, moreover, the best tool of medieval therapeutics, warding off calamities, insuring good harvests, curing sicknesses, epidemics and infirmities. Nothing was too rich to use in paying homage to these distinguished remains: gold, silver, precious uncut stones (the technique of faceting was not yet known), cloths and sundry other objects imported at great expense from distant lands. Accumulated in treasuries of the Church, these objects were museums in embryo which were frequented by pilgrims. All that had come near Christ was sacred, even the soil of the Holy Land which was made into broad, thin cakes stamped with pious images and called *terrae sigillatae*. Oil from lamps that had burned near sanctuaries in Palestine was also holy and was carried in ampoules of lead or silver. The Cathedral at Monza, Italy, houses antique specimens in silver from the seventh century on which are scenes recalling mosaic compositions that decorated Palestinian basilicas before their destruction by the Arabs. The cloths in which the relics were wrapped—the shrouds— had the same efficacy and from time to time pieces of them were distributed to the faithful. In Constantinople nothing was thought of dismembering or dividing relics to satisfy the demand while Rome, from the earliest Christian times, kept alive the traditions of respect that Roman paganism had

9. **The Shōsō-in in the To-daiji Monastery at Nara,** *near Kyoto, Japan. To contain the offerings sent from all over the world to the colossal bronze Buddha at Nara, a special store-house—the Shōsō-in—was built. After the death of Emperor Shomu in 756 A.D., his widow bequeathed all his treasures to it. Included were some invaluable T'ang pieces, then little known, as well as objects sent from the Middle East. Since 1873 the Shōsō-in has opened every November, that is to say, the beautiful season. It is the oldest museum in the world. The reinforced wood construction has been instrumental in preserving the objects through its natural regulation of the humidity.*

10. **Ivory Binding for a New Testament,** *traced to the Abbey of Lorsch, Germany. Victoria and Albert Museum, London. One of the most beautiful examples of those magnificent ivory plaques used as bindings for the four Gospels. The two leaves of the binding from Lorsch are today at Rome and London; the manuscripts are at Bucharest and the Vatican. Originating in the Ecole de la Cour de Charlemagne, these monumental plaques, made about 810, represent the most important ivory works of art which have been preserved. Inspiration for the style was drawn from remote antiquity.*

always shown for the bodies of the dead, even for those of the executed. The *Codex Theodosianus* forbade "troubling the rest of a deceased, even by disturbing the sarcophagus." Later, cloths that had touched saintly bodies were considered relics, which explains their multiplication; reverence was paid to no fewer than fifty-seven veils of the Virgin.

The consecrated bodies were preserved in gold or silver reliquaries, taking at first the shape of a casket, later, that of a church. When only a portion of the body had been conserved, the reliquary repeated its form—hand, arm, leg, foot, head or rib. Treasuries also contained frontals for altars in precious metal, portable altars, pieces of liturgical *orfèvrerie* (chalices, patens, ciboria, eucharistic doves), many of which were considered the attributes of some local saint, and manuscripts, primarily gospels. The splendid Carolingian gospels were much esteemed throughout the Middle Ages; they often were given sumptuous metal bindings, even as late as Gothic times. Liturgical vestments consecrated by former use were also kept with care. The treasury stored the sets of tapestries used to decorate the church during certain feast days in the year. In addition to all these objects of occidental craftsmanship, there were others from antiquity or from the Orient which for the medieval man signified the fabulously remote. Certain objects created by the civilizations of antiquity or Islam or the Far East, which the Middle Ages felt incapable of reproducing, were considered infinitely precious; acquired at great expense, they were incorporated into shrines or reliquaries. Thus, antique gems and cameos, for which the Middle Ages had a veritable passion, were kept intact for us. Without hesitation, sacred metalwork was ornamented with figures of Caesar, Germanicus, Jupiter or other gods no longer understood. The Reliquary of the Three Magi in Cologne is set with no fewer than two hundred antique stones. Suger, abbot of Saint-Denis near Paris, hunted as far as Sicily for cameos and sardonyx carvings. For shrouds, silks woven with gold (among them some rare Sassanian cloths) were imported from Islam or Byzantium. We owe to these treasuries what we now possess of Byzantine objects and also of very early oriental fabrics.

These treasuries were maintained in small rooms annexed to churches, cathedrals or monasteries, which were always vaulted to lessen the risk of fire. In the Cathedral of Bayeux the treasury room with its thirteenth-century cases is still intact. Upon occasion, a simple armoire within the church served as the treasury (Cathedral of Noyon, the Abbey of Souvigny). It sometimes happened that the treasury for precious objects was attached to another kind of repository, the archives which contained the "treasure of charters." There the abbey kept its property deeds and its documents justifying rights. Saint Louis had a small structure annexed to the *Palais de la cité* in Paris to shelter his most precious belongings; in the lower room were the relics of the Sainte-Chapelle and the crown jewels; in the upper room, his treasure of charters.

These treasuries were formed during the course of the Middle Ages in many stages. The first were assembled in the seventh and eighth centuries. One of the oldest is the treasury of the Cathedral of Monza, Italy, founded in the early seventh century by the pious Queen Theodolinda, Catholic wife of Agiluf, the Arian king of the Longobardi. But it was the Carolingian epoch which witnessed the first great treasures. Charlemagne's overwhelming piety had given new life to monasteries and cathedrals. His personal relations with the Byzantine basileus and the caliph Harun al-Rashid enabled him to acquire, through purchases or donations, a great number of relics and precious objects which were added to the booty captured from the Huns and the Arabs. Imitating Byzantine and Islamic practices, he commissioned from his ateliers sumptuous pieces of metalwork ornamented with gems and he vigorously encouraged sculpture in ivory. Cameos, antique intaglios, Byzantine or Moslem ivories, silks and cloth of gold, gems and objects in precious metals filled his coffers at Aix-la-Chapelle. Three years before his death Charlemagne decided to divide his treasures; keeping only one third for his heirs, he distributed the remaining two thirds among twenty-one great cities in the realm. According to legend he sent a different letter of the alphabet to each of the twenty-four largest abbeys. Scholars still wonder whether an A-shaped reliquary preserved in the Abbey of Conques in Rouergue, which houses some objects associated with Charlemagne, corroborates the legend. Curiously, these treasures have vanished and all that remain to claim a Carolingian provenance are the famous imperial crown in the Hofburg in Vienna (in reality no earlier than Ottonian or Romanesque in date) and the purple mantle with gold eagles that the emperor had given to the Cathedral in Metz and which is there still. Except for some manuscripts and ivory plaquettes the mantle is probably the only object contemporary with the great emperor that we have preserved. The post-Carolingian epoch saw the enrichment of numerous treasuries; that of the Abbey of Sainte Foy de Conques has one of the richest stores of objects from this great period. The treasury of the *Sancta Sanctorum* in the Lateran dates back to the same time. Although lacking in Carolingian objects, the treasury of Aix-la-Chapelle contains beautiful pieces from subsequent periods. All that recalled the Carolingian era was venerated as a relic equal to those of the saints. The oliphant which Roland burst when he blew it at the Battle of Roncevaux can be seen at Saint Seurin in Bordeaux. Even Roncevaux offered to the cult of pilgrims Charlemagne's chessboard and the rock cleft by Roland with his sword of steel so strong it resisted the shock; the latter was kept in the Abbey of Rocamadour.

The Romanesque period saw the formation of the great treasuries of Reichenau, whose most precious piece was the vase in which water had been changed to wine at the marriage in Cana; those of Hildesheim and Quedlinburg; and, in France, that of Sens, one of the richest in early textiles. Abbot Suger of Saint-Denis, minister of Louis VII, took the greatest care to enrich his collection of objects pertaining to the liturgy and the cult when his church was reconstructed. The treasury he established is today divided between the Bibliothèque Nationale and the Louvre; it contained many antique or exotic objects such as a sardonyx vase in the form of a ewer, one of porphyry in the shape of an eagle, an Arabian rock-crystal ewer and, most important of all, the rock-crystal chalice which had belonged to the Sassanide king, Khosrau I, and was known as the "plate of Solomon."

The enrichment resulting from the Crusades opened the second phase of the formation of treasuries in the Occident. The fabulous riches accumulated since antiquity by the Byzantine emperors aroused the covetousness of the crusaders. When the Venetians turned the forces of the fourth crusade on Constantinople and captured the city, King Baldwin I, dazzled by such luxury, said that all Christendom did not possess so much. Pillaging of the city lasted from the fourteenth to the sixteenth of April, 1204. Those who had done the actual plundering were forced to relinquish most of what they had in order to assure a more just distribution; half was given to the Venetians, half to the crusaders. Nine tenths of the Treasury of San Marco in Venice comes from this booty. Less obtuse than the crusaders, the Venetians coveted the bronze quadriga in the hippodrome, those original Greek statues from classical antiquity which had been stolen by the Romans from Greece before being taken to Byzantium. No longer capable of producing such works in bronze, the West carried them away and ended by placing them, like a trophy, high on the façade of San Marco. Another treasury built up by relics brought back by crusaders returning from the East is that of the Sainte-Chapelle in the Palais des Rois de France in Paris. Built by Saint Louis, the chapel itself was an immense reliquary of stone and colored glass, destined to shelter the numerous relics from the Passion sent by Baldwin II to the Saint-King as security for a loan. The king refrained from demanding repayment because he considered the security much more precious than the loan. Saint Louis commissioned magnificent *orfèvreries* to receive the relics and to serve in the performance of the liturgy. Of all these riches only two antique pieces remain today: the great cameo of Germanicus, taken to Constantinople by Emperor Constantine, and a consular scepter in sardonyx which served in Constantinople as the distinctive attribute of a dignitary at the court of the basileus. The gem was venerated as representing the triumph of Joseph at the court of Pharaoh; the scepter was used as a cantoral staff in the Sainte-Chapelle.

A great treasury linked to the history of France is that of the Cathedral of Reims. It dates back to the very origins of that history since it preserves the famous vase of Soissons which Clovis gave to the cathedral. One of the most beautiful pieces is the chalice which is supposed to have belonged to Saint Remi (437?-533) but which is actually no earlier than the twelfth century. Pillaged by the Normans in 822, by robbers in 941, by Carolingian princes in 991, it was rebuilt under the Capetians and the Valois. The coronation regalia for the kings of France were also stored at Reims.

These treasuries housed too many riches not to tempt public forces. Particularly in France they were squandered by the many appropriations of successive generations. In periods of war kings demanded the use of precious metals. At the time of the Norman

11. **A-shaped reliquary. Carolingian period.** *Treasury of the Abbey of Conques in Rouergue, France. For his collection of numerous relics acquired through his relations with Byzantine emperors, Charlemagne commissioned from the palace workshops magnificent pieces of* orfèvrerie *which often incorporated antique gems and cameos. These treasures have disappeared. According to legend, Charlemagne gave to twenty-four abbeys twenty-four reliquaries in the shape of different letters of the alphabet. This was once accepted as an explanation of the A-shape of this reliquary in the Abbey of Conques but detailed study has now revealed it to be not earlier than the abbacy of Begon (1087-1106).*

invasions Charles the Fat had already made requisitions, principally at Reims. During the Hundred Years' War the kings of France—Charles V, Charles VI and Charles VII—drained the treasuries as a primary source of revenue for the demands of the war. At the same time the monks of Mont Saint Michel did not hesitate to pledge at Saint Malo a part of the treasury of their abbey to help pay the expenses of the struggle against the English. In the sixteenth century Charles IX obtained from the pope the right to tax the churches of France, who melted down pieces from their treasury to feed the war against the Huguenots. However, the treasuries of French churches were still rich enough under Louis XIV to attract his greed. The final act of destruction came as a result of the famous edict of 1759, proclaimed by Louis XV by which all civil and religious pieces of metalwork were ordered sent to the foundry for the purpose of meeting the deficit in the royal treasury. The Revolution carried away the last vestiges. Thus can be explained why France is so poor in *orfèvreries* of precious metals while Germany, Italy and Spain are so rich. A vast exhibition of ecclesiastical treasures held in Paris in 1965 proved that without exception the churches of France have pieces of no more than secondary interest and often even of mediocre quality. Vandalism resulting from contempt for the Middle Ages added further to this "martyrology." With the suppression of the Order of Grammont in 1707, the Bishop of Limoges dispersed the famous treasury of the church; finding the main altar too cumbersome, he had the celebrated piece of Limousin metalcraft dismantled and sent to the foundry.

The "treasure" accumulated near a sanctuary is not an institution peculiar to Christianity; it existed in antiquity and is also found in Islam, China and Japan. In present-day Iran three museums were formerly treasuries. The most important is at Meshed in the center of the Khurasan district in northeast Iran, near the sanctuary which contains the body of Imam-Reza, the eighth Shiite imam, who was poisoned by Caliph Mamum in the eighth century. His tomb is a center of pilgrimage for the whole East; crowds from Iran, Pakistan, India, Iraq and Turkey converge to honor the saint. Over the centuries princely donors amassed there the precious objects which pilgrims come to venerate as sacred relics. About twenty years ago this treasure was installed as a museum in a specially constructed building at the edge of the tomb. Not far from Teheran the museum of Shah-Abdol-Azim was formed from gifts left at the tomb of this ninth-century martyr and descendant of the prophet. About 110 miles south of Teheran, near the tomb of Massouma-Ghom, sister of Imam-Reza, there is an historical museum particularly rich in objects of the Safawid period. In An Najaf, a holy city in Iraq, the great Ali, cousin and son-in-law of the prophet Mohammed and the first Shiite imam, is interred; there too the treasury is a museum.

In Japan temples were the first repositories of religious and even secular works of art. The Nipponese venerated great men—emperors, poets, artists—and in their honor erected temples in which were preserved objects that had belonged to or been created by them. During illustrious periods the museum was, so to speak, crystallized around the temple. Japan has kept intact such a treasury: Shōsō-in, founded in the eighth century in the monastery of Todaiji at Nara, near Kyoto. It still contains both utilitarian and precious objects which belonged to Emperor Shomu (who reigned from 724 until 756) and which his widow, Komyo, gave to the Todaiji monastery. The terms of the bequest stated that the empress, having collected all the national treasures left by the emperor, offered them to the Buddha Vairochana whose colossal effigy in bronze had been ordered melted down by the emperor a few years earlier. The gift included arms and armor, monk's habits, mirrors, screens, musical instruments, furniture, medicaments—in all, an inventory of some 650 articles. Within the grounds of the monastery a wooden building was constructed to receive the collection. Although it has been renovated several times, as often happens with wooden structures in Japan, it still exists and is the oldest museum in the world. Preserved in its halls are objects offered to Buddha from as far away as Iran, unique Chinese pieces from the T'ang Dynasty and in the storerooms 66,000 pieces of textiles have been catalogued.

At the beginning of the fourteenth century authority was not the only attribute of power. The *bourgeoisie* willingly paraded its new-found wealth. The upper class, intolerant of being outdistanced, answered with pageantry. The result was the prodigious development of the luxury crafts, especially of goldsmithery, of which only a few specimens remain. The inventories of the various mansions and châteaux which belonged to Charles V, King of France, can give us some idea of the pomp and ostentation. There were no fewer than forty-seven royal crowns and seven tiaras (for the princesses), belts of gold, seven dozen gold services, nineteen gold chandeliers, jeweled chests, seals and magical objects, among which were "the holy stone which helps women have children" and "the stone which cures gout." Antiquity was represented by a very large number of carved objects; these intaglios, certain of which served as seals, were in such great demand that there sprang up an active forgery trade. It is estimated that only one fourth of the intaglios said to be medieval are authentic. Other objects were reported to have been for "use across the sea" or were "Saracen," that is to say, Byzantine, Islamic or even Chinese. Among these treasures of a sacred character because they belonged to royalty were many jewels and metalwork pieces of an ecclesiastic nature: twenty-seven crosses of gold, nineteen gold statues of the Virgin and various saints, twenty-nine bejeweled reliquaries, a large chalice lavished with sapphires and rubies, twenty-seven silver crosses, six dozen silver statuettes or groups of statuettes, sixty-three complete "chapels" in various colors for the various feasts of the year—each "chapel" included all the liturgical vestments and vessels necessary for worship.

The treasures served as a reserve supply for metal and, in case of need, jewels were pawned and metals sent to the foundry. The King of France, Charles V, himself had to resort to this practice. Our less imaginative era stupidly hordes gold bars in the vaults of national banks; the more refined princes of the past had them worked by artists, thereby obtaining artistic enjoyment for themselves, but did not hesitate to sacrifice them when politics required it. This custom continued until the time of Louis XIV; he commissioned for the Hall of Mirrors and the great apartments at Versailles an admirable suite of furniture in silver which was completed by the beginning of 1660 but he was forced to have it melted down in 1689 to relieve the deficit in the treasury caused by the war with the League of Augsburg.

Such was the custom at the French court; foreign courts, however, took better care of their treasures. Of all the admirable French metalwork of the Middle Ages there remain no more than a few pieces preserved by their passage into foreign hands: for example, the enameled gold cup said to be from the kings of France and England and

now in the British Museum, London, and the ex voto to the Virgin, also of enameled gold, which was presented by Elizabeth of Bavaria to Charles VI of France on the occasion of their marriage on January 1, 1404, and which the following year was given as security by the king to his brother-in-law, Louis of Bavaria, from whom he had obtained a loan. Louis made a gift of it to the church at Altötting in Bavaria where it still remains. The only piece of French metalwork extant from the Renaissance is the gold cup of Saint Michel, given by Charles IX to his brother-in-law, Ferdinand of Tyrol at the time of his marriage in 1570.

These precious objects were kept in the "garderobe," a term not then restricted as it is now to a place where clothes are kept but which applied to the protection of all sorts of possessions, in the sense that the Italian word *roba* has retained.

In Pisanello we find a brillant reflection of the growing princely pomp of the cosmopolitan civilization of the early *quattrocento*. The grandees of that time appreciated the aesthetic value of their possessions fully as much as their price or rarity. The man who personifies all the refinement of that age is Jean, Duke of Berry (1340-1416), the brother of Charles V. The garderobe of Charles was that of a king; the duke's was the collection of an art lover whose taste was oriented toward the spirit of the Renaissance. His collections were disposed in the numerous châteaux of his immense fiefs, reproductions of which appear in illuminations made by the Brothers of Limbourg for the celebrated work listed in the inventories as the *Très riches heures de Monseigneur*. The library of Charles V was made for study; the library of the duke was that of a bibliophile, rich in superbly lettered and illuminated books. A true bibliophile, he borrowed books but did not willingly return them, as attested to by the quarrels he had over the *Grandes chroniques de France* which he borrowed from the abbey of Saint Denis. Only the intervention of his confessor induced him to return them. His brother Charles lent willingly but kept a register of loans, which still exists, and saw to their return. The duke received a considerable number (356) of *objets d'art* as gifts which came to him from all parts of the world, from Burgundian dukes, from his brother Charles V, from his nephew Charles VI, from popes and prelates, from the Count of Tripoli, from the Queen of England and even from officers in his household as well as from Genoese, Venetian and Florentine merchants who curried the favor of their clients by sending them gifts. He had many jewels, among them the "ruby of Alexander" and the "diamond of Saint-Louis"; exceedingly rare relics, such as Saint Joseph's wedding band; a profusion of rings; Florentine and English embroideries; fabrics from Cyprus, Venice and the Orient, listed as "the work of Greece"; tapestries; family souvenirs; collections of games; gold tableware; foot warmers; perfume flacons; three hundred manuscripts, some in the "style of Lombardy, or of Rome, or of Bologna"; enamels; and a host of small, often insignificant objects, proof of his insatiable curiosity. Princes had already become interested in the *bizarreries* of nature which were to become so popular in the sixteenth century; in that category were such antidotes against poison as the horns of unicorns (actually narwhal tusks), tongues of serpents and four bezoars. Horns of stag beetles were mounted in gilded silver. There was a knife that could "cut iron." The parks of his châteaux had menageries. The duke sought Byzantine vases, oriental cameos and medals. He prided himself on owning a gold portrait medallion of Constantine and Heraclius which inspired his miniaturists but was proved

12. **The Royal Gold Cup of the Kings of France and England,** *British Museum, London. Although stripped of some of its jewels, this solid gold cup decorated with translucent enamel in crimson, blue, black and yellow is one of the most precious vestiges of princely treasures from the fourteenth century. It was probably made in Paris about 1380 and was given by Charles VI, King of France, to his uncle, the Duke of Berry in 1391. The Duke of Bedford removed it to England in 1434; it was inherited by his nephew, the young King Henry VI, and figures in the inventory of Elizabeth I. In 1604 it became the property of the Constable of Castile, Juan de Velasco, to whom it was given by King James I; in 1610 the constable gave it to the Convent of Santa Clara a Medina de Pomar near Burgos. In 1803 the convent sold it to Baron Pichon; it remained in France until 1892 when the British Museum acquired it for the sum of £ 8,000.*

13. Portrait of the Duke de Berry by Hans Holbein the Younger. *Based on a Funeral Monument by Jean de Cambrai in the Cathedral of Bourges, France. Basel, Kunstmuseum. Kupferstichkabinett. This drawing preserves for us a record of the physical appearance of the Duke of Berry, whose statue was decapitated when it was taken from the Cathedral of Bourges during the Revolution. (The head was later remade from the drawing.) An impassioned art lover, the Duke of Berry, with his fabulous collection of objets d'art and precious books, was the first Maecenas of the Renaissance. His collection, for which we have a detailed inventory, forms the transition from the medieval treasury to the modern cabinet.*

a fraud by Scaliger and du Cange. It was sold to the duke on the second of November, 1402, by the Italian antiquarian Antonio Mancini and was doubtlessly made a few years earlier by some Netherlandish, Burgundian or French metalworker. Jean de Berry was also curious about history. He formed in his château at Bicêtre a collection of portraits of illustrious persons of his time, both lay and ecclesiastical, who figured beside princes of France and kings of the East and the West. The pictures hung in the main hall of the château and were destroyed when it burned in 1411. The gallery was inspired by the idea of glory peculiar to the Renaissance. The Duke of Berry was a Maecenas *à l'italienne*; with him began the transition of the treasury into the museum.

In the fifteenth century the taste for collecting became so widespread that it infected the *bourgeoisie*. Let us take for example the account which Guillebert de Metz, secretary and librarian for the Duke of Burgundy, gives of the town house of Jacques Duchié in his *Description de Paris*, written about 1430. In the courtyard there was a menagerie of peacocks and other birds of pleasure. The first floor salon was "embellished with paintings and instructive scriptures on the walls." The practice of decorating rooms with mottoes, in vogue by the end of the sixteenth century and continuing in the seventeenth, had already existed for some time. Another room was filled with musical instruments: harps, organs, psalteries, vielles, citterns and others, which the owner knew how to play. Beyond that was a room where all sorts of games were displayed. The chapel contained two beautiful lecterns and the walls of a study were covered with precious stones and "sweet-smelling spices." Rare furs were stored in one chamber; fabrics, rugs and metalwork in another. It is quite surprising to learn that this merchant who was interested in peaceful pursuits was also passionately interested in arms and armor with which he filled an entire room. There were crossbows, standards, banners, pennons, lances, halberds, floorings from trenches, axes, daggers, suits of armor in lead and iron, shields, escutcheons, cannons and other engines and "all manner of implements of war." In all this there were few pieces which could properly be called works of art; it was a collection of what was later to be called "curiosities," undoubtedly acquired at little expense but of sufficient importance to merit the attention of a chronicler.

Chapter

3

Renaissance

In 1162 an edict of the Roman Senate decreed that the Column of Trajan "must never be destroyed nor mutilated but must remain as it is to the honor of the Roman people until the end of the world." The decree undoubtedly marks the earliest attempt at the preservation of an historical monument in Western civilization. In truth, the memory of the grandeur of antiquity had never been lost in Rome, as attested to by the *Mirabilia urbis Romae,* a medieval guidebook for pilgrims which directed the city's visitors as much to ancient monuments as to churches. If the tidal wave of Gothicism had not submerged *trecento* Italy, the Renaissance would have arrived much earlier. In the thirteenth century Emperor Frederick II had imitations of antique statues made at Capua and Castel del Monte, thus proposing a new orientation to art that Niccolò Pisano was to follow; Niccolò's son, Giovanni, working on the pulpit for Pisa's *Duomo,* did not hesitate to borrow the attitude of the Capitoline Venus for his figure of Temperance. The emperor, who attempted a synthesis of divers cultures through the reconciliation of Christendom and Islam, also sponsored excavations at Augusta in Sicily. By the end of the twelfth century Cardinal Giordano Orsini had created in Rome a cabinet of antiquities which he then turned into a public museum for souvenirs of ancient Rome—if we can believe the assertion of a sixteenth-century panegyrist of the Orsini family. On the other hand, the antique inscriptions with which Rome abounded were for a long time as indecipherable as the Etruscan and Cretan languages remain for us today. The founder of epigraphy was a friend of Petrarch, Cola di Rienzo, who, obsessed with Rome to the point of mysticism, was hanged by his feet by an unruly Roman mob after self-aggrandizement deflected his avowed aims to restore liberty to the Eternal City and to Italy. In Florence the modern literary movement found its sources in antique literature but neither Petrarch nor Boccaccio was concerned with archeology. The situation was entirely different in Venetia. There, thanks to Venice, contact with antiquity had never been broken; passage from a Roman to a barbarian world had not been felt in that city which had never been invaded and which keeps alive even today the spirit of a Hellenistic city. From relations with Byzantium, heir to the Roman Empire, Venice drew the feeling of an uninterrupted succession of

14. **The Torso Belvedere.** *This work dating from the first century B. C. and signed by the Athenian Apollonius, might well portray Hercules, Marsyas or Philoctetes left wounded on the island of Lemnos. It is one of the first antique statues discovered in Italy and can be traced back to the Palazzo Colonna before 1463 and was mentioned as early as 1433; it was, perhaps, discovered during the reconstruction of the palace about 1420. Pope Clement VII had the torso transferred to the Belvedere Gardens at the Vatican where Maerten van Heemskerck sketched it turned over on its back about 1532-1535. This statue strongly influenced Michelangelo.*

15. The Cardinal Virtues-Temperance, by Giovanni Pisano *(c. 1250-1331). Pulpit in the Duomo, Pisa.*

16. The Capitoline Venus. *Copy after a Greek statue of the fourth century. Capitoline Museum, Rome.*

The Italians of the Middle Ages lived in an ambiance in which antiquity remained an ever-present force. In the thirteenth century Niccolò Pisano († 1280) turned to classical examples to learn to restore to sculpture its corporeal vitality; there are several examples of direct imitation of the antique in Pisano's pulpit in the baptistery in Pisa (1260). Forty years later Niccolò's son Giovanni, although more Gothic in spirit, continued the tradition; for his Temperance he imitated some antique monument which had itself been inspired by the Capitoline Venus.

42

historical periods. As early as the fifteeth century an active trade in antiquities, which must have been drawn in part from sources in the Orient, was being carried on in Venice. The earliest mention of a cabinet of antiquities concerns one in Treviso and is dated about 1335. We are fortunate to have an itemized bill of purchases made in Venice by a Trevisan citizen, one Oliviero Forza or Forzetta; he acquired manuscripts by Sallust, Seneca, Ovid, Cicero and Livy; fifty medallions, intaglios, pottery, bronzes, and statues in marble; children from San Vitale in Ravenna; and a lion, horses, oxen and male nudes. In 1375 a Paduan doctor, Giovanni Dondi, went to Rome to study antique monuments. The archeological tradition continued throughout the entire fifteenth century in the Veneto. Museums of antiquities soon became art schools, such as the collection formed around the mid-1400's by the Paduan painter, Francesco Squarcione. From his travels in Greece and Italy he brought back antiquities which he set up as models before his students. Under his tutelage Mantegna flourished, the only archeological artist to realize Alberti's dream of reviving the antique spirit; the Florentines drew their principles more from the study of nature than from works by the ancients. Following his master's example, Mantegna formed an archeological museum in his house at Mantua. It was fine enough to merit a visit from Lorenzo de' Medici. Collector-princes regarded Mantegna as an expert among connoisseurs. An art directly inspired by the antique was born in northern Italy: the art of the medal, as exemplified by Pisanello. A phrase of Valéry's is truly applicable to the Renaissance: "*on entre dans l'avenir à reculons.*" To free themselves of the restraints the Middle Ages had imposed on the flight of the intellect, Italians of the *quattrocento* looked to the antique, sough to re-establish ties with the Greco-Roman civilization, all the while adapting it to Christianity.

At first the interest of the Florentines in the antique focused on the examination of manuscripts buried in the archives of convents and this led to the revival of Roman and Greek belles-lettres. In their libraries, however, the humanists were fond of interspersing books with intaglios and medals. Aided by the Medicis, who inherited from his collections, Niccolò de Niccoli was one of the most active admirers of these little objects, so suited for exhibition among books. The great discoverer of manuscripts, Poggio Bracciolini, furthered the cause of antique art by finding works by Vitruvius, Frontinus, Pliny the Elder, Lucian, Pausanias and Philostratus. He himself had a collection of coins and sculpture and in his villa set aside a room for his museum. He boasted proudly that Donatello had seen and praised one of his pieces. It is not surprising to learn that Ghiberti had a collection of antique bronzes and marbles for, of all the Florentines, he was the one most moved by antiquity, in contrast to Donatello who was inspired most by his observation of nature.

The great bourgeois families—the Strozzi, the Ruccelai, the Pazzi, the Tornabuoni, the Martelli, the Capponi—filled their palaces with both ancient and modern *objets d'art* but the most important collections were put together by the Medicis whose power was founded on the greatest banking wealth of the time. The various inventories which remain intact help us to trace the evolution of their collections during the course of the century. The nature of our subject matter precludes our discussing here the numerous works of contemporary art that Cosimo the Elder commissioned for his *palazzo* on the Via Larga and for his country villas; we shall concentrate instead on the antique and foreign works he amassed. He was fond of reliefs and statues which he had Donatello, in the role of curator and expert, restore but he was more attracted by books and the intaglios and cameos which were *de rigueur* in humanist libraries. He was aided in the building up of his collections by his son Piero (Peter the Gouty) who was predisposed, perhaps, by his infirmities to such calm occupations. Piero spent entire days contemplating his father's treasures and commissioned sumptuous settings for the precious stones and intaglios. The oldest preserved inventories of the Medici collections were drawn up by Piero in 1456 and 1463, before his father's death. They list only objects of precious materials and omit, therefore, all paintings and sculptures. The record lists three hundred medals in silver and seventeen in gold, seventeen cameos and *tavole greche* or Byzantine icons. By 1463 the number of precious objects had doubled. The inventories also give an account of Flemish tapestries, musical instruments (most of which also came from Flanders) and Cordovan leathers. The third inventory, made out in 1465 after the death of Cosimo, reveals the considerable growth of the collection in two years.

The inventory of the palace on the Via Larga, drawn up in 1492 at the death of Lorenzo the Magnificent, shows some progress toward the evaluation of works of art for themselves. In some cases the artist who made a painting or sculpture is identified. Included in the list of pictures were some Flemish works, among them a *Deposition* by Rogier van der Weyden and a *St. Jerome* by Jan van Eyck which certain scholars consider identifiable with a painting of the same subject in the Detroit Institute of Arts (attributed by others to Petrus Christus). However, paintings were still esteemed for little in contrast to the value attached to jewels and oddities: thirty florins for the van Eyck. three florins for a work by the sculptor Desiderio da Settignano against 6,000 florins for the horn of a unicorn. The term *museum* appears at this time; Lorenzo's collection of books and gems is called *museo dei codici e cimeli artistici*.

It has recently been denied that Lorenzo the Magnificent was as active a patron of

17. **Tazza Farnese, Hellenistic period.** *Naples, Museo Nazionale. This splendid sardonyx cup, one of the largest of known cameos, probably came from the ruins of the Villa Adriana, Tivoli. It was one of the most prestigious objects in Lorenzo de' Medici's collection, rich in gems and antique cameos; he had bought it at Rome in 1471 where he had gone for the coronation of Sixtus IV; it had belonged to Pope Paul II, the former Cardinal Pietro Barbo who had brought from Venice to Rome a taste for the antique. The Tazza eventually passed into the Farnese collection which was removed to Naples in the eighteenth century. Representing an allegory of the Nile with Isis and Horus, the cup must have been made in Alexandria for the Ptolemies.*

the arts as his father, Cosimo. This pleasure seeker seems to have been a usufructuary rather than a creator; at any rate he was a more impassioned collector and searched for pieces all over the peninsula. He returned from Rome after the coronation of Sixtus IV with the finest of known antique stones, the famous *Tazza Farnese*. In 1471 at a sale ordered by Sixtus IV, he acquired for a small sum the collection of Pope Paul II, his rival in the quest for antiquities. In 1483 Lorenzo succeeded in obtaining the cabinet of Cardinal Gonzaga. Doubtlessly it was he who commissioned medallion reproductions of the most beautiful intaglios in the Medici collection for the *cortile* of the palace on the Via Larga.

Verrocchio assisted Lorenzo in matters of connoisseurship. The curator of antique marbles was a sculptor, the *bronzista* Bertoldo whose own creations were veritable pastiches of classical works. Sculptures ornamented the gardens, both the one adjoining the *palazzo* and the one within the great cloister of the Dominican Convent of San Marco, built by Cosimo and decorated with the mystical paintings of Fra Angelico. The monks felt no uneasiness at contemplating sacred images placed side by side with antique nudes for, at that moment in the Renaissance, the most enlightened spirits saw in the doctrine of divine revelation a continuation of antique wisdom and dreamed of reconciling the two, an attitude brutally denounced by Savonarola, precursor of the Reformation. In 1494, two years after Lorenzo's death, the revolt touched off by the arrival of French troops drove the Medicis from Florence; Lorenzo's son Piero fled to Naples, making away with only a few of the most precious cameos. The rabble pillaged the Medici palace and the garden of San Marco; the *Signoria* confiscated what remained of the collections, putting a part up for sale, an act which provoked passionate interest among all Italian art collectors.

In Rome the spirit of the Renaissance was kindled by Pope Nicolas V who, as Tommaso Parentucelli from Sarzana, had been a librarian for Cosimo the Elder. Pius II, of the noble Piccolomini family of Siena, had been educated in Florence and was a well-known philologist. As pope, he fought against the destruction of Rome's monuments by forbidding the use of antique stone or marble in new constructions but he was the first to violate his own edict. The first pope to be a real collector was the Venetian Pietro Barbo who became Paul II and who brought from the city of lagoons a taste for antiquity. In 1455 while still a cardinal, he began the construction of the immense Palazzo Venezia where he amassed his treasures, collecting series rather than single, beautiful pieces. An inventory of the palace drawn up in 1457 enumerates gems, cameos, series of coins, small bronzes (for which he had a particular fondness), tapestries, *oreficeria,* paintings with gold backgrounds, portable mosaics, reliquaries and Byzantine objects—especially ivory consular diptychs. The capture of Constantinople by the Turks in 1453 thrust upon Western markets great quantities of pillaged works of art with Venice serving as intermediary in their resale. Certain notations in the inventory reveal the subtleties of taste of a collector attracted by quality: "*optimis operis de aere, nec in ea est macula*" which indicated of certain bronzes that they were in "mint condition."

The successor of Paul II, Sixtus IV, did not manifest the same interest in works of art. He did, however, issue a papal bull forbidding the exploitation of antiques, an edict that was seldom respected. We owe to him the founding, in 1471, of the Museo

18. *The* **Apollo Belvedere** *as it appeared toward the end of the fifteenth century in a niche in the garden of San Pietro in Vincoli, Rome. From a drawing in the* Codex escurialensis. *The inscription "nel orto di sa piero in uinchola" indicates that the statue was found in the palace of Giuliano della Rovere, Cardinal of the Order of San Pietro in Vincoli from 1471 until his election as Pope Julius II in 1503. After his ascension to the pontifical throne, Julius had the statue removed to the garden of the Belvedere in the Vatican. Attributed by modern Hellenists to the fourth-century B.C. Greek sculptor Leochares, the work was found near Nettuno, at the present site of Anzio. It was restored in 1532 by Giovannangelo da Montorsoli, a pupil of Michelangelo, but has recently been stripped of his additions.*

48

20. **The She-wolf.** *Etruscan bronze in the Capitoline Museum, Rome. The famous Etruscan she-wolf of the Capitoline was part of the ceremonial gift made by Pope Sixtus IV to the Roman Senate in 1471, the year of his election. This gift comprised many antiques which had, until then, been conserved at the pontifical palace of the Lateran. It was at this time that the wolf was provided with the twins, Romulus and Remus. At the Capitoline the wolf was first placed above the entrance to the Palazzo dei Conservatori.*

◀ 19. **View of the Gardens and the Cortile of the Belvedere in Rome.** *Detail of a painting by Hendrick van Cleeve. Brussels Ancient Art Museum. This painting, dated 1589, was based on a drawing executed in Rome about 1550-1555. It shows how the Renaissance popes had disposed their antiquities to ornament the gardens of the Belvedere, a sort of pleasure villa built at some distance from the old Vatican palace to which it was connected by Julius II with two long galleries. Among the statues can be distinguished the* Tiber, *the* Nile, *the* Sleeping Ariadne *and the* Belvedere Torso, *provided with a head from another antique statue.*

Capitolino for antiquities. In that year, the year of his election, he made a gift to the Senate of four antique bronzes which were solemnly transferred from the Lateran to the Capitol to stand as "symbols of the virtue and excellence of the Roman people," but his act was more a political move than a declaration of his museological intentions. Among those bronzes were the *Spinario* and the famous Etruscan she-wolf with the twins Romulus and Remus, which was placed above the entrance, the same position it had occupied in the Lateran.

Like Louis XIV at a later time, Julius II was tormented by a love of glory. Although, unlike the Sun King, he did not have a long reign in which to realize his designs, nevertheless one is astounded at all that he did accomplish or outline in project form during the ten years of his pontificate. Wanting to make the papal city as glorious as the Rome of the Caesars, he left an indelible mark. In addition to the grandiose constructions he undertook and the cycles of frescoes he commissioned, he found time to amass a formidable collection of antiquities. While still a cardinal, Giuliano della Rovere succeeded in procuring a distinguished piece, the *Apollo Belvedere* which had been found at the end of the fifteenth century at Nettuno or Grottaferrata and which Poggio had seen in the palace of Prospero Colonna. When he became pope, Julius II transferred it from his *palazzo* near San Pietro in Vincoli to the Vatican. His most beautiful trophy was the *Laocoön*; this group of statuary was celebrated by the humanists even before they had seen it because it had been described by Pliny the Elder. In January 1506 it was found in a vineyard which covered the sites of the Baths of Titus and, below them, the *Domus Aureus* of Nero. Fearing the statue might be stolen, Julius II had it guarded at night. The *Laocoön* was truly the great discovery of the century; the day of its removal to the Vatican was proclaimed a holiday; the cannons of Castel Sant' Angelo thundered and church bells rang out over the entire city. Pope Julius displayed his antiquities in a garden laid out between the Belvedere Palace built by Innocent VIII and the new constructions of Bramante; clustered there were the *Apollo,* a *Hercules,* the famous *Torso*

Belvedere, a statue of *Commodus,* a *Sleeping Ariadne* and personifications of the *Tiber* and the *Nile.* The numerous drawings and paintings by Flemish artists depicting that garden of antiquities are proof of the attraction it had for foreigners who visited Rome. Leo X, succeeding Julius II, busied himself with organizing on a more national basis the conservation of monuments and the acquisition of statuary. He appointed Raphael superintendent of antiquities, putting under his direction the Capitoline and Vatican museums as well as the program for the excavation and conservation of antique monuments. The artist was further burdened with the task of surveying and drafting plans for a restoration of the antique city, a project he never had time to complete. From this period dates a report addressed to the pope about the vandalism which was destroying the ancient city; it is this report that contains the well-known criticism against "Gothic" *(Tedesco)* art as the art of the ignorant. Since 1799 tradition has been inclined to attribute the report to Raphael but recently the probability of his authorship has been disputed.

The most determined collector of antiquities in Rome was Pope Paul III. As Cardinal Farnese, he persuaded Alexander VI to allow his exploitation of ruins near San Lorenzo Fuori le Mura, preparatory to laying the foundations for his *palazzo.* They yielded a mine of antiquities; from the wall of one ancient fortress he recovered twenty busts of emperors. After having obtained from the pope the rights to all the statuary he could carry away in one night, he is said to have mobilized a force of seven hundred ox-drawn wagons to transport his windfall. Elected pope in 1534, he continued his investigations—that is he stripped several more sites and monuments: the gardens of Caesar, the Forum of Trajan, the Temple of Neptune, the Baths of Diocletian and the Baths of Caracalla, one monument which still retains some of its marble revetments. No more than treasure hunts, the excavations destroyed more history than they unearthed. The enormous collections amassed by Paul III were not destined to enrich the papacy; after passing through the hands of various Farnese heirs, most of them were eventually placed in the Museo Nazionale in Naples in 1787.

The embryo of the historical museum was contained in collections which, following the medieval fashion, brought together portraits of the twelve Caesars but now with more historical confidence. Petrarch had already grouped together coins of the Caesars which he offered to Emperor Charles IV. Numismatics had long provided the material for these series. The first rational undertaking of a museum of great men was that of Duke Federico da Montefeltro († 1482), the most accomplished prince of his century, a man of letters as well as of war, and such a paragon of refinement that all of Italy sent young nobles to him to learn the art of being a gentleman. He had laid out for himself in his palace at Urbino a little room or *studiolo,* designed not to store books but to serve as a place for meditation and reading; its walls were sumptuously fitted with marquetry which showed still lifes symbolizing literature, the arts, science and war; above them were hung portraits of twenty-eight intellectuals, the most celebrated poets, philosophers and theologians of antiquity, the Middle Ages and the contemporary period. Scholars have now established that Justus of Ghent (Joos van Wassenhove) painted these representations which are today divided between Urbino and the Louvre, following an apportionment made by the family in 1812.

21. **The Vision of Saint Augustine, by Vittore Carpaccio.** *Scuola di San Giorgio degli Schiavoni, Venice. Detail. Traditionally considered to represent Saint Jerome who, in the XVth century was the patron of the Humanists and whose history Carpaccio was commissioned to depict on the walls of the Scuola, this personage is now often considered to be Saint Augustine during an event in his life which corresponds to a similar episode in the life of Saint Jerome. Some scholars think that for the features of the saint Carpaccio's model was Cardinal Bessarion (1395?-1472) who, soon after its foundation, was one of the principal benefactors of the brotherhood. In any case, Carpaccio fashioned the saint's cell after the study of a Humanist during the Renaissance, filled with books, antique bronzes and scientific instruments.*

Collectors of antiquities were already numerous in Rome by the beginning of the sixteenth century. In 1509 Francesco Albertini drew up a long list of them in his *Opusculum de mirabilibus novae et veteris Urbis Romae*. The intense search for works of art gave rise to fierce competition. Giovanni Cristoforo Romano of Milan wrote. "A great many people are interested in these things [antiquities] but it is difficult to procure them. If one is fortunate enough to be the first to espy a piece, one must then buy it on the spot; they ask high prices..." In 1507 Giorgio Negroponte observed, "The moment an object is dug up, a host of buyers miraculously appears. They give eight or ten ducats for rusty medallions which they resell later for twenty-five or thirty..."

Fearing theft, owners often re-buried their antiquities. When an artist or collector died, there was a rush to loot his treasures. Italian princes felt no scruples about plundering war-torn cities of their countrymen for rare pieces. During the pillaging of Lorenzo de'Medici's collections in Florence, his own brother-in-law, Bernardo Rucellai, made off with choice antiques to ornament his famous *Orti oricellarii,* where the Academy of Plato convened. The sack of Rome, provoking the greediness of collectors all over Italy, touched off a redistribution of art treasures among the princely courts of the peninsula. When Duchess Isabella d'Este, wife of Giovan Francesco II Gonzaga of Mantua, was informed of Cesare Borgia's capture of Urbino and the subsequent flight of her sister-in-law, Elizabeth Gonzaga, she hurriedly wrote to her brother Ippolito d'Este to procure for her from the ducal palace a Venus and a Cupid which she wanted for her own *studiolo*. In the absence of originals, collectors contented themselves with copies, often in miniature; Isabella d'Este filled her *grotta* with a collection of small-scale bronze reproductions of celebrated antique statues. The duchess was passionately fond of works of art but lacked the funds to buy them. She compensated for her pecuniary difficulties with obstinacy and ruthless opportunism, even at the expense of relatives ruined or banished from their duchies by the vicissitudes of politics. Her letters detail for us her many disappointments; we learn of her unsuccessful attempts to procure a Giorgione and a van Eyck; because of their prices she was forced to pass up some coveted intaglios, vases and cameos. She was inconsolable at having been robbed by Barbary pirates of precious objects she had on her person when she fled during the sack of Rome by imperial troops in 1527; she succeeded in buying back some pieces when they turned up on the Venetian market and asked travelers to Tunis to look for a Hercules and a Venus in marble which she was especially eager to redeem. This imperious woman was often unkind to her artists, threatening them with imprisonment when they were slow to perform. For a long while Isabella schemed to get a marble bust of the Empress Faustina in the collection of Mantegna, the favorite painter of the Gonzagas and the one who had decorated her *studiolo* with two of its most beautiful paintings; it was the very piece the artist most preferred but, sick and in debt, he was finally forced to give in to her demands; six weeks later he died, at the age of seventy-five.

The whole of Isabella's museum was divided between the *studiolo* and the *grotta* directly below it. Confined to one part of the immense ducal palace, with a minuscule *giardino segreto* adjoining it, the retreat was not intended for use as living quarters but as a place for delectation where the duchess went to pass calm hours in an atmosphere of luxury and beauty resting from the fatigues of her active life. Now stripped of its works of art, this *ritiro* evokes in its abandon a melancholy memory of a knowledgeable and refined woman who set the style for her time. A virtuous wife, impassioned mother and veritable statesman who governed for her weak husband, Isabella succeeded in avoiding the political imbroglio in Italy and in the general tumult caused by the French invasion and the rivalries of Milan, Venice, Florence and Rome, was adroit enough to save the duchy of the Gonzagas.

RITRATTO DEL MVSEO DI FERRANTE IMPERATO

Chapter 4

Mannerism

In the last few years the concept of the Renaissance era has been severely constrained so that it no longer encompasses both the fifteenth and the sixteenth centuries. If the term is taken to mean the movement of ideas which, after having promoted rationalism found its artistic conclusion in classicism, then the Renaissance knew its "primitivism" in the *quattrocento* and its apogee under the pontificates of Julius II and Leo X.

It is natural to limit the scope of a term to the generations that invented it. Sustained by his belief in the enlightenment generated by the restoration of the ideas of antiquity, the man of 1430 truly had the impression of experiencing a "rebirth" after the dark shadows of the Middle Ages. For an Italian in 1530 the Middle Ages were already too remote in time for him to feel consciously opposed to that period of barbarism. For him, "Barbarism" had a geographical rather than a chronological significance. Like the Greeks, the Italians tended to attach the epithet to all that was not Italian, especially to northern Europe. Events of considerable importance supervened, profoundly modifying the equilibrium of the human soul. The man of the *quattrocento,* living within the confines of the city, could conceivably feel that he was at the center of the universe and that his thought dominated the world. Then, in 1492 Christopher Columbus discovered America; other men and other lands arose from the unknown and the field of human consciousness was abruptly widened. Forty years later another, infinitely more serious shock unsettled the simple humanism of the time. Copernicus, in 1543, published his *De Revolutionibus orbium cœlestium Libri VI*. Not only was man no longer the center of the world but the world itself, which until then he had believed to be the axis of the universe, was dispossessed from its privileged position by the sun.

Man, the deposed king, could regain his sovereignty only by attempting to embrace the infinite in thought. Henceforth a humanist was truly a "universalist," priding himself on his possession of the world through the intellect. His omnivorous appetite for knowledge extended to all kinds of questions about the earth and the heavens but a science still in its infancy could supply few answers to his ardent demands. He experienced anguish before such incomprehensibility and to him the world seemed a mystery, a situation which explains the revival of magic and sorcery and the sudden

22. **The Natural History cabinet of the Neapolitan naturalist and chemist Ferrante Imperato.** *After an engraving in his* Dell'Historia Naturale *(Naples, 1599). Paris, Bibliothèque Nationale. This is an example of the natural history cabinets where humanists assembled collections of animals, fossils and minerals.*

prosperity of alchemists and astrologers. Irrationality began a vehement offensive against the beautiful, rational edifice of fifteenth-century thought, pure as a church by Giuliano da Sangallo and a recent historian could characterize this epoch as an "anti-Renaissance."

Even architecture was to bear traces of this bizarre taste. Sixteenth-century man, escaping his severe palaces closed in upon themselves, began in the humanist period to create houses and gardens filled with fantasy, the *palazzi del giardino*, the *delizie*, each an attempt at a *mundus symbolicus*. A fine example is the Villa d'Este at Tivoli which is well preserved today, unlike the villa which Buontalenti built for Francesco I de' Medici, Grand Duke of Tuscany, at Pratolino where stones, trees and rocky ground yielded themselves to all the intellectual subtleties of which Florentines of the Mannerist period were capable. The *Apennino* of Giovanni da Bologna, in the English garden laid out in the eighteenth century by the Lorraine, remains today as a lone example of the games which men of that time believed approached in some measure the reality of things whose meaning escaped them. A still more remarkable example is the cabinet of Francesco I in the Palazzo Vecchio in Florence; it is an obscure room, almost a cavern, consecrated by the duke, fascinated with alchemy and astrology, to the four elements.

Man, in all of this, lost none of his arrogance. A new curiosity about the past incited humanists of the time to examine history which seemed to them to have been created by great men rather than by nations. Such feelings inspired an astonishing collection, that of a prelate in Como, Paolo Giovio, humanist, historian and Latinist (1483-1552). About 1520 he began building up an immense collection of portraits in his residence at Como; it was divided into four categories, one grouping effigies of dead poets and scholars; another, those of living poets and scholars; a third, those of artists; and the fourth, those of men in politics: great militarists, statesmen, papal sovereigns and monarchs. Paolo Giovio's sport was hunting icons. Agents throughout Europe tracked down documents for him; renowned contemporary figures, such as Hernando Cortez who sent him his portrait, vied for a place in his museum. There were few originals among the paintings in the gallery; most of the portraits were copies or even reconstitutions based on medals, frescoes or miniatures. Paolo Giovio called his museum "*Sanctissimo tempio dell'immortal virtù sede sacrata.*" Under each portrait there were Latin inscriptions (*Elogia*). The museum quickly became famous; its contents were widely known through engravings published at Florence (1551), at Paris (1552) and at Basel (1577). Paolo Giovio's initiative was one of the elements which inspired Vasari to undertake a history of Italian art by the biographical method (his *Lives of the Most Excellent Architects, Painters and Sculptors* appeared in 1550). Princes, like Cosimo I de' Medici and Ferdinand of Tyrol, sent artists to copy the paintings. The *museum jovianum* was, for a long while, the established iconography of celebrated personages; the organizers of the historical museum at Versailles during the time of Louis-Philippe returned to it as their model. As recently as thirty years ago history texts in European schools were influenced by it. Only the taste for original documents which developed after World War II was able to sweep away its last traces.

In the sixteenth century amateurism became one of the requisites of the princely life, so indispensable to what we would call today a "man of the world" that treatises on *savoir-vivre* offered counsel on the subject.

23. **Portrait of Paolo Giovio.** *From the Basel edition of the* Elogia virorum bellica virtute illustrium *(1575-1577). The first historical museum was assembled by this humanist in his residence at Como.*

Related to the great Baldassare Castiglione who was the author of the famous *Il Cortegiano* (1528), Sabba de Castiglione, a Milanese gentleman who died in 1554 at the age of sixty-nine, conceived his memoirs (*Ricordi*) as lessons in good breeding for the use of gentlemen. *Ricordo* 109 is entitled "*Circa gli ornamenti della casa.*" One's house, according to one's own taste could contain different kinds of cabinets which grouped together: *a*) musical instruments; *b*) antique sculptures or, lacking them, works by Donatello; *c*) sculptures by Michelangelo or Giovanni Cristoforo Romano or their contemporaries; *d*) antique medallions or, if need be, modern ones in gold, silver or bronze; *e*) portraits or paintings by Fra Filippo Lippi, Mantegna, Bellini, Perugino, Raphael, Leonardo, Giulio Romano; *f*) intarsias by Fra Giovanni di Monte Oliveto or Fra Raffaello da Brescia; *g*) hangings from Arras, tapestries from Flanders, carpets from Turkey or Barbary or painted fabrics; *h*) copper engravings or woodcuts by Italian and German artists, particularly Albrecht Dürer and Lucas van Leyden.

Modern works figured only in the absence of antiquities in this ideal collection; though Michelangelo might enjoy the privilege of being represented as himself, Donatello was no more than a substitute for the ancients. The Antique retained its prestige in the presence of the Natural. Antiquities were searched for with passion; forgeries were made, particularly for export; sumptuous galleries were built to house sculptures exhumed from Italian soil. The oldest building still in existence which was constructed for use as a museum is an *antiquarium*; an annex to the *Casino del Giardino* in the curious town of Sabbioneta, it is almost an evocation in miniature of Mantuan pageantry which was built by the youngest of the Gonzaga family, Vespasiano, Duke of Sabbioneta (1531-1591). In a long gallery constructed between 1580 and 1584, Vespasiano placed statues, bas-reliefs and busts which were, for the most part, spoils brought back by his father, Rodomonte, from the sack of Rome in 1527. The decoration, completed in 1590, was conceived to complement the antiquities (which were, however, carried off to Mantua in 1774 at the time of the Austrian rule); the effect of perspective in the gallery was accentuated by two *trompe-l'œil* paintings.

57

Sabba de Castiglione, born about 1485, was, when he wrote his memoirs, somewhat reactionary, even *démodé*. The kind of collection he recommended contained only works of art but the collections formed by the grand dukes of Tuscany in Florence (which, frustrated by Rome in her role as pioneer in the world of the arts, became the great center of Mannerism in Italy) give us a more exact idea of the complexity of the *ornamenti della casa* during that period. The first grand duke, Cosimo I, found it difficult to retrieve the ancestral collections, victims of three pillages: in 1492 when the rabble invaded the palace of Lorenzo the Magnificent, in 1527 when the reassembled collections were sacked by Leo X and in 1537 when Alessandro was assassinated and his palace devastated. To the works he was able to recover, Cosimo added artifacts found in excavations of Etruscan sites; in 1554 he acquired the *Chimera* of Arezzo and ten years later a likeness of the orator Aulus Metullus which was discovered near Lake Trasimeno. This interest in Etruria revealed the desire of the Florentines to resurrect an antiquity of their own, different from that of the Romans and more ancient. Engrossed in history, Cosimo I sent the painter Cristofano dell'Altissimo to Como to copy the 280 portraits in the *museum jovianum* ; Cristofano worked there for sixteen years (from 1552 to 1568) and the fruit of his labors was the famous *Museo mediceo* which, until World War II, graced the corridor which links the Palazzo Pitti with the Uffizi. Cosimo found ill-suited to ducal dignity the modest bourgeois palace built on the Via Larga by Michelozzo for Cosimo the Elder. He installed himself in the Palazzo Vecchio and, in 1559, commissioned another palace opposite it to house the administrative offices of the Tuscan state: *il palazzo degli Uffizi*. For the marriage of Francesco de'Medici, Vasari constructed within five months in 1564 the immense corridor which (in imitation of the one mentioned in *The Iliad* which connected Hector's palace to that of Priam) spanned the Arno River and connected the Uffizi to the Palazzo Pitti, a *palazzo del giardino* bought by Cosimo's wife, Eleanora de Toledo in 1549 and, at the duke's wish, enlarged by Bartolommeo Ammanati.

After the death of Cosimo I in 1574, the Grand Duke Francesco I decided to regroup the collections, using for exhibition space the upper stories of the Uffizi where Cosimo had installed his artisans. Buontalenti was the mastermind for the project; he had the halls decorated with vivid paintings and he himself designed the marble decor for the famous *tribuna,* the composition of which we know through a description in an inventory drawn up in 1589, two years after the death of Francesco I. The walls were covered with works by Piero di Cosimo, Andrea del Sarto, Pontormo, Sodoma, Cristoforo Allori, Raphael (*Portrait of Leo X, John the Baptist, Madonna della Sedia*). Antiquities were dispersed through the halls. The successor of Francesco I was his brother Ferdinand I, in 1587; the latter while a cardinal in Rome, erected a magnificent residence, the Villa Medici, a sort of *villa-museo* with façades encrusted with innumerable antique bas-reliefs. The interior was filled with admirable antiquities which were transported to Florence in 1775: the famous Medici *Venus* found at Hadrian's Villa at Tivoli, the *Arrotino* and the group of Niobids, copies in the style of Scopas which were discovered in 1583 near the Porta San Paolo.

A commentary by Filippo Pigafetta on a *canzone* by G. B. Elicona, composed on the occasion of the marriage of Marie de'Medici to Henry IV of France, contains a description of the museum in the Uffizi in 1600. In the east loggia were antique and Renaissance sculptures and the historical museum of portraits of the Medici family, painted by

24. **The Antiquarium,** *annex to the* Casino del Giardino *in Sabbioneta, near Mantua, Italy. This long gallery was laid out between 1580 and 1584 by the youngest of the Gonzaga family, Vespasiano, to house his collection of antique statues and reliefs. It adjoins his pleasure palace, the* Casino del Giardino.

25. **The Chimera of Arezzo.** *Fifth-century Etruscan bronze. Archeological Museum, Florence. Believing that ancient Tuscany had boasted a civilization different from that of Rome, Florentine Humanists began searching for Etruscan works of art towards the end of the 15th century. The* Chimera of Arezzo *was acquired by Grand Duke Cosimo I in 1554.*

Bronzino either from life or retrospectively, and the *"giovannina"* collection made up of copies from the *museum jovianum*. The *tribuna* housed the most celebrated paintings and Greek and Roman medallions and coins. In another room were "precious objects from nature and art." The attic stored antique and modern armor, both domestic and foreign, and sundry instruments for mathematics, physics, geometry and astronomy. In the *loggia dei lanzi* the grand duke established a laboratory for alchemy.

To these riches must be added the "Medici treasury," comprising objects in silver, gold, cut glass and porphyry as well as cameos, antique intaglios, gems and enamels. This collection was started by Lorenzo the Magnificent and added to by the first grand dukes. Florentine goldsmiths, as well as many foreigners working in the city, prospered under lavish ducal patronage. Although subjected to many expropriations over the course of the centuries, especially by the Austrians, the diminished treasure still arouses the admiration of visitors to the *Museo degli Argenti* in the Pitti Palace. Gem cutting became a specialty of Florence; artisans virtuosic in the art were summoned from Spain and France. Francesco I spurred his artists and alchemists to discover new techniques and he himself found a laboratory method for smelting rock crystal. Thanks to him, the art of porcelain manufacture was discovered in Florence and was ready to spread to the rest of Europe by the end of the *cinquecento*. Known through imports from China since the fourteenth century, this translucent material which combined the qualities of porcelain and glass seemed magical. By the beginning of the sixteenth century, perhaps earlier, alchemists and artisans in Venice were endeavoring to make *porcellana ficta*. Around 1575 Bernardo Buontalenti, working for Francesco I, discovered the secret of making the paste, the recipe for which has been preserved. Ceramists immediately began to exploit his discovery but, at the death of the grand duke, manufacture was curtailed and pieces produced up until that time became exceedingly rare. Francesco himself did not disdain working as an artisan; the

26. **The Tribuna of the Uffizi,** *Florence, as it looked before 1914. Decorated by Bernardino Poccetti with a dado of precious marble and crowned with a curious cupola encrusted with shells, the Tribuna housed, from the end of the XVIth century to the beginning of the XXth century, the rarest pieces of the grand ducal collection.*

Frenchman Montaigne, visiting Florence in 1580, observed that the grand duke delighted "in trying to copy Oriental stones or to work crystal, being a prince who is interested in everything from architecture and the mechanical arts to alchemy."

Cosimo II undertook the colossal enterprise of decorating with a mosaic of precious stones the entire inner walls of a rotunda more than ninety feet in diameter, the *capella dei Principi de San Lorenzo,* a gigantic chapel faced with lapis lazuli, marble, bronze, nacre and coral where all that is suited to a *bibelot* is shown on a monumental scale. The ateliers established to carry out this enormous task, started in 1604, are the basis of the *opificio delle pietre dure,* a factory still active in Florence.

Art, history, nature—each had its place in the Medici collections which, taken as a whole, were the quintessence of that *teatro totale* of which humanists in the mannerist epoch dreamed. Cosimo I formed a cabinet devoted to natural history, containing actual animals, shells, fossils and minerals as well as casts made from nature by Della Robbia and Riccio in the beginning of the sixteenth century; there were albums of botanical and zoological drawings, many by Francesco d'Umbertino, il Bacchiacca, who was employed by the grand duke expressly for this work. The most remarkable of these draftsmen near the end of the century was the Veronese, Jacopo Ligozzi, who became court painter for the grand dukes; his seventy-odd water colors preserved in the *Gabinetto Disegni e stampi* in Florence number among the most beautiful ever executed in that realistic style which attempted to hold up a mirror to nature. The archdukes helped the Bolognese naturalist Ulisse Aldrovandi to assemble his famous *Natural History* which comprised at least 2,000 drawings of plants, 2,000 of animals and 4,500 of minerals and gems, in large part the work of mediocre illustrators whose poverty of talent grieved Aldrovandi.

Although European flora and fauna were not neglected, it was the botany and zoology of the "Indies," introduced into the princely gardens, that most attracted scholars. Aldrovandi was a great admirer of Mexican feathered pieces, going so far as to find them "more beautiful than works by Apelles." All these exotic manifestations were associated with, in the imaginations of the erudite of the time, the *Historia Naturalis* of Pliny, which encouraged a taste for the monstrous but which is not so much, as Baltrusaïtis said, a resurgence of medievalism but rather a specific expression of the mannerist period which was obsessed with penetrating the mysteries of nature and was prepared by the *Metamorphoses* of Ovid to expect the faculty of limitless creation to manifest its profound essence more explicitly in monsters than in normal creatures. The Italy of that time was a center for prodigious activity in diametrically opposed directions. After the experience of classicism, the humanists of the peninsula gave free rein to the most irrational speculations about nature. The prestige of the works of art then produced in Italy exposes us to the danger of a distorted view of the collections there during the second half of the sixteenth century; we would be too much inclined to find, for the most part, art museums as opposed to the German collections which would be richer in natural curiosities. In fact, Italian princes were no less passionate than the Germans in their quest for the rare and *al peregrino,* filling whole rooms in their palaces with curiosities—mineralogical, botanical, zoological, teratological, mathematical, physical and chemical. Such a room was not thought of, as in Germany, as a *Wunderkammer* which is the exact equivalent of the French *chambre des merveilles*. Despite all his interest in natural phenomena the Italian reserved his wonder for works by man, calling this kind of cabinet simply: *museo naturale*. One historian counted no fewer than two hundred and fifty such museums of natural history in sixteenth-century Italy.

France was the first country in northern Europe to be influenced profoundly by the new spirit. For her the conquest of Italy was the opportunity to show herself for the first time as a major European power in wars of invasion; even the delusion of grandeur which led her to confront the Holy Roman Empire did not, in the end, harm her politically. The first contact took place during the Neopolitan expedition of Charles VIII; when he retreated from Italy, he was able to save only a small part of booty, having been forced to abandon his immense baggage, supplies and the royal treasure in order to escape the troops of the Italian League under the command of Francesco Gonzaga at Fornovo in July 1495. However, the "specialists" with whom he had surrounded himself followed Charles to France; the records of payment to Italian workers at Amboise in 1497 and 1498 inform us about this eccentric band which was composed of a few true artists and artisans but also included hairdressers, *parfumeurs* and *"des hommes habiles à faire éclore les poulets."*

62

By the beginning of the sixteenth century Italian paintings were finding their way to France. A *Madonna of the Spindles* by Leonardo—lost today—provoked great excitement when it was bought by the financier Florimond Robertet. Louis XII, unsuccessful at procuring the services of the great painter, was obliged to seek him out in Milan. It is quite possible that the king brought back some works by Leonardo to France; some historians think such was the case with the *Madonna of the Rocks,* now in the Louvre. However, the impulse to collect was strongest in Francis I, whom Louis Dimier calls "the father of curiosity in France," a description which somewhat diminishes his role. Francis, like Louis XIV a little later, wanted to be the first in everything, in war as in love and in the patronage of literature and the arts. Without doubt he is the paragon of a sixteenth-century prince, as Duke Federico da Montefeltro of Urbino had been for the fifteenth century. In 1516 Francis I, victor at Marignano, succeeded where Louis XII had failed; he lured Leonardo da Vinci to the castle of Cloux near Amboise, where the artist died in 1519. The atelier of Leonardo formed the nucleus

27. **Leda and the Swan, after Michelangelo.** *National Gallery, London. This version of a picture by Michelangelo was carried to France by one of his pupils. It was sold to King Francis I. In 1625 Cassiano del Pozzo is said to have seen at Fontainebleau a painting on this subject which was attributed to Il Rosso. According to Piles and Florent Le Comte, Michelangelo's original was destroyed by des Noyer, Superintendent of Buildings from 1638 to 1643, who was overly prudish. Mariette refutes this opinion, saying that he had seen the painting attributed to Michelangelo and that it was sent to England. In truth one finds at the sale of the Sir Joshua Reynolds collection on March 17, 1795, under the name of Michelangelo, a* Leda *which showed indications that it had been in royal French collections and also in the collection of the Earl of Spencer. The latter bought it in 1742. The painting was offered to the National Gallery by the Duke of Northumberland in 1838.*

of the royal cabinet of paintings; although we cannot assign an exact date to the king's taking possession of the paintings, we do know that his collections included *La Gioconda,* the *Saint Anne* and a *John the Baptist,* which might have been the half-length representation of the saint or the one transformed into a Bacchus in the seventeenth century. Another Leonardo owned by the king was a *Leda* which was later destroyed as immoral. In 1536 he bought still another *Leda,* a work by Il Rosso in the style of Michelangelo but this too disappeared, another victim of prudery. The king acquired many pictures by Andrea del Sarto who worked at the court; he commissioned Titian to paint his portrait from a medal; he obtained a *Visitation* by Sebastiano del Piombo. Diplomatic gifts further swelled the collection; Pope Leo X offered him *The Holy Family* and *Saint Michael* by Raphael (dated 1517 and 1518) through Lorenzo II de'Medici, Duke of Urbino, as intermediary. The king received as a gift from Cardinal Bibiena Raphael's *Portrait of Joanna of Aragon,* which after a recent cleaning under my direction reveals itself as an unrestored work of admirable quality, contradicting the tradition which attributes it to a collaborative effort with Giulio Romano. According to Vasari, Cosimo I, Grand Duke of Tuscany, commissioned from Bronzino *An Allegory of Time and Love* (now in the National Gallery, London) as a gift to the French king.

More than anything, however, Francis I wanted *antiquailles,* those trifling curiosities without which no collection at that time was considered complete. He sent Andrea del Sarto on a buying mission to Rome but the artist never returned, kept the money and sent nothing. The king fared better with Francesco Primaticcio, who arrived at Fontainebleau in 1532, one year after Il Rosso. Dispatched to Rome in 1540, the Bolognese returned with one hundred thirty-three cases containing one hundred twenty-five statues, busts and torsos as well as molds of the most celebrated antiquities in Rome. Giacomo da Vignola, then a young and unknown architect who had accompanied Primaticcio to Fontainebleau, supervised the casting of rather crude bronzes from the molds. In the seventeenth century the Kellers, foundry workers for Louis XIV, were to bring perfection to this art. The Louvre preserves some of the casts, among them the *Laocoön, Ariadne Sleeping,* the *Hercules Commodus* and the *Spinario.* Only one original has thus far been identified, the *Diane à la biche* carried off to the Château at Meudon by Anne de Pisseleu, Duchesse d'Étampes. An unknown painter at work during the reign of Henry II must have drawn inspiration from it for his *Diana the Huntress* at the Louvre, doubtlessly an allegorical portrait of Diane de Poiters.

Antiquities were immediately restored or, so to speak, "completed," as was the custom in Italy since the fifteenth century. The interest in bronze copies was nourished by the Neoplatonic concept of the Beautiful, current until the eighteenth century, whose advocates promulgated the Idea as opposed to Matter and consequently preferred replicas of masterpieces to mediocre originals.

There was an active trade in antiquities by the end of the fifteenth century, with French nobles avidly seeking them, especially busts of Roman emperors for their châteaux. One of the inescapable laws of curiosity manifested itself at that time: success breeds forgery. A remark made by the humanist Henri II Estienne is worth citing for its humorous denunciation of the impudence of counterfeiters; he coined the term *antiquaille,* based on the Italian *anticaglie,* a word which, when uttered, he said "makes one automatically reach for one's pocketbook." The Hellenist mocked the snobbery attached to antiquities: "Today the world is full of collectors of *antiquailles* at whose expense forgers prosper." Estienne recounted the adventure of one fool who, particularly attracted to a certain piece, found he had selected the hopeful dealer's eighty-year-old wife.

All the works amassed by the king were kept in the château at Fontainebleau: tapestries, precious metalwork, and contemporary Italian creations, such as the bronze *Nymph* of the Florentine Benvenuto Cellini who lived at the court. The palace, a creation of Francis I, was situated in a game-filled forest thirty miles east of Paris; later Vasari was to call it the "Rome of the North." Antique sculptures and bronze replicas graced the gardens. The most precious pictures were set into stucco in five vaulted chambers by Il Rosso. Cool in summer, easy to heat in winter, these rooms, laid out between 1541 and 1547 by Primaticcio, constituted the "baths" (which disappeared with Louis XV). There the sensuous monarch sought to refresh both body and spirit. It was a singular place for the conservation of paintings and the effects of injudicious restoration could already be seen. Before going to Rome, between 1538 and 1540, Primaticcio had cleaned a *Saint Michael,* a *Virgin* and a *Saint Margaret* by Raphael.

If the presentation was "mannerist," the composition of the collection of Francis I was classical, completely in the spirit of the Renaissance. The monarchs who succeeded him were to be more eclectic. The taste for things Italian waned under Henry II with the attitude prevailing that France had been able to create her own national style. When Henry II received as a gift from Roberto Strozzi in 1550 the two *Slaves* conceived by Michelangelo for the tomb of Julius II, he hastened to give them away to his favorite, Anne de Montmorency. Portrait collections became the vogue. At the French court the Clouets started the fashion for "having one's portrait done" either *aux trois craïons* or in oil, with the likenesses reduced to bust and face, expressive of man's consciousness of himself, concomitant with the Reformation and the impetus behind the moralistic literature of Montaigne. The representation in painting of the psychic life could have originated only in France. The taste for portraiture spread to all of Europe, with princely families exchanging likenesses; for that purpose several oil or chalk copies were made from the original portrait. The walls of small, specially designed salons were covered with these likenesses. Catherine de' Medici, who knew how to "*esquicher et pourtraire elle même,*" accumulated in her mansion (later the *hôtel de Soissons*) more than four hundred portraits, excluding her own crayon studies. They were installed in a number of apartments where they were set into the wood-paneled walls. In one room thirty-two portraits were paired with thirty-two Limoges enamels; in a "room of mirrors" eighty-three hung next to one hundred nineteen Venetian mirrors. In my installations for the Louvre in 1953 I tried to evoke one of these portrait galleries by using original frames and, in some cases, by making borders from old silver mirrors to recall discreetly the *cabinet des glaces.* A great number of the five hundred fifty-one portrait drawings owned by Catherine have been preserved for France as the result of a curious detour. They had been bequeathed by Catherine to Christine of Lorraine, the daughter of Ferdinand I de' Medici.

In the eighteenth century the English collector Sir Henry Howard bought three

28. **South American Rat, by Jacopo Ligozzi** (*c. 1547-1626*). *Water color. Cabinet of Drawings and Prints, Uffizi Museum, Florence. A leaf from the natural history collection executed by Ligozzi for Grand Duke Ferdinand II of Tuscany.*

29. **The Alchemist, by Giovanni Stradano.** *Detail. This picture figures in the cabinet of the Palazzo Vecchio, dedicated to the four elements and recalling the scientific and alchemistic researches of Grand Duke Francesco I of Tuscany.*

66

30. **Elisabeth de Valois, daughter of Henry II of France, drawing by François Clouet.** *Musée Condé, Chantilly, formerly in the cabinet of Catherine de' Medici. This is typical of the small portraits* aux trois craïons *or in oil that were the vogue at the time of Henry II and Henry III. Collectors accumulated them by the hundreds.*

hundred eleven of them which remained in the Howard castle until 1890 when the duke of Aumale purchased them for the collections of the Count of Carlisle at Chantilly.

Many princes followed Catherine's example but none outshone her. The taste for collections of historical portraits also spread through France. The *museum jovianum,* known through engravings, inspired emulation. André Thévet, a Franciscan friar, published a collection of copperplate engravings in 1584 entitled *Pourtraits et vie des Hommes illustres,* the fruit of careful documentation in which he criticized Paolo Giovo for the inadequacy of his historical method.

In the second half of the century "curiosities" began to accumulate at Fontainebleau, next to the works of art brought together by Francis I. These curiosities were kept in a cabinet in the donjon. Brother André Thévet, who had traveled in the Near East and Brazil, was named as their custodian by Charles IX. All the bric-a-brac inherent in this type of museum was kept in the cabinet; in addition to the Saint Servin cameo, there were many Chinese and Turkish objects as well as esoterica brought back by explorers and merchants from countries the world over and by Thévet himself from Brazil (for example, the Mexican robe of ibis feathers now in the Musée de l'Homme, Paris). The most extraordinary object was unquestionably a seven-headed hydra, the gift of the Venetian Republic to the king. In his 1642 inventory of the "treasury of wonders at Fontainebleau," Father Dan, caretaker of the château, listed the ruins of the hydra, noting that rats had eaten one of the heads. The hydra was, of course, the fabrication of some charlatan. Clever forgers supplied a knowledgeable but easily deceived clientele with monsters; the cockatrice, an animal with the head of a cock and tail of a serpent, widely used in medieval bestiaries as a symbol of the devil, was very much in demand. During the second half of the century an Italian by the name of Tartaglio turned them out in quantities as well as other kinds of stripe-skinned monsters.

The *"cabinet de curiositez"* was all the rage at court; Diane de Poitiers and the Montmorency and

33. **Slave, by Michelangelo.** *Louvre Museum, Paris. Conceived originally for the tomb of Julius II, two Slaves were sent as a gift to Henry II of France by Roberto Strozzi. They came to the Louvre as revolutionary plunder from the collections of the Duke de Richelieu.*

◀ 31. **Saint Anne, by Leonardo da Vinci.** *Detail. Louvre Museum, Paris. This is one of the three paintings mentioned by the secretary of the cardinal of Aragon as being in Leonardo's studio in the castle of Cloux at Amboise in 1517. Bought for Francis I, it was removed from the royal collections by Richelieu.*

◀ 32. **An Allegory of Time and Love, by Bronzino.** *National Gallery, London. This painting is undoubtedly identifiable with a work by Bronzino which Vasari is said to have sent to Francis I of France. It did not remain long in the royal collections and was acquired in Paris in 1860 by the National Gallery of London.*

Guise families all had one. The ceramist Bernard Palissy, who was the first to make geologic studies in France, had a cabinet of fossils, enamels and pottery. At Catherine de'Medici's *hôtel de Soissons* not far from the portraits and among the bibelots which filled the house from cellar to attic, one found crocodile skins, a chameleon, nuts from India, lacquers from China and mummies, whose ground-up ashes were supposed to ward off accidents.

The humanists imitated princes to whatever extent they were able. Not content to keep only the king's "*cabinet des raretez,*" Brother Thévet had his own collection of historical portraits (for the most part antique medallions and chalk drawings); to this he added natural curiosities brought back from his own voyages.

The introduction of the term *curieux* into the French language, with the connotation of amateur, can be dated exactly; it is found in a lexicon edited by Robert Estienne in 1538. He translates the term *antiquarius* as *ung homme curieux d'avoir ou sçavoir choses antiques;* it designates, therefore, a learned person as well as a collector and pertains to works of art of the past, principally to those of antiquity. In the second half of the century the meaning was broadened to include natural creations, which was ultimately to evolve as its primary meaning. *Antiquaire* in the seventeenth and eighteenth centuries referred to a connoisseur of antiquities rather than a collector. (In France the *Antiquaires de Normandie* and the *Société des antiquaires de France* have retained this meaning.) In English the term can be traced back at least to 1533 when John Leland was appointed royal antiquarian by Henry VIII. The word *amateur* (from the Latin *amator,* a lover, admirer or devotee) might be equated with the Latin *musarum cultor,* a cultivator or supporter of the muses. From *cavea,* which in Latin meant a hollow place or cavity, developed *cabinet,* a piece of furniture for the safekeeping of small objects, jewels, letters and intimate papers, later expanded to include small rooms where precious and rare objects were kept. By the eighteenth century the word also applied, in France, to gardens compartmented by shrubbery and in England to summer-

houses or bowers. *Cabinet* in French and English corresponds to the German *kammer* and is now associated with the idea of an art collection. Cabinets aroused such an interest among tourists that guides listed the collections and galleries to be seen in the cities they visited. At the end of the sixteenth century a certain Lacroix du Maine published a compendium of celebrated cabinets, of which we possess no more than its eloquent title: "The most renowned libraries and cabinets (which some call chambers of marvels) of France, with a listing of rare books, medallions, portraits, statues or effigies, precious gems or other niceties and curiosities seen in the houses of princes who collect such magnificences." Educated travelers, crisscrossing the whole of Europe, were attracted to all kinds of collections, libraries and galleries. Formed, for the most part, by artists, amateurs, aristocrats and scholars, they were liberally open to the public. One Gabriel Symeoni, on a visit to Rome in 1557, described in detail the new Villa Giulia, even recording the rules posted at the entrance for visitors; it seems there was, at certain hours, an admission fee. Pierre de Bourdeilles, seigneur de Brantôme, reports the same about the Paris residence of the Florentine Ghiaceti (or d'Adjacet). Overflowing with works of art, it was, according to the author of *Vies des dames galantes,* "the most beautiful, most superb house of the last century. Anyone could go to see it for a sou."

Heirs to Burgundian extravagance, the Hapsburgs found themselves in a position, by virtue of the location of their realms, to realize a synthesis of the different artistic currents in Europe. As early as the beginning of the sixteenth century, Margaret of Austria, regent of the Netherlands, set an example for refined taste by encouraging music, literature and painting; though her library was eclectic, her collection (which boasted Jan van Eyck's *The Marriage of Giovanni Arnolfini and Giovanna Cenami* now in London's National Gallery) contained only paintings by artists from the Low Countries.

Crowned emperor by the pope in 1530, Charles V played the role of a Maecenas more from necessity than from temperament; in his eyes it behooved the state to support artists. To be sure, he liked Titian but he did not set about collecting to satisfy any artistic taste nor to nourish a connoisseur's instinct. He was first and foremost a political man, preoccupied with maintaining an immense empire, the equilibrium of which was constantly being threatened by wars and religious struggles. The Fugger family, bourgeois Augsburg bankers, were more amateurs than was Charles, whose election they secured by bribing the electors.

Munich was the scene of the birth of amateurism in Central Europe. William IV, duke of Bavaria (reigning from 1508 to 1550), formed a cabinet of curiosities and commissioned humanist paintings like Altdorfer's *The Battle of Alexander on the Nissus River* (1529), one of the most philosophical pictures of the century. His successor Albert V (reigning from 1550 to 1579), married to Anne, daughter of Emperor Ferdinand (brother of Emperor Charles V), was profoundly affected by an Italian sojourn in his youth. This was the time when contact with Italian civilization was deemed indispensable to the forming of a prince. Albert resolutely introduced ultramontanism, or extended papal supremacy, into Munich. He set about collecting, without much personal taste however, an extraordinary group of curios and objects, totaling no fewer than 3,407 items, according to a catalog drawn up by Fickler in 1598: paintings,

34. **Gemma Augustea,** *cameo, circa 10 B.C. Kunsthistorisches Museum, Vienna. Purchased by Rudolf II, this cameo is the most beautiful piece from the emperor's* Schatzkammer. *It is a representation of the Emperor Augustus with a personification of Rome as a goddess, crowned by the* Orbis Romanus, *in commemoration of the victory of Tiberius over the Pannonians.*

35. **Nautilus mounted in a goldsmithery setting.** *Residenzmuseum, Munich. Made about 1570 by Wenzel Jamnitzer (1518-1585) for Duke Albert V of Bavaria. An example of the manner in which natural curiosities were often given an extravagant presentation.*

drawings, engravings, coins, ivories, armor and glassware. We are especially indebted to him for his encouragement of the minor arts, particularly goldsmithing. He bought countless antiques (among them a great number of counterfeits) and had a large gallery built to hold them, which his successors transformed into a ballroom between 1586 and 1600, following plans by Friedrich Sustris. This oldest museological structure in Europe was partly destroyed in the 1944 bombings but has since been rebuilt. The antiquities, even more than at Sabbioneta, are here incorporated into a mannerist decor, somewhat like cameos set in a coffer. The Bavarian world is joined to an evocation of antiquity through a series of frescoes representing cities and villages of the duchy.

The first Hapsburg who seems to have been possessed by the demon of collecting was an archduke of Austria, Ferdinand of Tyrol (1529-1595); he was given Castle Ambras near Innsbruck by his father, Emperor Ferdinand I in 1563. He filled the castle with divers collections which, until most were removed to Vienna in 1806, constituted, so to speak, a sanctuary of mannerism in Europe. All the elements of a princely cabinet of the time were there: a *Kunstkammer* or art gallery, a *Schatzkammer* or treasury of objects in precious metals, a *Wunderkammer* or cabinet devoted to natural curiosities, a *Rüstkammer* or wardrobe for parade armor and a history museum. The art gallery was the least developed. One of the most precious treasures in the *Schatzkammer* was a gold saltcellar made by Benvenuto Cellini which had been bought by Francis I and given by Charles IX to his brother-in-law Ferdinand upon the occasion of his marriage to Elizabeth of Austria; Charles also presented a gold chalice; tapestries from the Fontainebleau atelier, which today are unique pieces; and the monarch's own portrait by François Clouet. It is fortunate that the famous saltcellar left France where, during the course of the centuries, most objects in precious metal were melted down; the gift made by Charles IX has preserved it for our admiration.

The history museum contained copies made for Ferdinand between 1576 and 1579 and was based on the *museum jovianum* at Como. The *Rüstkammer* is a peculiarly Germanic type of collection and is strongly appreciated in Eastern Europe. The Kremlin Museum owes its origins to a *Rüstkammer* and is still called an "arms museum." During the mannerist period European princes were fond of elaborately tooled and damascened armor which took years to make. Innsbruck was one of the great centers of production, rivaling Milan and Nuremberg. The catalog of the *Rüstkammer* at Ambras was published in 1601 under the title *Armameritiorum heroicum serenissimi principis Ferdinandi Archiduci*. The collection included a whole array of the prince's own parade and tournament armor; Turkish armatures; the ceremonial helmet, shield and sword of Emperor Charles V; suits of fluted Maximilian armor as well as others *à la polonaise*; and Alessandro Farnese's parade armor designed by Piccinino. Almost all of the pieces are now in Vienna, with the exception of one very beautiful suit preserved in the Musée de l'Armée in Paris, the gilt armor which belonged to Francis I. This sumptuous armor was commissioned in 1539 from the Innsbruck workshop of Jörg Seusenhofer by Emperor Charles V's brother, Ferdinand I, king of Bohemia and Hungary and archduke of Austria, as a gift for the king of France; however, an armature of such splendor took a long time to execute; before it was finished, Charles was at war with Francis and so the French king never received it.

36. **Gallery of Antiques in the Residenz, Munich.** *Built for Duke Albert V between 1569 and 1571, this gallery was transformed into a reception hall between 1586 and 1600 with lavish new decorations which incorporated the statues into the decor.*

In 1583 it was listed in an inventory of Ambras Castle. On February 9, 1806 it was noticed by Napoleon as he returned to Vienna at the head of his armies and was ordered sent to Paris where it was eventually united with the sword surrendered by Francis I at Pavia and carried off to Madrid and finally given royal honors by Napoleon. Hitler had the celebrated armature returned to Austria in 1940; when French troops found it near Innsbruck in 1945, they returned the coveted trophy to Paris, to the Musée des Invalides.

Without doubt the richest collection in Ambras Castle was that of the *Wunderkammer*; it contained a superabundance of everything which was supposed to be in this kind of collection: optical tools, musical tools, instruments and mechanical clocks which were made by German artisans and were vied for throughout all Europe. There were collections of various games, costumes and exotic objects. The castle's 1596 inventory mentioned two "*Indianisch tuech*" which are the two Chinese paintings of the Ming Period (a landscape and aquatic birds) still preserved in the Museum of Natural History in Vienna. Among the exotic objects were ivory horns and spoons from Benin, an African kingdom discovered by the Portuguese which had an active trade with Europe at this time in ironwork and carved ivory. The *naturalia* included a great number of freaks or monsters, the accidents of nature which were thought to have a quasi-metaphysical character which might give an insight into the secret of the universe. Abnormal fetuses, which were very much in demand, were well represented; if they were human, they were believed to have been produced by dreams during conception or pregnancy, a belief still held by some, even today. The strange attraction for dwarfs and fools, a taste the Spanish court kept until the eighteenth century, was explained thus: these deformed creatures were "marvels of nature." At Ambras there was a section of portraiture devoted to dwarfs, giants and cripples; the portraits of some of these *Wundermenschen* still survive, among them that of Früher von München and his daughter, veritable "dog people" with an overdeveloped pilose system.

37. **Various objects in silver at Ambras Castle.** *Amongst these objects can be seen in the background a carved rhinoceros horn; in the center is a bezoar (calcareous stone from the stomach of Tibetan goats) set in silver. The rhinoceros horn and the bezoar were said to be protections against poison and sickness.*

Mannerism was at its glittering best on the eve of its waning at the court of Emperor Rudolf II at the end of the century. Archduke of Austria, king of Hungary and of Bohemia, he chose Prague as his official imperial residence upon his election as king of the Romans in 1576. He was a wretched statesman; in concession after concession he lost his domains and was finally deposed by his brother Matthias who succeeded him in 1612. Disinterested in power, this Saturnian prince devoted himself to learning; preoccupied with astrology, he protected the Danish astronomer Tycho Brahe and the great Johannes Kepler who was his astrologer and imperial mathematician; at that time observation of the stars was linked with the art of foretelling the future. Artists from all over Europe, especially from the Netherlands, Germany and Italy, converged on Rudolf's court at Prague. At Hradcany Castle he formed a fabulous collection which was to have a disastrous fate. A true Hapsburg, he was interested in many kinds of European art, in Titian's *Danaë* as much as in Dürer's *Martyrdom of the 10,000 Christians*; he particularly liked Dürer and Bruegel, whose works he had in abundance. His most glorious trophy had been Dürer's *Madonna of the Rosary*, painted for the Church of San Bartolommeo in Venice; he paid an enormous sum for it and, because of its fragility, took great precautions in transporting it: enveloped in sheets, linen and carpeting, it was carried by hand from Venice to Prague. Rudolf's *Schatzkammer* contained some of the most precious examples of German metalwork as well as admirable antique pieces; it was he who bought the famous *Gemma augustea*. He commissioned a crown and scepter for himself (today conserved in the treasury of the Hofburg, Vienna) which were among the last great works produced by mannerist goldsmiths.

His preferred painters reveal to us something of his intellectual interests. He sent to Milan for Arcimboldo, who was his master of ceremonies for festivals and who, for the edification of the court, painted those "composite heads" which were not meant as clever conceits but represented an effort to express the existence of a profound unity between man and the world. It was probably not on his own initiative that the Milanese painter undertook these bizarre figures because his work before he left Italy was quite modest, but was rather at the instigation of the emperor or of some erudite at court who was tormented by the problem of the essence of things. Rudolf's melancholy spirit found itself in intimate accord with Dürer's. The art of Bruegel corresponded exactly to the philosophical position of mannerist humanism with its universalist tendencies. Other artists at Rudolf's court ardently studied natural creations with the hope of understanding the essence of nature itself through the analysis of its forms. Two such artists were the nomadic Fleming Joris Hoefnagel, whose motto was *"Natura sola magister,"* and the Nuremberger Hoffmann, to whom reality meant Dürer. He so completely adopted the latter's style that he eventually made pastiches dated and signed with the famous monogram, thus supplying the great market demand for Dürers.

It is not surprising that Rudolf II, surrounded as he was by alchemists and astrologers, had at Hradcany one of the most fabulous *Wunderkammern* of the epoch. He collected tools of magic, mandrake roots, deformed fetuses, bizarre animals, monsters and bezoars. Calcareous concretions formed in the stomachs of a certain kind of Persian mountain goat *(capra aegagrus),* bezoars are very rare because their formation depends on the diet of the animal. Through the use of special formulas, it is possible, however, to "cultivate" them in the stomachs of more common ruminants. Valued for their antidotal powers, bezoars were much sought after in a period when princes lived in terror of being poisoned by their enemies; one did not venture abroad without a bezoar on one's person. They were even given sumptuous gold mountings. Curiously enough, modern science has corroborated to a certain degree their therapeutic powers. As late as 1808 the Shah of Persia could find no more precious gift than three bezoars to send to Napoleon.

Unlike his aristocratic contemporaries who were eager to show off their collections, the mentally ill Rudolf, a life-long celibate, jealously hid his. Reserved for a privileged few, a visit to his treasures had all the character of an initiation; the paintings were hung behind draperies in a room where the windows were opened only for the emperor.

Prague succumbed to a sad fate in the seventeenth century. During the first fifty years, the treasures of Emperor Rudolf were pillaged several times. During the course of the Thirty Years' War, certain pieces were sold at Nuremberg in order to meet military expenses. Others were sent to Vienna. After Tilly's victory at White Mountain, Maximilian of Bavaria, in command of the imperial troops, left Prague with fifteen wagonloads of spoils which were to enrich the collections at Munich. In 1631 Prague was occupied by the Saxons; this time fifty carts and several boats carried off captured trophies to Dresden.

The reputation of Prague was legendary and as the Thirty Years' War drew to a close, enough art still remained to arouse the covetousness of Koenigsmark. With negotiations for peace already under way, the celebrated general led the Swedish army on a forced march to Prague and entered the city on July 25, 1648, seizing Hradcany and the Mala Strana quarter. He was unable to take everything, thanks to the keeper of the collections, the sculptor Eusebius Miseron, who had succeeded in removing some of the paintings to Vienna; he had to be tortured before he would reveal where

38. **The Tower of Babel, by Pieter Bruegel the Elder.** *Kunsthistorisches Museum, Vienna. From Rudolf II's collection at Hradcany Castle, Prague. Bruegel's art corresponded exactly to the philosophical position of Manneristic Humanism.*

76

the keys to the treasury were hidden. Boats laden with spoils moved on the Elbe and the Moldau towards Mecklenburg where they added to loot brought by an overland route; from there, all was expedited to Stockholm. Queen Christina ordered an inventory drawn up by her librarian, Freinshemi, and her curator, the Marquis of Fresne; the report covered no fewer than 137 pages in folio. In contrast, the inventory taken at Prague on the order of Emperor Ferdinand III after the Swedish invasion listed no more than ten paintings and a handful of objects. The treasures of Prague seem truly inexhaustible; emperors as late as Joseph II in the eighteenth century still found things to sell. Recently the art world was startled by the discovery of seventy paintings that had long lain forgotten in the attic of Hradcany Castle; the majority, however, were acquisitions made after the time of Rudolf II.

Only a small number of the pieces captured by the Swedes remained in Stockholm. As the goods of the crown were the personal property of the sovereign, Christina, when she abdicated, took along her collections, in great part comprised of loot from Hradcany. Trunk after trunk accompanied her on her triumphal procession across Europe which ended eventually at Rome. There the queen, already enamored of art and the sciences (and who had hastened the death of Descartes by persuading him to move to her cold country), proved herself an ardent archeologist as well and amassed a fine collection of antiquities. After her death her collections were sold in lots by her heirs to the Spanish Crown and to Roman princes. In 1720 the financier Pierre Crozat acquired for Philippe II, Duke of Orléans and Regent of France, the most beautiful paintings belonging to the Odescalchi family; these were sold in London when the duke's collections were liquidated during the French Revolution.

Thus are collections made and unmade. Gathered together by one man, whose personality they reflect, pieces, once they are dispersed, fall into other, equally ephemeral groupings. The dismantling of the Prague collections is, however, very regrettable; their assemblage was the fruit of a certain kind of culture which flourished in Europe at the end of the sixteenth century, a culture which lives today only in the imagination. The work of the enigmatic Rudolf II is gone forever.

Koenigsmark captured at Prague other works of art which postdated Rudolf's reign. He carried off, for example, some of the bronzes made by the sculptor Adriaen de Vries for the palace of another great militarist: Wallenstein. The monumental fountain that Christian IV, king of Denmark and Norway, commissioned from the same sculptor was seized by the Swedes in 1660; it is in the park at Drottningholm, outside Stockholm, where one can best study the *œuvre* of this Dutch artist who did not work in his own country. The unity of Europe is created out of such movements of flux and reflux which very often behave like whirlpools, depositing alluvia far from the source.

The Hapsburg family was responsible for a great concentration of works of art beginning to form at this time in another of their European realms. This collection was not to know the misfortune which befell that of Rudolf; it remained more or less intact, eventually becoming the nucleus of Madrid's Prado Museum. Philip II of Spain had much more artistic feeling than his father, Emperor Charles V. Titian lived long enough to paint portraits of both father and son; favored by Charles, he was also extensively patronized by Philip. The latter, true to the Hapsburg instinct for the universal, amassed works from all over Europe in his palaces: the Escorial, the

39. **One of the capitulary rooms of the Escorial Palace,** *near Madrid. In the Royal Monastery of Saint Lawrence of the Escorial which consisted of a monastery, a church, a palace and a mausoleum, Philip II of Spain brought together his books for the library and his works of art which had been purchased throughout Europe. Originally shown in the capitulary rooms and the sacristy, the Escorial paintings have recently been regrouped in a special museum.*

Alcazar and the Prado. In his collections Flemings such as Rogier van der Weyden, Patinir, Quentin Massys, Bosch and Jan Gossaert (called Mabuse) hung beside Germans like Baldung-Grien, Cranach and Dürer. As for the Escorial, it is indeed an institution in the mannerist spirit, a *teatro totale* embracing a monastry, a royal residence, a hospital and a university; it is an image of the harmony of the world brought about by the accord between God and monarch. The library served all branches of learning; as the focal point of the sanctuary, its location at the entrance to the mass of granite buildings and its church-like façade are symbolic: the temple of learning prepares one for the temple of faith, seat of the highest knowledge. Without a museum, this *teatro totale* would not have been complete; Philip II grew old there, surrounded by some of his most beautiful paintings, principally Flemish ones, which were reverenced almost as sacred images. Rogier van der Weyden's *Descent from the Cross,* acquired by Maria of Hungary, sister of Emperor Charles V, and sent to Spain, was the most distinguished piece; it was put up in the Escorial in 1574. The king dreamed of even more; he tried to procure van Eyck's *Ghent Altarpiece* from the Saint Bavo church. Unsuccessful, he had to content himself with a copy made by Michiel Coxcie in 1557 at the request of the church vestry.

Mannerism has recovered from the condemnation meted out by Romain Rolland in his Latin thesis of 1895. It could not be otherwise; the anticlassical tendencies of our era have helped critics and historians to see the value of the movement. For some, like Bousquet, it is the true western tradition, and it is classicism which is guilty of bringing creativity to a standstill. Without going to either of these extremes, one must acknowledge the great speculative worth of mannerism. If it engendered many mediocre works, it also produced masterpieces but, above all, it was the painful gestation of the modern world. In the years between 1530 and 1600 the museum evolved an extensible form that would never stop growing. The following centuries were to bring new orientations of taste and greater interest in the work of art *per se*. The seventeenth century witnessed keen competition among European amateurs. New centers sprang up and museums took on greater significance in culture and pedagogy. It was reserved, however, for the eighteenth century to turn it into a public institution.

Chapter

5

Royal Art

In the seventeenth century the great collections formed in the north of Europe and not, as before, in Italy. Overflowing with antique and Renaissance treasures, Italy, however, proved to be an inexhaustible reservoir for dealers and amateurs. Ardent competition pushed prices high and works of art changed hands all over Europe; sometimes entire collections were affected. The Reynst brothers in Amsterdam, sons of a shipowner who made a fortune in the Indies, succeeded in acquiring the cabinet formed by the Doge Vendramin at Venice. Christina of Sweden took with her to Rome her collection, largely comprised of spoils from Prague. One of the most important transactions ever made in works of art was the purchase en bloc of the Gonzaga cabinet at Mantua; this was effected in 1627 by Daniel Nys, a Flemish dealer established in Venice, on behalf of King Charles I of England. The agent's letters to his Britannic Majesty are well worth reading for the way in which he boasts of his adroitness, details the enormous expenses he went to and declares that he earned nothing from the deal, having done all for the glory of the king; the Correggios alone, he said, were worth what he had charged for the entire group. Ruined by the extravagance of his family and the expensive fondness for horses that had been traditional with the Gonzagas for a hundred years, the duke offered for sale the whole of the Mantuan collection, quite possibly the most beautiful of those formed during the Renaissance; he kept only the *Triumphs* of Mantegna, which were also acquired by the Stuart king only two years later. The sale stunned all of Italy and filled the inhabitants of Mantua with consternation. "They would have put up double the price," wrote Daniel Nys, "if the duke had been given the slightest opportunity to buy back his treasures from England."

40. **View of Arco, water color and gouache by Albrecht Dürer.** *Louvre Museum, Paris. This admirable water color was found among the group of 5,542 drawings which the minister Colbert bought for Louis XIV from the financier Jabach in 1671. This purchase was the basis for the finest such collection in the world.*

Just as it happens today, entire collections changed countries; such was the case with the Earl of Arundel's famous collection of paintings and *objets d'art*; following his exile in 1642, the nobleman had it removed from London to the Netherlands, where it was sold after his death.

The greatest sale of works of art in the seventeenth century involved the collections of Charles I; confiscated by the Puritan government after his execution in 1649, they were liquidated between 1650 and 1653 through private sales and public auctions. The

41. **The Market Place** *at Prague. Detail of a picture in the Würzburg Museum. During the XVIIth century it was often possible to obtain paintings or curiosities from baskets in the open air or from the shops in the market place.*

king of Spain, Queen Christina of Sweden, Archduke Leopold-Wilhelm, governor of the Netherlands, Cardinal Mazarin and the Parisian banker Jabach shared the booty.

The purchase of works of art was generally handled by courtiers who sometimes indulged in all sorts of unscrupulous dealings. Alfonso Lopez, sent by Louis XIII to Holland to buy ships and war materials, profited from the stay by acquiring paintings destined for Richelieu and forming a collection of his own. The Dutch traded on an international scale; the Fleming, Daniel Nys, set up in Venice, effected the sale of the Gonzaga cabinet to Charles I. Guillaume Forchoudt of Antwerp had branches in Paris, Vienna and Cadiz. Certain subjects which were in fashion at the time were more salable than others. In 1677 the Forchoudt brothers wrote their father: "Business flourishes in Vienna and we would sell many more paintings if we had a greater stock of *The Four Elements, Landscapes* and *Battles.*"

During the course of the seventeenth century the art trade organized itself. Paintings were still sold at fairs but more and more these were only second-rate works. The fairs at Saint-Germain, Paris, and at Leipzig kept, however, a certain luster down to the eighteenth century. Heirs to the commercial methods of the Italians, the bourgeois of northern Europe were clever enough to corner for themselves the profitable art market. By the sixteenth century the city of Antwerp was regulating the sale of art objects; only the guild of Saint Luke was authorized to issue licenses for the sales. For the express purpose of selling their works, painters banded together in exhibitions, the first of which was held in 1540. Trade in antiques was set up on the stock exchange. The most active of all was the *Schilders-Band* which exported Flemish paintings and imported Italian works. Art dealers in Antwerp were affiliated with the guild of Saint Luke in an accessory position, like the gilders and framers. In the city of Amsterdam art dealers were likewise obliged to comply with the rulings of the brotherhood of Saint Luke. There and at the Hague private associations of artists obtained the right to hold exhibitions, with a view to selling pictures by their members. During the course of the seventeenth century, Amsterdam became the trade capital of the art world, especially for paintings. It witnessed the first modern auctions, complete with appraisers selected by the burgomaster, auctioneers and sales catalogs. One townhouse, the *Heer logement,* was set aside for these sales, which were held in the open air, altogether in keeping with this kind of transaction. "To auction off" in Portuguese is *por en praca,* literally, "to set up in the public square." To close a sale, the auctioneer tapped a copper basin with his ring; eighteenth-century London instituted the ivory mallet. In order to be seen by all the public, the auctioneer was at first mounted on horseback and later was put on a stage. During the van Uffelen sale in 1639 Rembrandt did a rapid sketch of Raphael's *Portrait of Baldassare Castiglione,* one of the chief attractions under the hammer; in this drawing one senses, even after three hundred years, something of the fever of a great sale.

Ambassadors whose functions took them all over the globe often became involved in dealing in art. Lord Dudley Carleton, Great Britain's ambassador to the Netherlands, had a multitude of agents and clerks. He amassed in Italy a veritable countinghouse of antiquities, planning to export them to London. Named to a post at the Hague, he sought to trade antiquities for paintings. He began negotiating with Rubens and soon each was trying to cheat the other. After a round of epic bargaining, the ambassador sent the artist some mediocre and much-restored antique works in exchange for eighteen paintings by Rubens. The artist included in the lot several works by his pupils and later managed to rid himself of some of the antiquities by selling them to the Duke of Buckingham for the considerable sum of 100,000 florins.

The great collectors themselves did not disdain plying the dealer's trade. Mazarin, for instance, greatly enjoyed being in the center of art transactions. He would choose the best of what was sent him from Italy and liquidate the remainder at auction.

Amsterdam owed its reputation to the severity of its commercial customs. The story of Gerrit Uylenburgh is a case in point; this dealer had sold to the Elector of Brandenburg thirteen old masters, chiefly Italian, which a painter at the Berlin court, one Hendrick van Fromantiou, thought were forgeries; the paintings were returned to Amsterdam in 1672, arousing great excitement in all the artists' quarters because each faction called in painters to support its opinion. Thirty-one of the fifty-one consulted decided the works were authentic. Nevertheless, the dealer was discredited; he went into bankruptcy and retired to England after a public auction of all his goods.

Experts were as divided then as they are now and, in the Latin countries, were often less than scrupulous. When Jabach sold the Duke of Liancourt a small *Virgin* by Annibale Carracci and a *Portrait of Gaston de Foix* by Giorgione for 150,000 livres each although they were unquestionably copies by Sébastien Bourdon, the public made sport of the financier's trickery. Bourdon, a dealer himself, did not hesitate to add to his store of art by exploiting his talent for copying; he turned out quite good pastiches of Poussin and Le Nain. In his *Mémoires* Loménie de Brienne warned against the flood of copies in circulation; some merchants even managed to sell the same painting several times. Trade in counterfeit antiquities stimulated the market while trade in forged paintings inundated it because it was so profitable. Rome abounded with forgers who hired poor young artists to work for just enough to keep themselves alive. Terenzio da Urbino, an imitator of Raphael, went so far as to execute his pastiches on old, worm-eaten panels, coating the finished picture with tinted varnishes. These practices were in use by the beginning of the seventeenth century, proof of how active the art market was at that time. Forgers found easy prey for their tricks, especially among their clientele in northern Europe where people had not yet learned to be connoisseurs. Giulio Mancini, the pope's physician, who wrote his *Considerazioni sulla pittura* in 1620, devoted an entire paragraph to aids for distinguishing copies from originals. He remarked, "Those who wish to pass off copies as originals often blacken them with smoke from damp straw to remove from the colors all trace of newness; this gives an appearance of age to the pictures and, to perfect the deceit, they paint on old wood." Later, the Neopolitan Luca Giordano (so well-known for his rapid work that he was called "Luca Fapresto" or "Luca the Speedy") showed himself capable of imitating everything, ancients as well as moderns: Ribera, Cambiaso, Pietro da Cortona, Guido Reni, Lanfranco, the Carracci, Tintoretto, Bassano, Raphael, Caravaggio and even, it seems, Rubens and Rembrandt.

Painters often supplemented their incomes by acting as dealers; the Carracci were doing this as early as the sixteenth century. Rembrandt was not very successful at it but Rubens, painter, courtier, connoisseur, made a fortune in dealing. Artists often performed expertise or gave artistic counsel to great personages, the position we call "adviser." Court painter to Vicenzo I, Duke of Mantua, Rubens advised the ruler on his purchases; in 1617 the painter brought off a brilliant coup with the acquisition of Caravaggio's *Death of the Virgin* which had been refused by the church of the Madonna della Scala despite the admiration its novelty had aroused in artistic circles in Rome. We possess all the correspondence exchanged on the subject between Rubens in Rome and the duke in Mantua; the painter himself supervised all the formalities of packing and transport. Rubens served also as counsel for Philip IV of Spain; he left Madrid for Flanders in 1639 with a royal commission to buy paintings. The purpose behind the trip made by Velázquez in 1649 to 1651 was the purchase of old masters and antiquities for the king; the artist was, however, not too successful because, succumbing to the charm of Italy, he applied himself, it seems, to things other than his mission.

A curious story revolves around Nicolo Renieri, a French-born artist living in Venice, who, while working as a painter, simultaneously acted for forty years as a not-so-scrupulous dealer in Venetian art; it has been told that he tried to pass off as a Giorgione a Pietro della Vecchia which he himself had commissioned. In 1655, in order to keep his collection within the "glorious Venetian state" (or so he said), he asked the Council of Ten for authorization to raffle it off. The catalog from this lottery is one of the oldest printed sales lists we have.

A taste for works of art was not the sole motive for buying. Speculation began at this time. In August 1675 the abbot of Coulanges wrote to Madame de Sévigné, "Paintings are as good as ready cash; there never was a better investment. You can sell them whenever you wish at double the price you paid."

Collectors now specialized more than they did during the preceding epoch. Curio cabinets aroused greater interest than ever; scientific discoveries were being made but leaders in that field were seldom art collectors. However, an extensive museum related to science was organized in the seventeenth century at the College of Rome by the Jesuit priest Athanasius Kircher (1601?-1680). In rooms decorated to evoke the terrestrial and celestial spheres, the father disposed among a collection of antiquities and pre-Christian objects, ethnographic artifacts brought back from all over the world by Jesuit missionaries who were noted for their immense knowledge of linguistics, geography and ethnography. This museum, whose holdings were dispersed in 1870 and again in 1915, formed the nucleus of the present-day Museo Pigorini in Rome with its ethnographical collections and was a materialization of the intellectual, scientific and spiritual empire symbolized in Jesuit iconography by the image of St. Ignatius of Loyola.

Nicolas Claude Fabri de Peiresc (1580-1637) serves as an example of one of the most picturesque *"curieux"* of the seventeenth century. A member of the parliament of Aix-en-Provence, he filled his mansion with an extraordinary number of objects pertaining to natural history, numismatics, linguistics, archeology, history, ethnography and astronomy. He maintained emissaries in Asia, Africa and America; when a foreign ship arrived in Marseilles, Peiresc ran down to the docks to see if he could procure some rare token from a distant land for himself. An observatory surmounted his house. He lived among columns of books and curiosities of all sorts in every salon: statues, mummies, stuffed animals. Peiresc kept an army of cats for which he had a great affection; the enemies of rats, they were, as Bonnafé remarked, "the conservators of his library." A scholar of repute, Peiresc corresponded with all of Europe. Some of his letters to Rubens have been preserved; he was one of the men who negotiated the contract with the artist for the Medici Gallery in the Palais du Luxembourg.

The art collector became a connoisseur or, in Italian, *conoscitore* or *cognoscente*; the Spanish painter and art historian Palomino spoke of the *aficionado* or amateur. *Curieux* remained the preferred term in France, Loménie de Brienne listed the requisite qualities of the *curieux*: he must paint, have money, know Greek and Latin and cultivate connoisseurship to avoid being duped "by underhanded picture dealers."

Latinisms such as *cimaliarchium, cimelium, cimeliotheca* and *rarotheca* were sometimes used to designate a collection of art and curiosities. The word cabinet, before its adoption in Great Britain had its English equivalent in *closet,* in a sense that is now archaic. The Germans created a whole gamut of expressions based on the purpose of the collection: *Raritätenkabinett, Curiositätenkabinett, Naturalienkabinett, Munzkabinett* (collection of medallions), *Mineralienkabinett*; *Kabinett* was used concurrently with *Kammer,* a word which was still in use.

The arrival in Paris of a painting from Italy was an event. News spread quickly and collectors gathered at the unpacking. When Poussin's *Four Seasons* arrived in Paris, an audience formed at the residence of the Duke of Richelieu; in a long and scholarly discourse Le Brun and Sébastien Bourdon celebrated the merits of the pictures. The education of the amateur was then in an experimental stage; no works on the history of art existed, only biographies of great national artists compiled by historiographers in their respective countries. Engravings were the only mnemonic aids available for retaining the memory of a work of art and were extensively used in expensive volumes in which masterpieces were grouped according to an iconographic format. The Ridolfi Brothers in 1646 published a work on the Venetian painters entitled *Meraviglie d'arte*. Archduke Leopold-Wilhelm, in order to publicize his gallery, of which he was very proud, commissioned Teniers to prepared an engraved publication of its principal paintings. The artist made small-scale reproductions of the works—called *"poncifs"* or "pas-

tiches"—to serve as models for the engravers. This was a labor of patience which undoubtedly lasted for years since two hundred forty-five copies had to be made. These "pastiches de Teniers" aroused the interest of amateurs; the Duke of Marlborough succeeded in bringing together one hundred twenty of them and they still turn up here and there in museums today. In 1658, two years after the archduke had left Brussels, the volume of engravings appeared under the title *Theatrum pictorium Davidis Teniers antverpensis*. An exhibition of the most beautiful paintings in all of Europe was organized by the Dutch collector Jean de Bischop who commissioned hundreds of copies as well as drawings after the originals.

The treatment occasionally inflicted on works of art would seem to us most disrespectful; mutilated antiquities were rather badly completed and the critical study of originals was not yet a matter of course. Restorations were entrusted to the most talented artists. Bernini began his career as a restorer of antiques; one of the most remarkable examples of his virtuosity is the Lodovisi *Ares* in the Museo delle Terme in the National Museum, Rome; the *Eros* he added to the statue is somewhat baroque. When the city of Arles presented Louis XIV with the *Venus* found in the amphitheatre, François Girardon was commissioned to give it arms; his completed work flatly contradicted the original sense of the statue. Paintings were often transformed, that is, cut down or enlarged to fit their settings. At the end of the Sun King's reign, the new austerity which followed an epoch of libertinism stirred up a wave of prudery which destroyed or mutilated countless mythological paintings; works by Poussin, Titian and Rubens suffered. The garrulous Loménie de Brienne tells us that his *Venus* by Poussin caused him many worries whenever he entered his private chapel because the position of the legs "revealed too much of the seat of love." Although he had seen many others like it in Italy in cardinals' houses, he continues, he felt obliged to reduce his *Venus* to a bust by cutting off the legs.

During the seventeenth century the greatest artists made fortunes and enjoyed a consideration which permitted them to live in a princely fashion, a situation they were to lose in the eighteenth century when aristocratic and bourgeois snobbism returned them to their former status as artisans. However, during their golden age, they too formed collections which were often quite revealing about their own artistic tendencies. For example, it is not surprising to learn that Anthony van Dyck owned nineteen Titians and that Rubens had ten, in addition to the thirty-two copies he had made during his stay in Madrid—what an indefatigable worker! At Antwerp Rubens built a palace *à l'italienne* (which has recently been reconstructed); for it he built a rotunda in imitation of the Pantheon to house his antiquities.

Although they were in private hands, all these cabinets, museums and galleries were accessible to the public, as corroborated in the innumerable guides and itineraries compiled for travelers at that time. Let us mention a few of the earliest publications on northern collections: *Itinerarium Galliae* in 1612, the *Ulysses Belgico-Gallicus* of 1631 (published by Zinzerling and Abraham Gölnitz), the *Voyage de France pour l'instruction et la commodité tant des français que des étrangers* (1639). This type of guide enjoyed great popularity in Italy; the *Nota delli Musei, galerie e ornamenti di Statue e pitture ne' palazzi e ne' giardini di Roma* appeared in 1664. The Bibliothèque Nationale at Paris contains an international compendium, dated 1645 and in manuscript form, which lists *Curieux des diverses villes*.

42. **The Collection of Archduke Leopold-Wilhelm at the Coudenberg Castle, Brussels, by David Teniers.** *Detail. Kunsthistorisches Museum, Vienna. The arrangement of the archduke's collection is well known to us thanks to the numerous copies painted by David Teniers the Younger, the ruler's curator and adviser. The representation of an art lover's cabinets was one of the most successful subjects for painting in the Netherlands.*

42

England's first great amateur was the Stuart king, Charles I. The Tudors had a passion for jewels and sumptuous vestments but they hardly bothered about art. An accomplished but politically inept prince, Charles brought England to the fore as a cultivated nation. Among his outstanding achievements were his acquisition of the Gonzaga cabinet at Mantua, his commissions to Rubens for great cycles of decoration and his purchase, following the advice of Rubens, of Raphael's original cartoons for *The Acts of the Apostles,* at that time still in the possession of the tapestry works where they had served as models for the hangings ordered by Leo X. The keeper of the collections of Charles I was a Dutchman, Abraham van der Doort, who was so scrupulous that, unable to find a miniature the moment the king called for it, he hanged himself. The catalog of the royal collections listed 1,387 paintings (460 of which were at Whitehall) and 399 sculptures; this scientific work was brought out by Vertue-Berthée in 1757 and has recently been republished.

Some of the notables at the English court imitated their prince, among them the famous Duke of Buckingham and, in particular, Thomas Howard, Earl of Arundel, who was an excellent connoisseur. The king acquired the paintings in the Gonzaga cabinet and, through the same agent, Arundel managed to buy the drawings. In his youth he spent several years in Italy with the architect Inigo Jones and became infected with a passion for archeology. At a time when most antiquarians had eyes only for Italy, Arundel sensed the importance of Greece and Asia Minor. Precursor of Lord Elgin, he dreamed of unearthing the bas-reliefs of the mausoleum at Halicarnassus and tried to obtain permission from the Sublime Porte to cart off to London the reliefs from the Golden Gate of Constantinople. The mirage of ancient Troy lured him long before it haunted Heinrich Schliemann. The salons, galleries and garden of Arundel House were filled with antiquities. Savants and men of taste congregated there; Bacon was a frequent visitor.

Save for the Greek and Roman works, Lord Arundel removed all his collections to the Netherlands. The government of the Commonwealth dispersed the royal collections, keeping at Cromwell's request only the *Triumphs* of Mantegna and the Raphael cartoons. Most of the art found its way to the continent. Alonzo de Cardenas, ambassador from Spain, had to hire eighteen mules to bring the works bought by the Spanish king from La Coruña to Madrid.

The 1697 fire at Whitehall destroyed whatever else remained of the collections of Charles Stuart. The scepter of amateurism passed from England to France. King Henry IV, fanatic builder, restorer of the State, showed little taste for this kind of royal activity. It was he, however, who initiated a program for the conservation of the Italian masterpieces at Fontainebleau; he had them moved from the insalubrious bathing chambers (where they were replaced by copies) to a main wing. A Dutchman, Jean de Hoey, whose maternal grandfather was Lucas van Leyden, was keeper of the collections of Henry IV. In 1608 he was entrusted with the restoration of "paintings and old pictures, whether on panel or canvas, belonging to His Majesty at the Château of Fontainebleau, and was at the same time to clean the borders of all frescoes in the chambers, galleries and cabinets of that château." His family continued as conservators to the king until the royal collections were transported to the Louvre under Louis XIV. It was an Italian,

43. **Portrait of Abraham van der Doort, by William Dobson.** *Hermitage Museum, Leningrad. This man, keeper of the collections of Charles I of England, committed suicide because he was unable to find part of the collection as quickly as he thought he should.*

43

Queen Marie de'Medici, who renewed traditions of pageantry at the French court. When she was regent for Louis XIII, she commissioned from Rubens a gallery retracing her exploits for her Palais du Luxembourg. Louis XIII appointed artists to decorate the royal residences but showed no interest in collecting. During his reign Cardinal Richelieu, who assumed the task of governing, filled his Château de Richelieu in Poitou and the Palais-Cardinal in Paris with French and Italian paintings. During the Piedmont campaign in 1629, he succeeded in buying Leonardo da Vinci's *Saint Anne*; it is a mystery how it escaped the royal collections. Those who sought the favor of the powerful minister and knew his passion for collecting gave him works of art. For example, the Duke of Montmorency presented him in 1632 with a truly royal gift, Michelangelo's two *Slaves* from his family's château at Ecouen; however, the implacable statesman did not hesitate to have the duke beheaded when he joined a conspiracy against the king. It was undoubtedly through a gift that Richelieu acquired before England's Charles I one of the prizes of the Gonzaga cabinet, the five pictures from the *studiolo* of Isabella d'Este, among them two Mantegnas and one Perugino. The Gonzaga Duke Vicenzo II was intriguing at that time to obtain an honorary title from the French court; quite probably to win the favor of the Cardinal, he sent him this princely gift on the advice of his representative in Paris. Richelieu bequeathed to the Crown his collections in the Palais-Cardinal along with the palace itself (now known as the Palais Royale), out of devotion to the person of the king who had resided there during one of the Frondes. One can argue that politics as much as taste motivated Richelieu's collecting, if one bears in mind that he willed his library to his nephew Armand de Vignerod "to serve not only the family but also the public" and that he added the sum of 400 livres for the librarian's salary and 1,000 livres for acquisitions.

Cardinal Mazarin was not then, as Pierre du Colombier claimed, "the man who introduced into France the virus of collecting." He did, however, have an insane passion for art and typified the fanatic collector. He loved jewels and, like an oriental prince, delighted in letting them flow over his hands; but above all he craved paintings. His life as a collector was shattered in 1651 when the leaders of the Fronde of the Princes confiscated his art and books (40,000 items in all) and subsequently sold them to provide the reward offered for his capture; later, through secret agents, he succeeded in repurchasing most of them. Mazarin was one of the most eager purchasers of the collections of Charles I when they were put up for sale in London; the financier Jabach, who bought for himself as well, acted as his agent. The cardinal's collections were divided between his apartment in the Louvre and the two-story gallery of his mansion, incorporated today in the Bibliothèque Nationale. Inventories attest to the incredible luxury of his lodgings: 21 cabinets, 411 tapestries, Florentine tables and buffets, lacquer chests from China, chests in ebony and mirrors of all kinds. The prelate did not recoil from indelicate maneuvers to procure for himself a rare piece. He persuaded Cardinal Barberini to give the queen Correggio's *Mystical Marriage of Saint Catherine*; Anne of Austria received it with pleasure but was forced to relinquish it to the minister the next day. At Mazarin's death Cardinal Barberini, who had not appreciated the trick, had the painting restored to the Crown. Like all collectors, Mazarin was exceedingly jealous of his collections and feared depredations by visitors. When Queen Christina of Sweden asked to see his apartments in the Louvre, the cardinal, who was away, wrote to Colbert to beg him to

44. **Antiope, by Correggio.**
Detail. Louvre Museum, Paris. In 1627 this painting was acquired by Charles I of England along with other works from the collections of the duke of Mantua. When the king's collections were sold, Antiope was bought by Jabach who in turn sold it to Cardinal Mazarin from whose heirs it was purchased by Louis XIV.

46. Portrait of Jabach and his Family, by Charles le Brun.
Formerly in a Berlin Museum. Destroyed during the bombing of Berlin in 1945, this painting portrays the family of the financier Evrard Jabach who was without a doubt the greatest collector in France at the time of Louis XIV. Almost all of his most beautiful works passed into the royal collections and are today at the Louvre.

◄
45. Cardinal Mazarin in the Gallery of his Town House.
The so-called "Mazarine Gallery," which occupied two floors of the cardinal's mansion, was constructed by Mansart and is today incorporated in the Bibliothèque Nationale of Paris. The collections which were displayed here are now for the most part at the Louvre and were purchased by Louis XIV from the cardinal's heirs.

"keep the crazy woman out of my cabinets at the Louvre for one could so easily take some of my small paintings." Colbert answered that he had taken the necessary precautions and had had the queen watched. If one can believe his secretary, Loménie de Brienne, a fantastic character who led a most adventuresome life, on the eve of his death the cardinal was far from preparing himself for an encounter with his Maker by meditating on the transitoriness of this world; instead, there he was in his nightshirt, pacing up and down in the middle of his collections, lamenting to himself: "I must leave all this. What trouble I had to acquire these things! I'll never see them again where I'm going!" Did he fear he was headed for Hell or did eternal happiness seem to him a mere trifle beside the joys his art had given him?

At Mazarin's death on March 9, 1661, Louis XIV ordered an inventory taken of his possessions. His apartments contained 877 paintings, 386 of which were masterpieces. The king bought the most beautiful pieces for his own collection. Later Colbert succeeded in producing for the Crown, under advantageous conditions, the Jabach chefs d'œuvres. Originally from Cologne, a banker and businessman, Jabach epitomizes a type of amateur that came to the fore in the eighteenth century—the great financier. Director of the Compagnie des Indes and sole supplier of buff leather to the royal armies, he built a great fortune and filled his mansion on the Rue Neuve Saint Merry with art. He bought widely at the London sale of the collections of Charles I. He had one of the finest collections of drawings at a time when an interest in drawings was evidence of refined taste. The first to amass a collection of this kind was Giorgio Vasari who used them to illustrate, after a fashion, his history of art and had them mounted in magnificent mannerist frames. Later dispersed, these drawings are today the pride of several cabinets. When Bernini arrived in Paris in 1665, Jabach entertained him, along with some of the greatest Parisian amateurs, at a dinner in his mansion on the Rue Neuve Saint Merry; after the feast the collection was admired. Portfolio after portfolio was opened and

after scrutinizing the drawings for a long time, Bernini, reports Chantelou, got up brusquely, saying that he had worn out his eyes with looking at so many beautiful things. According to recent investigations, some of Jabach's finest paintings were acquired at this time by the king but the conditions of the transaction are vague. In 1671 the banker was facing grave financial difficulties when Colbert bought from him 101 paintings (for which the inventory is lost) and all his drawings (5,542) for a price that made Jabach groan. Ill and on the verge of bankruptcy, he beseeched Colbert, who was dragging out the negotiations, to "consider, in the name of God, that I find myself before the mouth of Hell and that I am fighting forces that spare no one." Jabach made a financial comeback and set about forming another collection, which proves that he bought works of art for aesthetic reasons and not merely for ostentation. The inventory compiled after his death lists 687 paintings most of which were, it is true, of secondary quality. His real passion was for drawings; at the time of his death he owned more than 4,000, some of which were exceedingly beautiful.

The Richelieu, Mazarin and Jabach collections and the cabinet of the Gonzaga family in Mantua, which Charles I had enjoyed for twenty years, all eventually came into the possession of the king of France. Here are some of the works in the Louvre today which came originally from one or the other of these collections: the small *St. George* and *St. Michael* of Raphael; Correggio's *Allegories and Antiope*; Giorgione's *Concert Champêtre*; Titian's *Man with a Glove, The Entombment, Supper at Emmaus, Woman at her Toilet,* the pseudo *Allegory of Avalos* and the *Pardo Venus*; Caravaggio's *Death of the Virgin*. All the Holbeins in the Louvre came, via the royal collections, from Jabach who had bought many of them from Arundel. As for Leonardo's *St. John the Baptist,* given by Louis XII to Charles I, it re-entered the French royal collections, as had the *Saint Anne* thirty years earlier, through Richelieu. Until the very end of his reign the collections of Louis XIV were continually being enriched by gifts or acquisitions. The city of Venice, desiring the favor of the monarch, offered him Veronese's *Supper in the House of Simon*. Most of the Poussins in the Louvre came from the Sun King who acquired many of them from the Duke of Richelieu who, according to contemporary sources, was obliged to forfeit them in payment of a gambling debt. Near the end of the reign some paintings by the artists of northern schools finally entered the royal collections: the *Kermesse, Queen Thomyris* and *Madonna of the Innocents* by Rubens and Rembrandt's *Portrait of the Artist as an Old Man*. These acquisitions attest to the gradually widening influence the "partisans of color" were achieving in their struggle against the entrenched aesthetic of form.

Charles Le Brun, *premier peintre* to Louis XIV, was put in charge of superintending the royal collections. The pictures were at first grouped in the Louvre where the cabinet from Fontainebleau had been brought. Later, they were taken to Versailles where the most precious were placed in the king's chambers while others decorated the many grand apartments. At the Louvre they had been confined to veritable storerooms with great numbers of them arranged on movable shutters. The most valuable had been kept in armoires.

The drawings acquired from Jabach in 1671 formed the basis of the drawings cabinet at the Louvre, today one of the richest in the world. The cultural policies of Louis XIV were truly worthy of a great king; blessed with logic, foresight and a sense

47. **Kermesse, by Peter Paul Rubens.** *Detail. Louvre Museum, Paris. Not until the closing years of the XVIIth century did the first paintings by artists of the northern school come into the French royal collections. Kermesse by Rubens was purchased by Louis XIV from the Marquis de Hauterive in 1685.*

48. **Bacchanal, by Titian.** *Prado Museum, Madrid. This is one of the bacchanals ordered first from Bellini and then from Titian for Duke Alfonso d'Este for his camerino d'alabastro in the ducal palace at Ferrara. It entered the collection of King Philip IV of Spain after going to the Ludovisi family of Rome.*

49. **The Three Philosophers, by Giorgione.** *Detail. Kunsthistorisches Museum, Vienna. One of the most precious paintings from the collection of Archduke Leopold-Wilhelm whose aide-de-camp and keeper of the collection was David Teniers the Younger. The Archduke's collection became the property of the Austrian Crown.*

of economy and with Colbert as his able minister who well knew how to take advantage of any situation, the king sought to provide the State with all institutions necessary for the progress of the arts and advancement of the work of artists and scholars—libraries, museums, academies and manufactures. It would be a digression to detail here the founding of the Royal Library, nucleus of the present Bibliothèque Nationale but we shall discuss one of its finest departments which grew into today's consummate *Cabinet des Estampes.* It owes its origins to the acquisition in 1665 or 1666 of the massive collection of 235,000 engravings brought together by the Abbot of Marolles. This erudite exemplifies yet another type of collector, one who tracks down complete series. La Bruyère in his *Caractères* presents *Démocède ou le curieux* as a parody of this type and has him say, "I have all of Callot save one which is not even a significant piece; quite the contrary, it's one of his poorest works but it would complete Callot for me. I have hunted twenty years for this engraving and despair of ever finding it; what a pity." Many have believed that Michel de Marolles was the model for this Démocède while others have pointed to another fanatical amateur, Charles de l'Orme. The abbot had a passion for classification; he volunteered to catalog the archives of his friends for the pleasure of it. Within five months he completed an inventory of the Nevers family library of more than 19,000 volumes, classifying the titles according to a numerical system of his own invention. Even he was stupefied by the finished work and said he

would not have believed it if he had been told the story by someone. He sold his engravings en bloc to the king to avoid their being dispersed after his death and so that "a body which grew slowly and with difficulty should not be dismembered." At every stage in the history of the museum the public has profited from this instinct of the amateur to seek immortality through the inviolate collection. Immediately after the sale of the 580 volumes of engravings, the abbot began collecting again and at his death in 1681 left 111,424 new items, of which 10,576 were drawings.

Philip IV of Spain was an exceedingly poor statesman; he brought about the downfall of his kingdom by entrusting the reins of government to the incapable Olivares. A man of learning and culture, Philip was a patron of the arts and a great collector. The friendship he tendered Velázquez and the honors and title he bestowed on him can be cited as an example of the high esteem princes had for artists in the seventeenth century especially if one considers the snobbery and severity of etiquette cultivated at the Madrid Court. The king had a passion for paintings, gave lavish commissions to Velázquez and Claude Lorrain and bought works by Correggio, Titian, Veronese, Tintoretto and Raphael. One of the principal jewels of the Italian Renaissance, the *Bacchanals* painted by Titian for the *camerino d'alabastro* in the ducal palace at Ferrara, was given him by Cardinal Ludovisi. Eclectic in the Hapsburg tradition, Philip was also interested in Flemish art, buying works by Velvet Brueghel and profiting from Rubens's ambassadorship at Madrid by giving him massive commissions.

Ties between the courts at Madrid and Vienna enriched the latter with magnificent works by Velázquez; however, it was the admirable collection of paintings, principally Venetian, assembled by Archduke Leopold-Wilhelm which guaranteed a priviliged position to Vienna's Kunsthistorisches Museum. Both a Prince of the Church and a man of war, this son of Emperor Ferdinand II was attached at first to the Madrid Court, later named representative to Portugal and then, in 1646, made governor of the Netherlands. He had Coudenberg (since destroyed by fire) built as his official residence and his collection of 517 Italian masterpieces was installed there. The painting we now consider his most important is Giorgione's enigmatic *The Three Philosophers*. He appointed the painter David Teniers the Younger as keeper of his collection and aide-de-camp. Following the artist's counsel, he acquired many fine Flemish paintings, including Jan van Eyck's *Cardinal Niccoló Albergati*, Hugo van der Goes's *Adam and Eve* and an incomparable series of works by Pieter Bruegel the Elder. The pictures were placed among statuary, intaglios, medallions and tapestries. Gravely ill in 1656, Leopold-Wilhelm resigned from his official duties and left for Vienna, taking his works of art with him. Upon his death in 1662, his collections went to his brother, Emperor Ferdinand III. Just as works by Leonardo gravitated to Paris, those by Bruegel seemed destined to converge at Vienna, where the Brussels pictures joined those of Rudolf II from Prague.

The end of the seventeenth century and beginning of the eighteenth witnessed the flowering of the Wittelsbach collections. Duke Maximilian I (1597-1651), especially fond of Dürer and other sixteenth-century Germans, began an assemblage of masterpieces that was to make Munich one of the museological capitals of Europe. Interrupted by the Thirty Years' War, this effort was resumed by Max Emanuel (1679-1726) and continues into the present.

50. **Portrait of John the Good of France,** *French School, XIVth century. Louvre Museum, Paris. This painting, the oldest known portrait in European painting, was bought by the scholar Roger de Gaignières at the Château at Oiron. In 1717 it was withdrawn from the sale of Gaignières' collections, which he had given to the Crown but which he was allowed to enjoy for the remainder of his life. The portrait was at that time installed in the royal library.*

At the same time Roman princes and cardinals were building up collections particularly rich in contemporary paintings. This was the formative period of the famous Borghese, Doria, Colonna, Spada and Pallavicini galleries, today all public or private museums. The archeologist Cassiano del Pozzo had a house full of famous antiquities, where Pietro da Cortona and Poussin, from whom Pozzo commissioned a *Seven Sacraments*, went to absorb history and inspiration. In Milan Cardinal Federico Borromeo founded a library, the Biblioteca Ambrosiana, and in 1625 a painting and sculpture academy with an adjoining pinakotheke. At Genoa, too, most of the great princely collections were formed in the *seicento*, certain of which are still in private hands. One of the most beautiful, that of the Brignole-Sale family, was given to the city in 1874, along with the Palazzo Rosso, by the Marchioness Maria; it became the nucleus of Genoa's *Museo Civico*.

The impetus given to historical studies in the seventeenth century resulted in the creation of great collections devoted entirely to portraiture. Henry IV amassed in the little gallery of the Louvre (the Apollo Gallery) portraits of the kings and queens of France, of which there remains but a single, splendid vestige, the *Portrait of Marie de' Medici* by Pourbus the Younger. For his Palais-Cardinal, Richelieu commissioned from Simon Vouet and Philippe de Champaigne a series of twenty-six historical portraits having a very special connotation in regard to the statesman's politics; the choice was limited to those French statesmen, militarists and ecclesiastics who had unfailingly supported the Capetian monarchy. The collection constituted, therefore, an affirmation of the fierce loyalty to the royal person imposed by the cardinal on a France split by civil and religious struggles. In addition Richelieu's library contained fifty-eight portraits of illustrious men. The inventory of Cardinal Mazarin's collection lists 241 portraits of popes from St. Peter to the minister's contemporaries. In 1675 Grand Duke Ferdinand de' Medici inherited the collections of his brother, Cardinal Leopold. They included a series of portraits of artists which became the nucleus of that iconographical museum which was long one of the innovations of the Uffizi; the portraits are no longer all hung together. France has kept rigorously intact a seventeenth-century historical museum, a rare accomplishment for a country so ravaged by vandalism. This gallery is that of the Château de Beauregard in the Loire valley. The museum was the work of the lawyer, Paul Ardier, who bought Beauregard in 1617, retired there in 1631 and died in 1638. Before retirement Ardier had served as "Secretary of Defense," handling administrative matters for the French army. He installed his historical museum in a long gallery; the floor was paved with Delft tiles depicting in great detail the French army—its dress, arms, insignias and musical instruments. Because of these "incunabula" of Delft faïence, the château became more celebrated in Holland than in France. On the walls the history of France unfolded in 363 portraits, disposed by reigns. Around each king of France were grouped the statesmen who served him as well as contemporary foreign princes, popes, emperors and sultans. Each panel bore the dates of the reign, accompanied by mottoes and devices. These likenesses are all rather monotonous, bust-length portraits with the exception of two equestrian ones of the monarchs who were contemporaries of Ardier: Henry IV and Louis XIII. The kind of idea which motivated Paul Ardier was later to inspire King Louis-Philippe to create the Musée de Versailles: to affirm the continuity of French history, accomplished at Versailles despite the vicissi-

51. **View of the History Gallery of the Château of Beauregard,** near Blois. *This gallery of the history of France which groups the illustrious men of his time around each king, was made by a lawyer, Paul Ardier, who had served as the minister of war and retired to the château in 1631. In 1627 the floor was paved with Delft tiles representing various army corps (after the engravings by Jacob de Gheyn).*

tudes of the different regimes and at Beauregard because of the allegiance of subjects to their dynasty. We begin to realize that museology is not a new thing and that its forms perpetuate themselves across the centuries.

Another, still almost intact, *musée historique* in France was the fantasy of a great lord exiled from court by the royal authority he had defied; to enliven the tedium of banishment to the distant reaches of his province, he converted his château into a museum of portraiture. A correspondent of his cousin Madame de Sévigné, the bizarre and turbulent Bussy-Rabutin had a gallant pen that he used with elegance in his lively, satirical observations. When Madame de Sévigné remained in Paris while the city was besieged by the king's army, he wrote to her: "How weary I am of all this; were it not for the hope of pleasing you somewhat with the sack of Paris and of having you fall into my hands, I believe I would desert; but this life mitigates my peevishness." Disgraced, he was imprisoned in the Bastille until 1666 and was then compelled to live at his château in Burgundy where he remained until his return to favor in 1682. He chose museology as a divertisement. One entered the château through a "salon of heraldry" decorated with reproductions of the great houses of France paired with their emblemata, those canting arms or rebuses which were the delight of Latinists from the sixteenth century on. Other rooms were devoted to the kings of France, distinguished militarists from Du Guesclin to Bussy-Rabutin himself, royal mistresses, great statesmen, men of letters and the dukes of Burgundy. The theme in one rotunda was the glorification of women; there one could admire the most beautiful ladies at court, from many of whom Bussy-Rabutin boasted of having obtained favors, and in the center was enthroned the gallant author of *Histoire amoureuse des Gaules* himself, in Roman costume and blond peruke.

Such a gallery of beauties was not unique in its time; the château of Pibrac, near Toulouse, contains one, albeit incomplete, which dates from the period of Louis XIII[1]. Charles Emmanuel II, duke of Savoy, commissioned from the Frenchman Ferdinand Voet portraits of thirty-six contemporary beauties; the gallery so pleased Cardinal Fabio Chigi that he had it copied for his own villa by a certain Veglia. About the same time, the Constable of Naples, Lorenzo Colonna, married to Marie Mancini, a niece of Mazarin, installed a similar gallery in his palazzo in Rome; the artist was probably Paul Mignard, son of Nicolas Mignard and nephew of Pierre. This type of gallery was fashionable even before the seventeenth century; one was formed by Duke Ferdinand of Tyrol at his château at Ruhelust in the sixteenth century and Frans Pourbus the Younger painted one for Vicenzo Gonzaga at Mantua early in the seventeenth century. By the eighteenth century the vogue has spread to Russia; Catherine the Great acquired Prince Yussupov's collection and had it installed in her palace at Peterhof in the "Cabinet of Muses and Graces"[2].

Savants collected portraits of their friends or of great contemporaries; these pictures generally hung in their libraries. One has only to read the correspondence of Peiresc to learn how the portraits were obtained; the amateurs at that time showed no more discretion than those who collect the photographs of celebrities today.

The vogue for historical galleries spread throughout France. In his townhouse in Le Mans a certain de Tessé had the baroque idea of hanging in one cabinet portraits of the horses in the royal stables and in a second, portraits of queens of France and royal mistresses on horseback. The two series are on exhibition today in the museum at

Le Mans. Equestrian iconography was an old tradition at that time, having appeared at the end of the fifteenth century in the Palazzo Schifanoia at Ferrara and in the sixteenth in the Palazzo del Te at Mantua.

In a like vein was the sculpture collection in the eighteenth-century *galerie des illustres* in the *Capitole* in Toulouse; lamentably, it was destroyed some fifty years ago to make room for a gallery of history created by the worst official painters of the time.

All these galleries derive from the example set by Paolo Giovio a century earlier. One collection which has been kept intact and continues to grow proceeds directly from it: the gallery of artists' portraits in the Uffizi Museum in Florence; it was started by Cardinal Leopold de'Medici in his apartment in the Pitti Palace and, along with other paintings in the cardinal's *quadreria,* was inherited by Grand Duke Cosimo III, in 1675.

During the reign of Louis XIV France gave birth to a modern concept of history, no longer based on quasi-legendary chronicles but on actual events and on written or visual records. Toward the end of the 1600's the scholar Roger de Gaignières wished to found a colossal national historical museum; he amassed thousands of documents for the "clarification of French history": either original engravings, drawings and paintings, or drawings after paintings; stained-glass windows and funerary monuments executed by a team of copyists in his employ. Gaignières had direct contact with the Benedictine college of Bernard de Montfaucon, who at that time was attempting to define the critical bases of French history. Jean Adhémar has shown that one of the motives behind Gaignières's forming his collection was to teach history to the Duke of Burgundy whose tutor he was; because of this the royal treasury covered many of the expenses incurred during the establishment of this documentation. Gaignières was a methodical scholar; he classed the documents in series, intending to make them into a *catalogue raisonné* eventually. In addition he had a collection of three centuries of playing cards, a topographical series on principal European cities, costume drawings dating from the time of St. Louis and a file of autographs. He had 27,000 portraits, including many sixteenth-century miniatures and some medieval portraits; in a single purchase he bought twenty-one from the Benedictines at Oiron, including what was unquestionably the finest piece in the château: the oldest portrait in occidental painting, that of the French king, John the Good, now in the Louvre. In 1711 Gaignières, acknowledging that the Duke of Burgundy and his governess Madame de Montespan had provided the funds for his museum, made a gift of it to the king; the latter, in recognition, granted him a pension and the right of perfect usufruct. When the scholar died in 1715, the documents and some portraits, notably that of King John II, were transferred to the royal library. In 1717 the majority of the portraits were, unfortunately, sold. Clérambault, "keeper of the cabinet of nobiliary titles," at the Couvent des Grands Augustins, was entrusted with the Gaignières inventory; he managed to withdraw some portraits from sale, filing them among the papers of the relevant families—and alloting some pieces to himself in the process. Thus, most of the sixteenth-century miniatures in the Louvre have been resurrected from a long entombment among old documents.

Chapter 6

Museographia

The prodigious growth of amateurism during the eighteenth century was a direct consequence of an economic prosperity and the social transformation it initiated. Whereas the old aristocracy founded its wealth on the exploitation of land, a new class of society owed its affluence to a sudden expansion of trade and to the slow rise of industry which permitted better use of capital through the formation of corporate partnerships and a more rational organization of labor. Commerce in money, in other words the banking business, proved the most fertile field for the rapid build-up of colossal fortunes. The *bourgeoisie* profited from these advantages, particularly in France where commercial activity of any kind was forbidden the nobility, an interdict not so rigorously upheld in England. Italy and central Europe were the last to succumb to the socio-economic revolution and throughout the whole of the century collecting in those countries remained what it always was, an affair for princes. In France and England the number of "consumers" was considerably swelled by the increase in wealth and its wider distribution; during the entire century the result was a constant rise in the price of art objects, determined not only by the increased demand but also by a more or less avowed speculative intention, which also affected many other sectors of the economy.

The vogue for public sales was as great then as it is now. Amsterdam kept her position of importance but was first challenged by and then, in the second half of the century, eclipsed by Paris. In the seventeenth century the various guilds, exercising their rights to sell all objects similar in kind to those they themselves manufactured, paralyzed auctions in France. Gersaint, Watteau's dealer, introduced the Dutch system of sales; there was an expert who prepared the sale, edited the catalog, saw to the publicity and hired the services of an auctioneer who was paid by the day but was also given a percentage. Sales were usually held under porte-cocheres, often at the dealer's place of business but by the last third of the century there existed special halls, like those in the Hotel Bullion, the Hotel d'Alligre or in the townhouse of the artist-dealer Lebrun, husband of Madame Vigée-Lebrun. Upon occasion the king lent his palace for certain sensational sales; for example, the Jean de Julienne collection was auctioned off in the Salon Carré of the Louvre in 1767; the de Lassay sale in 1775 had for its

52. **L'Enseigne de Gersaint, by Jean-Antoine Watteau.** *Charlottenburg Palace, Berlin. In 1720 the Parisian merchant Gersaint commissioned this painting from Watteau to serve as a signboard for his shop on the Notre Dame bridge; it was completed in eight days. The sign did not remain in place very long; it was first purchased by the amateur Jean de Julienne and then, before 1760, by King Frederick II of Prussia who had a passionate love for contemporary French works. When the painting was removed from the shop, its format was changed.*

53

54

55

setting a room in the Tuileries. These auctions attracted not only collectors and dealers but also secondhand shop owners and idlers. As happens today, a fever gripped the public as it watched the prices rise and saw masterpieces change hands in the gradual stripping of the salesroom. Artists like Beaudoin, Cochin and Gabriel de Saint Aubin made quick sketches during the transactions. Saint Aubin, who lived with pencil in hand, drawing whatever impressed him in the street or in the salon, never missed a sale; with a few cursive strokes he could record a painting in the margin of a catalog while it was being auctioned off. Aubin's illustrated catalogs offer modern scholars a fund of information on pedigrees and attributions.

Businesses of questionable merit sprang up around the well-known auction houses. An equivocal character, the secondhand dealer prospered from dubious transactions. *Confessions of a Secondhand Dealer,* a pamphlet published in 1776, reviews the tricks of the trade. The profession was already practicing collusion; that is, a group would agree to refrain from bidding against each other in order to divide the loot later for a good price; in the event of a dispute, accomplices were quick to arrange a second auction.

In the second half of the century, the growing financial crisis in France made Paris a place for selling rather than for buying. Like Italy, France was mined for art treasures by German princes, English lords, Russian boyars and Dutch merchants. The Revolution extinguished this brilliant trade. England, collecting all during the eighteenth century, profited immeasurably from the liquidation of the French collections after 1789. France did not recover her position of eminence until a century later.

London's two great auction houses, Christie's and Sotheby, were founded in the eighteenth century. In 1744 Samuel Baker established the auction house which at his death assumed the name of his nephew, John Sotheby. Christie's was opened at 125 Pall Mall in 1766 by the thirty-six-year-old James Christie; its salons were used not only for public sales but also for exhibitions devoted to

56. Sir James Christie, by Thomas Gainsborough. *Paul Getty Collection, Sutton Place. In 1766 James Christie opened at 125 Pall Mall in London a public hall for exhibiting and selling the works of English artists.*

53. A Sale at Christies in London about 1805. Thomas Rowlandson. *As a result of the French Revolution, London became the main art dealing center in Europe ; many collections were brought from France to England for safety.*

54. Prince Eugene of Savoy at Somer's, the art dealer, in Amsterdam. Van den Berge. *Rijksmuseum, Amsterdam. Similar to* L'Enseigne de Gersaint, *this drawing shows Prince Eugene kneeling down to examine a picture shown to him by the painter Van den Berge, at Somer's, the art dealer (extreme right).*

55. Portrait of Samuel Baker, by Charles Grignon. *Detail. Sotheby Collection, London. In 1744 Samuel Baker began at Russel Street, Covent Garden, the first in a series of sales which eventually brought about the establishment of Sotheby's as an auction house.*

56

living artists, among them Gainsborough, a personal friend of James. The exodus of art from revolutionary France provoked great activity in the London market. In 1791, on the eve of the Reign of Terror, the Duke of Orléans, one of the most violent agitators of the Revolution, foreseeing the events about to convulse the French nation, sold in several lots to the English the celebrated collection in the Palais Royal; he benefited but little from the transaction, for this sans-culotte duke who called himself Philippe Egalité and was instrumental in having his cousin Louis XVI beheaded, was himself guillotined in 1793. The sale was a veritable liquidation, profiting only the buyers; the pre-auction exhibition of the paintings caused a sensation in London. This dispersal of France's finest princely cabinet consummated the fall of Paris and the ascension of London as the world's art market.

Eighteenth-century France boasted several expert dealers whose opinions were sought by foreigners: Gersaint, Basan, Glomy, Rémy. The most erudite was Jean Pierre Mariette (1694-1774), print dealer and engraver, who had inherited the business from his family. Knowledgeable and well-traveled, at the age of twenty-three he was recommended by Prince Eugene of Savoy to Emperor Charles VI to catalog the print collection at Vienna. He was responsible for several publications, in particular a *Traité des pierres gravées* (1750), which was the finest synthesis of dactyliologic knowledge at that period, and his *Abecedario,* a collection of biographical notes on artists of all time, in imitation of the *Abecedario pittorico* by the ecclesiastic Antonio Orlandi (1709). The business of refuting the Italian's errors took Mariette a lifetime. The manuscript of this monument to scholarly criticism, so different from the usual anecdotal biographies of artists, was withheld from the market by the dealer's family after his death and deposited in the royal print cabinet. There Chennevières and Montaiglon discovered it and eventually published it, an enterprise which took ten years to complete (1853-1863). Mariette had also envisaged publishing a corpus of the work of all engravers; the following century Bartsch drew copiously from his notes for his own monumental work, the *Peintre Graveur.* Mariette did not content himself with accumulating historical documents; he also sought to analyze the individual style of each artist, as is proven by his *Reflections on the drawing styles of principal painters* (1741). The keeper of the royal print cabinet invited him to collaborate on the remounting of the collection and his erudition opened for him the door to the Royal Academy of Painting and Sculpture, which he entered in 1750. Mariette collected not only prints but also drawings, a magnificent group which was dispersed in several celebrated sales in 1775 and 1776. Jealous of his collections, which served him in his scholarly research, he refused to show them; it was said of him that "he was like a miser hiding his gold; he opened his portfolio only for those whose love of art he knew or who were at least initiated into its mysteries."

Joseph Smith, generally called "Consul Smith" although he did not serve as England's consul to the Venetian Doge until near the end of his life, exemplifies another type of dealer. Born about 1675, the British subject had established himself in Venice by the beginning of the eighteenth century and entered into a partnership with an English merchant, Williams. After the latter's retirement in 1712, Consul Smith conducted the business alone. For the most part his first clients were English tourists

57. **Agony in the Garden, by Giovanni Bellini.** *Detail. National Gallery, London. Purchased in 1863 by the National Gallery, this work was undoubtedly among those taken from Venice by the British consul to that city, Joseph Smith, who was a professional art dealer in the XVIIIth century. The painting seems to have figured in the sale of the collection of the artist Sir Joshua Reynolds on March 13, 1745.*

in Venice whose ardent souvenir hunting touched off the mass production of *vedute*, in Rome as well as in Venice. Somewhat later Francesco Guardi began to paint such views; a number of his small-scale *vedute* and *capricci* still remain in English collections. Countrymen tended to patronize their fellow countrymen: French painters in Rome turned out views for French travelers; English painters, for English travelers. The cicerone who guided tourists in London procured works of art for them by such Englishmen as Colin Morison and James Byres.

At this time the industrious Joseph Smith worked diligently to recruit new customers; even the great Elector of Saxony became a client. Aware that Canaletto's *vedute* seemed to have special appeal for the British, he sent the artist to paint in England. His contract with Canaletto seems to have been quite similar to the arrangements current by the end of the nineteenth century; it reserved for him the right of first choice and provided for a commission on each painting sold. Smith also handled rare books and drawings; according to rumor, his integrity left something to be desired. He collected art for pleasure and the crowning achievement of his career was the sale of his entire collection to George III of England in 1762. Among the paintings, which included a number of seventeenth-century Venetian works, figured the singular *Agony in the Garden* by Giovanni Bellini, the *quattrocento* master who was little appreciated then; this picture is today one of the jewels of London's National Gallery.

Dealers combed Europe in search of lucrative business. One of the most picturesque of these agents—who denied being one—was Count Francesco Algarotti, the son of a Venetian banker and a man of great culture and refinement. After rounding out his education with stays in London and Paris, he betook himself to St. Petersburg in the company of Lord Baltimore. He afterwards divided his time between the courts of Prussia and Saxony, receiving the title of count from Frederick the Great; he advised the Elector of Saxony on supplementing and re-arranging his collections and procured for him many beautiful paintings. Algarotti lived in Berlin from 1747 to 1753; he died in Venice in 1764 at the age of fifty-two.

In this feverish world of art speculation, intellectuals did not disdain to act as intermediaries upon occasion, hoping to profit from the commissions paid them; Diderot, Grimm and Madame Geoffrin fulfilled such roles in Paris for Catherine II of Russia. Grimm procured for the czarina the entire collection of the Comte de Baudoin. The prudent Diderot sought the counsel of his painter friends Vernet, Cochin, Vien and Chardin; in 1772 he succeeded in buying en bloc the celebrated Crozat collection for the sum of 460,000 livres which, he wrote to Falconet, at that time engaged in casting a statue of Peter the Great at St. Petersburg, "is not the half of its worth." The deal was negotiated privately, thereby avoiding a public sale. A cynic, Diderot flattered his august client by belittling his own country: "We (French) are as poor as church mice; we sell our diamonds and strip our galleries to pay the controller general." As in the preceding century, artists willingly served as advisers to the illustrious; Hyacinthe Rigaud counseled Augustus of Saxony, King of Poland, whose portrait he had painted in Paris in 1715, the Duke of Savoy and the King of France himself. The American painter Gavin Hamilton, one of the early champions of the neoclassical aesthetic, handled antiquities in Rome, selling chiefly to England; much of what he traded came

58. **The Holy Family, by Rembrandt.** *Hermitage Museum, Leningrad. This work was purchased in Paris for Catherine II along with the collection of 119 paintings of the Comte de Baudoin in 1784. Diderot, Grimm and Madame Geoffrin acted as agents for Catherine in Paris.*

59. **Catherine II walking in the Tsarkoye Selo Park, by V. Borovikovski.** *Russian National Museum, Moscow. It was Catherine II who, with her purchases of entire collections throughout Europe, founded the imperial collections of the Hermitage.*

from sites he had excavated himself in the city or its environs.

As today, news concerning the sale of works of art and the high prices they commanded provoked passionate opinions. The removal of Raphael's *Sistine Madonna* from the Convent of Saint Sixtus at Parma by Augustus II of Saxony caused a sensation all over Europe. More than a year of bitter negotiations preceded the sale; a law forbidding its exportation, imposed by Philip, Duke of Parma, had to be lifted; the price paid—25,000 *écus*—seemed enormous. The prestigious work arrived in Dresden at the end of winter 1754. According to tradition, the entranced King of Poland yielded his throne to it because the lighting in that particular spot showed the painting to its best advantage. "Let one make room for the sublime Raphael," he supposedly cried out.

The loss of rich collections to foreigners was deeply felt. Paris deplored losing the Crozat collection to Catherine of Russia. In his *Memoires secrets* Bachaumont wrote on March 25, 1771, "The Russian Empress has obtained all the paintings in the collection of Monsieur the Count of Thiers (¹)... Monsieur de Marigny, lacking the funds to acquire them for the king, has had the misfortune of seeing these riches pass into the hands of a foreigner." In his preface for the catalog of the Tallard sale in Paris (which required thirty-three sessions from March 22 to May 14, 1756) the connoisseur Rémy appealed in a pathetic tone to all French collectors: "Can we not hope that the sale of this precious cabinet will attract the notice of our amateurs and that there will be a renascence of this great taste which not long ago prevailed in France... Already our too frequent losses have sufficiently warned us that foreigners have prodigiously enriched themselves at our expense and that, if we do not take precautions, they will succeed in stripping us of all our excellent paintings which have been the glory of our country and which were procured in Italy only after great effort and cost." Was Rémy sincere or clever? At the time of the sale the financial crisis was not yet so grave in France; but the taste for collecting had modified. One by-passed the noble compositions of the Renaissance and of the preceding century, preferring in their stead small Dutch pictures, *fêtes galantes,* porcelains, bronzes, precious furniture and *chinoiseries.*

The purchases of Catherine II provoked another scandal, this time in England. In 1778 Horace Walpole put up for sale the celebrated collection his father Lord Robert Walpole, Whig prime minister to two kings for twenty-five years, had assembled at his country house, Houghton Hall (Norfolk). Collectors in London waxed indignant when the czarina declared, "I have already laid my hands on them and I will not let go my prey any more than a cat would a mouse." John Wilkes convened the House of Commons and proposed raising funds to acquire the collection of Houghton Hall, which would form the nucleus of a national picture gallery within the British Museum; Parliament was not of the same opinion and the credits were refused.

Collecting was so in vogue that treatises were published to guide the amateur. The oldest of these bears the date 1727; entitled *Museographia,* it was written in Latin, which assured it an international distribution. Its author was a Hamburg dealer, Caspar F. Neickel. He advised on the choice of likely locations for finding objects, on the procedure for caring for them in a controlled climate, on problems of classification. He suggested placing a table in the middle of each salon on which pieces taken from the *repositorii* could be examined. He grouped objects under two headings: *naturalia* and *curiosa artificialia*; paintings and *objets d'art* formed part of the latter category and were prized not for their aesthetic qualities but as objects. The collections Neickel extolled were closer to the old curio cabinets than to the more modern cabinets of art. Both were cultivated to an equal degree throughout the century.

The museum also invaded the monastery. In the eighteenth century, abbeys tended to evolve into vast centers of culture, particularly in Central Europe where their metamorphosis into sumptuous palaces expressed the close association of Church and State. Located near the refectory, the imperial apartments, the theatre and the library and decorated like a temple to human learning, the museum was indispensable. Each monastery had its *Bildersaal* and its *Wunderkammer*; the monastery at Seitenstetten in Austria has preserved intact a cabinet of curiosities with all its objects and baroque armoires. In its *Mathematische Turm* the monastery at Kremsmünster has a veritable scientific museum and an observatory where the first meteorological notations were taken. The monasteries at Herzogenburg, Melk, Kremsmünster and Heiligenkreuz in Austria still have their *Bildersäale* where the walls are covered with paintings locked frame to frame. The monastery at Sankt Florian contains two museums; one, installed in 1767 is baroque and is composed of contemporary works either bought or received as gifts; the other is devoted to medieval and Renaissance pictures carefully arranged in a baroque setting, a juxtaposition of periods which reveals a remarkable museological sense. It is to this monastery that we owe the conservation of the major portion of the *œuvre* of Albrecht Altdorfer who shares with Dürer the distinction of being Germany's finest sixteenth-century painter. Austria retains some fine examples of the monastic museum; the museological form was not unknown to the rest of Europe (excepting Spain) but it fell victim to the vandalism that ravaged wherever the effects of the French Revolution made themselves felt. Let us mention in passing the museum of the *Benedittini* in Catania, founded by the prelate Vito Amico and Father Placidio Scammacca.

It contained antique and Paleo-Christian objects turned up in local excavations or purchased in Naples or Rome, as well as Chinese and Japanese curiosities brought back by missionaries. After the last World War, the collection joined that of Prince Biscari in the municipal museum at Castello Ursino, once the Catanian residence of Frederick II, King of Sicily. The *couvent des Génovefains* in Paris boasted a fine cabinet of curiosities, which grew out of several magnificent gifts; the scholar Peiresc gave a portion of his antiquities and the Comte de Caylus bequeathed his collection. In 1753 Louis d'Orléans provided the abbey with superb rococo style cabinets to hold its collection, to which he added his own. Louis d'Orléans was as pious and virtuous as his father was dissolute; he lived a secluded life within the convent his generosities had so handsomely enriched. Now a *lycée,* it still retains its cabinets but they are empty—the collections were confiscated during the Revolution. The celebrated series of glyphs is today in the *Cabinet des Médailles.*

As connoisseurship evolved into an art, the question of authenticity became an essential factor in determining the value of works of art; in his treatise Caspar Neickel recommended extreme caution in the matter. All this, however, did not prevent the copy from finding collectors and even partisans. "I do not fret over acquiring originals by the great masters," declared Charles de Brosses. "For certain reasons of my own, I make no case for having originals by minor masters; I prefer beautiful copies of famous paintings, available at a price I can afford." Impoverished artists found in copy work a way to survive. Between 1730 and 1745 Gian Antonio Guardi eked out a living tirelessly copying Venetian masterpieces, including Veronese's *Marriage at Cana* for Mattia von Schulenburg, the Doge's marshal. Picture galleries were formed with choice copies. The great French jurist and president of the *Cour des Comptes,* Paulin Pondre, created for his château at Guermantes, near Paris, a gallery that he had decorated in 1709 with paintings by Merelles after the old masters. This picture gallery, which still exists, documents artistic tastes at the end of the reign of Louis XIV. There are reproductions of Raphael's *Parnassus* and *School of Athens*; Guido Reni's *David and Goliath*; Il Domenichino's *Judith and Holofernes*; van Dyck's *Bacchus and Ariadne, Venus Requesting Arms for Aeneas, the Bagpipe Player* and a *Portrait of a Man*; a *Bacchanal* by Rubens and a *Saskia* by Rembrandt. This vogue for copies explains the abundance of so-called "original replicas" which have been troubling the art market since the eighteenth century. This interest in the reproduction surprises us today and yet the taste reflourishes under our eyes. An amateur like Carlos de Beistegui, who could well have afforded originals, preferred for his château at Groussaye a melange of period rooms, all of contemporary manufacture. For this type of collector the commissioning of copies undoubtedly satisfied the creative impulse better than the mere acquisition of old pieces.

The pervasive rationalism of the eighteenth century manifested itself museologically through advances in the fields of restoration and conservation. The trend was still to "complete" antiquities; however, the progress made in archeology, due principally to the excavations in the Campania, brought with it a better respect for the original document. The Comte de Caylus was fond of saying that when he formed a cabinet, he was not concerned with showpieces but that his interest was in "shards of agate, stone, pottery and glass which served better to re-establish the original use or the artist's intention." He carefully cleaned each of his fragments, analyzed its material to determine the composition and authenticity and often consulted chemists or mathematicians for help in his researches. He was an early champion of the scientific study of archeological documents and would have liked to see this mode of experimental investigation applied to paintings to corroborate the connoisseur's judgment.

As for paintings, the significant improvement of methods of restoration added to their longevity. One finds mention of conservators of paintings from the sixteenth century on; it was common practice at that time to summon the greatest artists to recondition the masterpieces of their predecessors. For example, Primaticcio cleaned and revarnished the Fontainebleau Raphaels—*The Holy Family* and *Saint Michael*—between 1537 and 1540. In 1603 the young Rubens journeyed to Valladolid with copies of Raphael paintings by Pietro Facchetti, a gift from the Duke of Mantua to the King of Spain. Finding them at the time of their unpacking greatly damaged by the humidity, the artist set about restoring them. "All the injuries they had sustained," he wrote the duke's secretary, "had given them the look of age." Works that had suffered terribly from long and difficult transports or radical changes in climate imposed upon them by commercial transactions were subjected to restoration. Old paintings had their darkened varnishes removed; they underwent cleaning, retouching, treatment for craquelure—interventions often carried to the extreme. In the seventeenth century the Florentine Baldinucci complained about the hazards of even careful restoration: "One runs the risk of losing the velatura, the half tones and even the retouches which are the final strokes responsible for a great part of the perfection of a work."

By the seventeenth century paintings whose supports had decayed were being reinforced with new backings bonded to the old. The technique of transferring a layer of paint by "lifting" it from its original canvas to a new one was invented during the following century. The process had been used with frescoes even earlier in Italy; documentary evidence dated 1507 proves its existence in Naples. It is true, however, that a portion of the wall was removed in these early attempts. The transfer of mural paintings became an acute problem with the discovery of Herculaneum and Pompeii. It seems strange that despite the presence of specialists in Naples, the Bourbons summoned François Canast whose crude technique was to quarter the *intonaco* and re-assemble the sections on a bed of gesso. Later, Giocchino was able to transfer a fresco in one piece. To Italy goes the credit for developing the process in the beginning of the eighteenth century and making it possible to transfer even panel paintings to canvas supports. The first conservators to use the process in France were Picault and Godefroy and, later, the latter's widow. In 1750 at the first exhibition of the king's paintings held in the Palais du Luxembourg, the astounded public could admire Andrea del Sarto's *Charity* on canvas, displayed next to its original wood support.

The program to follow in the restoration of any painting was the object of painstaking studies and conferences among experts before the work was entrusted to the conservator. In France, the Academy of Painting and Sculpture was called upon to give advice. By the beginning of the seventeenth century, Naples had a conservation center. The one at Venice, founded in 1778 with public funds, was particularly active; work proceeded in a room in the convent attached to San Zanipolo under the direction of Pietro Edwards. Even before the opening of this workshop, the Venetian government was seeing to the conservation of its masterpieces; from 1725 to 1777 reports were made on 751 "sick" paintings. Between 1779 and 1785 Edwards had restored, under the Accademia's watchful eye, 405 paintings. The Accademia Clementina at Bologna likewise supervised the restoration of pictures. These interventions often excited ardent debate. The value of patina—whether or not to remove it—was already being disputed. It is striking how close the methods of conservation and restoration and the controversies they aroused then are to those of today.

In the first half of the century the great French collections took shape. Not entirely aloof from the market, the king participated only upon occasion and at little expense. The most beautiful collections in France were eventually to pass into the hands of foreigners. The Duke d'Orléans boasted the richest cabinet, which was installed in the Palais Royal in an area with overhead lighting. This prince, who rivaled Augustus the Strong of Saxony in the number of bastards he fathered, hunted art as passionately as he hunted women. He had for a son a hypocritical prince who all but sold the entire collection after his father's death, destroyed some works he deemed licentious and bought only a few devotional pictures. The regent began collecting toward the end of the preceding century, devoting himself wholeheartedly to the task after the death of his father in 1701. His greatest coup was the purchase, negotiated in Rome by the financier Crozat, of a block of paintings belonging to Christina of Sweden. In time he amassed 478 paintings and an admirable collection of engraved gems.

Royal favorite against her will, offered in the prime of life by her husband to Victor Amadeus II of Savoy, the Countess de Verrue escaped the ducal court in 1700, building a townhouse for herself in Paris. To console her bitterness, she began assembling a collection; more modern than the regent's, its four hundred pictures included Dutch masters and contemporary French and Italian works. Everything was auctioned off in March and April of 1737; the English bought widely at this sale which interested the entire art world.

Originally from Toulouse, Pierre Crozat made his fortune in a banking venture with his brother Antoine Crozat, Marquis of Chatel. While the latter continued to pursue his career, Pierre Crozat retired at forty to enjoy his fortune. An enormously rich man, he was called "*Crozat le pauvre*" to distinguish him from his even richer brother. His was the finest collection of the century. Encompassing "all aspects of the rare in art," it comprised 1,500 intaglios, 400 paintings and 19,000 drawings; an important part came from Venice where the regent had sent him on a buying expedition for paintings. These treasures and the proceeds from the sale of a portion of them were divided among his heirs after his death in 1740. The engraved stones were bought en bloc by the Duke d'Orléans; the drawings were put up for public sale; the oldest of his nephews, Louis-François Crozat, Marquis of Chatel, inherited the sculptures. The paintings were divided into three lots, the most important of which went to the younger brother of the Marquis, Louis Antoine Crozat who sold them to Catherine of Russia in 1772. As for the paintings bought by the regent, they were eventually sold in London, where they had been sent in 1791.

The eighteenth century witnessed the flowering of amateurism in England. The loose control of a foreign monarchy fostered a broad and intense development of society life which enjoyed great luxury because of the general economic prosperity.

60. **The Sistine Madonna, by Raphael.** *Gemäldegalerie, Dresden. In 1753, after long and difficult negotiations, Frederick Augustus II of Saxony, succeeded in obtaining this painting from the Convent of Saint Sixtus at Plaisance for a considerable sum, thus provoking a great sensation among the princely amateurs of Europe. The famous work arrived in Dresden in 1754.*

118

London was not the sole beneficiary; provincial life, centering around the great country houses, also flourished. Among the twenty-eight most important collections enumerated in his *English Connoisseur* (1776), Thomas Martyn credited no fewer than four to the Duke of Devonshire: Chatsworth, Hardwick Hall, Chiswick and, in London, Devonshire House. Englishmen traveling in Europe bought up masterpieces everywhere: Rome, Venice, Paris, Amsterdam. This passion for the painting of the past ended up by incurring the wrath of the moderns who rebelled against the "grand style." Hogarth used his talent for polemics to further the cause. Out of this movement of protest emerged the Royal Academy of Arts, founded in 1769 to defend the rights of artists; it originated in an export trade to benefit the Foundling Hospital. The society's first president was Sir Joshua Reynolds who, more than any other artist, manifested a lively taste for earlier schools of painting!

Another passion gripped elegant English society—the taste for antiquities. More than other Europeans, the English were responsible for reviving an antique influence which was to convulse the evolution of styles and lead to neoclassicism. An association was founded in London in 1739 to propagate the classical taste: The Society of Dilettanti; in the beginning this was a group of jovial drinkers who met for dinner the first Sunday of each month, at which time they exchanged *lazzi* and epigrams in Latin. Sir William Hamilton, husband of the celebrated and scandalous Emma Lyon, Nelson's mistress, brought back an archeological collection from Naples where he had been ambassador. The finest ensemble of antiquities graced the Westminster home of Charles Towneley, intimate friend of Hamilton; this *maison-musée* became a meeting place for connoisseurs and artists. Charles Towneley was especially interested in sculpture while Payne Knight collected medals, intaglios and small bronzes. The Hamilton, Towneley and Knight collections eventually enriched the British Museum.

In eighteenth-century Germany amateurism remained an attribute of the royalty of the various principalities but the passion for collecting was second to the desire to dazzle with splendid buildings. Certain capitals, however, because of their enlightened monarchs, began to amass works of art. At Brunswick, Duke Charles William Ferdinand consolidated into a museum the collections brought together by Anton Ulrich during the seventeenth century and enriched it which his own acquisitions. The prince of Hesse-Kassel formed an admirable picture gallery which the vicissitudes of history later removed en bloc to Leningrad. At Düsseldorf William of Pfalz-Neuberg (who reigned from 1690 to 1716) collected paintings by Rubens and van Dyck and managed to acquire Rembrandt's celebrated cycle of *The Passion,* which had been commissioned by Frederick Henry, Prince of Nassau and Stadholder of the United Netherlands. Düsseldorf lost this cabinet to Munich at the beginning of the nineteenth century. At an even earlier date, the Bavarian capital received the Mannheim collections, rich in the Netherlandish school, when in 1777 the Wittelsbach line died out and the duchy passed to the Palatinate. Fortune favored Munich; not only did the collections of others converge upon this metropolis in southern Germany but the city boasted an admirable gallery of its own based on the collection of the Elector Max Emanuel. The elector had a particular liking for the Flemings and collected so zealously that he went into debt. In a single transaction on September 17, 1698 he bought from Ghisbert von Ceulen 120 works for 90,000 florins. The lot included twelve paintings by Rubens (including

Helena Fourment and *The Rape of the Daughters of Leucippus*), fifteen van Dycks, ten Velvet Brueghels and eight Brouwers. Later, he bought paintings by Poussin, Murillo and Titian. Conforming to an eighteenth-century vogue, he built a special edifice to house his collections: Schloss Schleissheim, near Munich, the work of an Italian architect, Zuccali. For his paintings he commissioned beautiful and elegant frames, all patterned after a single model.

Frederick the Great of Prussia infused with new life the rudimentary *Kunstkammer* inherited from his ancestors. His taste for things French inclined him toward the Parisian painters of the eighteenth century. He bought thirteen Watteaus, twenty-six Lancrets, thirty-seven Paters, four Chardins and works by Boucher and de Troy. He had wanted to broaden the range of his collections but the necessities of war obliged him to curb his desires. In 1763 Catherine II acquired in Berlin a group of northern paintings originally intended for him. Frederick envied the Elector of Saxony who preferred art to soldiers but who was to repent his choice when Frederick's troups occupied his territory.

The museological capital of eighteenth-century Germany was incontestably Dresden. In her two successive electors, both called Frederick Augustus and both elected kings of Poland, were combined the virtues of East and West. Each had the occidental's refined taste as well as the oriental's sense of superabundance. Frederick Augustus I (Augustus the Strong or Augustus II as king of Poland) made his *Kavalierstour* through Europe (1687-1689) as a young crown prince. The trip left a deep impression on him; he was determined to cut the figure of a great monarch and resolved to make his court at Dresden the equal of the glittering European capitals. He plunged into a massive building program, threw splendid parties and bought art on a large scale —a policy which was to prove ruinous for Saxony. His son, Augustus III, followed suit; his misgovernment ended in the catastrophic Seven Years' War which put Saxony at the feet of Prussia. History has been severe in its judgment of the two rules but contemporary thought tends to show more indulgence toward these inept monarchs who preferred artists to soldiers. Augustus II made a trade with the soldier-king, Frederick William I of Prussia, of six hundred dragoons in exchange for a series of Chinese vases which so took his fancy that he built in Dresden a veritable "temple of porcelain" and had no peace until Saxony herself had discovered the secret of hard-paste porcelain. He founded the royal porcelain manufacture in Albrechtsburg Castle in Meissen in 1710. As for Frederick William I, he had no hesitation about bartering his works of art for rare specimens of soldiery; he "sold" to Catherine II of Russia an entire cabinet of Baltic amber, which he had just had made for himself, in exchange for one hundred grenadiers six and a half feet tall.

Innumerable agents and canvassers, including Count Francesco Algarotti, combed Europe on behalf of the Elector of Saxony. Augustus II began his collecting with a masterly coup, acquiring in 1698 from Le Roy, a Parisian dealer, fifteen paintings, among them the *Sleeping Venus* by Giorgione. Count Brühl, who formed a collection of his own that was later bought by Catherine II, served as prime minister under Augustus III in a government which accorded first place to "cultural affairs." Under his ministry, art from all over Europe converged upon the Saxon capital. A few statistics will give an idea of the lavishness of this prince: Augustus III, being exceed-

ingly fond of pastels by Rosalba, owned no fewer than 157 of her works; in 1745 he purchased the *quadreria* of Duke Francesco III of Modena (one hundred paintings) and in 1753 he acquired Raphael's *Sistine Madonna*. These trophies entered Dresden only a short time before disaster erupted, the result of the policy of luxury and pleasure; in 1756 the Seven Years' War broke out and with it ended the vigorous life of the *Gemäldegalerie*.

In 1722 a general inventory taken of paintings divided among the various royal churches, chapels and palaces listed 4,700 pictures, of which 3,110 were works of value. (In 1707 only 535 works had been counted.) After a fire in the royal residence in 1705, the cabinets containing the collection of curiosities, happily spared, were moved; the paintings were taken down at the same time and re-installed in the ballroom. By 1722 larger quarters were needed so the buildings near the *Jüdenhof* were remodeled for that purpose. Between 1744 and 1746, the galleries were enlarged and given wide, arched bays that permitted a better lighting for the paintings.

Heinecken, curator of the gallery, undertook publication of a work on the chief masterpieces in the collection, the first volume of which appeared in 1753. The notes accompanying each painting, reproduced in engravings, and the preface, which traced the history of the collection, were in French, the international language of amateurs and collectors.

Contact with the West introduced Peter the Great, imitator of European monarchs, to collecting. Until then, the czars had maintained only a garderobe in which accumulated the arms, armor, precious cloths, jewels and the gold and silver plate it behooved a czar to own; the present-day Kremlin museum had its origins in such a repository and still retains the name of "Arms Museum." The amateurism of Peter the Great only went halfway; the collections he formed were more like those of a sixteenth-century German prince than those of a monarch in the Age of Enlightenment. Do we not see in him a Rudolf II, interested in the freaks of nature, ordering that fetuses and monsters preserved in alcohol be sent to him? His cabinet at Saint Petersburg was, then, primarily a curiosities cabinet. The most "curious" objects were undoubtedly the pieces of solid gold jewelry found in tombs in Siberia which were sent to him as a gift on the occasion of his son's birth by Nikita Demidov, the son of a serf who had become the richest miner in the Urals. Since gold extracted from prehistoric tombs was included in the total yield of the mines, these early monuments were subjected to exploitation by specially trained prospectors. Why, unless he knew of his sovereign's interest in all sorts of curiosities, did Nikita Demidov make a gift of these bizarre objects instead of having them melted down, as was the usual practice? In any event, the jewelry had a great effect; the czar, captivated by the beauty of the objects and by the aura of mystery they evoked as relics of barbarian civilizations, immediately promulgated a ukase to protect the Siberian monuments; he further decreed that whatever was found in the earth, including fossils, be sent to him. To win his master's favor, the governor of Siberia, one Prince Gagarine, financed special expeditions which yielded about one hundred exquisitely formed pieces of this gold jewelry. They were sent in several lots to St. Petersburg where today they number among the most precious objects in the Treasure of the Hermitage. An analogous find has not been made since.

61. **Helena Fourment, by Peter Paul Rubens.** *Alte Pinakothek, Munich. This picture, painted on the occasion of Ruben's marriage (December 6, 1630) was part of the sale of more than one hundred works (including 12 by Rubens) by the merchant Ghisbert von Ceulen to the Elector Max Emanuel in 1698.*

Peter the Great also had a few antique sculptures, among them a *Venus*, said to be by Tauriscus, and some paintings; it is not surprising that these were from the Dutch School because it was through Holland that Peter, who wanted to work as a carpenter in the shipbuilding yards in Amsterdam, came into contact with western civilization. In fact, the first plan for the new city of Saint Petersburg had been inspired by that of Amsterdam. Among the paintings was an especially fine Rembrandt, *David and Jonathan,* which the czar had bought in Amsterdam in 1716.

Peter's cabinet of curiosities was installed at first in the building of the twelve colleges, a vast administrative complex that housed the different ministries; the collection was open to the public—indeed, the czar, who desired the enlightenment of his compatriots, encouraged visitors to come and had snacks and vodka served to them! In 1734 the cabinet was moved to the Academy of Sciences where it was given a national museological installation; the collections devoted to natural history and ethnography remain there yet. The others are now in the Hermitage, incorporated into the museum collections or presented in a special gallery, over which a wax likeness of Peter the Great presides, dressed in robes once worn by the czar himself.

Catherine II, informed by Raffenstein, her agent in Rome, of the talent of Signora Maron, sister of Raphael Mengs, for making miniatures, wrote her correspondent: "Order me several, several, as though they were little pastries to fill a basket." She was completely serious in this pronouncement, this czarina who called herself a "*gloutonne*" where art was concerned. A princess from one of the smallest German houses who attained at thirty-three an imperial career through a *coup d'état* she perpetrated on the very person of her husband, Catherine was an adventuress of genius; she was never sated by yet another military campaign, another lover, another masterpiece. Her unquenchable thirst for culture was a sort of barbarian instinct whose avidity knew no bounds; her imagination was limitless. She was just the monarch needed at that crucial moment in the expansion of the Russian empire. She bought everything en bloc: Diderot's library and that of Voltaire; all the portfolios of drawings by Clérisseau; at Dresden, the entire collection of Count Brühl (1769); at Paris, the entire Crozat collection (1771; 400 paintings) as well as that of the Comte de Baudoin (1784; 119 paintings) and the regent's collection of 1,500 intaglios; at London, the whole Walpole cabinet (1779; 498 paintings). She was represented at all the sales, with courtiers bidding or buying for her in Paris, London, Amsterdam and Brussels; her ambassadors and "philosophers" acted as her agents. The moment a great collector died, she was notified. Ships crossed the seas with cargoes of masterpieces for her; in 1780 one ship sank in the Baltic with the loss of a group of paintings from the Gerrit Braamkamp collection in Amsterdam. Dealers from all over the world flocked to Saint Petersburg to show their paltry goods; they were usually badly received as Catherine preferred paintings with illustrious pedigrees that could inspire her with confidence. She commissioned copies of works she could not have. Knowing full well what a trip outside Russia might cost her, she refrained from going to Rome, lured though she was by its mirage. Undeterred, she had all the Raphaels in the Vatican copied for her palace; from this insane project, which Raffenstein supervised, there remain the copies of the loggie, done between 1778 and 1785; the architect Quarenghi built a special gallery for them in 1788. Hardly had her armies reached the Black Sea

62. **Peter the Great.** *Wax figure dressed in the czar's robes. Gallery of Peter the Great, Hermitage Museum, Leningrad. In spite of his haste to modernize Russia, Peter the Great did not neglect the formation of those collections which add to the glory of a monarch and are indispensable instruments for progress in the sciences and the arts in a modern state. He accumulated books and curiosities and bought the first paintings for the imperial collections.*

when she ordered excavations; she enriched her treasury with a find of marvelous gold jewelry executed centuries earlier by Greek goldsmiths working on the coast. She commissioned splendid pieces of *orfèvrerie* from the Parisian artisans Germain, August and Gouthière, occasionally giving them as gifts to her favorites. She inspired emulation; the Orlov, Demidov, Yussupov, Stroganov and Cheremetiev families began to collect. They eventually contributed to the national wealth of Russia, since their collections, along with hers, were confiscated by the Soviets.

The first catalog of Catherine's collection appeared in French in 1774; it detailed 2,080 entries and of its seventy-six pages, six had been left blank; in the copy in the Hermitage, these blank pages bear handwritten mention of 125 new paintings. At about the same time, Count Ernest Munnich was compiling, at the czarina's order, a more detailed catalog which was never printed; the third volume, dated 1785, lists 2,658 paintings.

To house these masterpieces, an entire museum had to be built. Catherine at first contented herself with disposing them throughout her private apartments in the Palais d'Hiver and in a pleasure pavilion, an "*ermitage*" built for her by the Frenchman Vallin de La Mothe from 1765 to 1768, on the banks of the Neva; this hermitage was connected to her apartments by a long gallery. She withdrew there to rest, beyond the reach of etiquette, with her intimates, among her paintings, her parrots and her favorite animals; a roll-away table allowed the czarina and her guests to dine without the presence of servants. Unfortunately, this retreat was completely renovated in 1858 to 1859 and was given a decor in poor taste. In 1775 Catherine ordered Felten to build an annex to the pleasure pavilion, intended from the first as a museum; it was called the "*grand ermitage*" to distinguish it from the "*petit ermitage*" built ten years earlier by Vallin de La Mothe and known now as the "old hermitage."

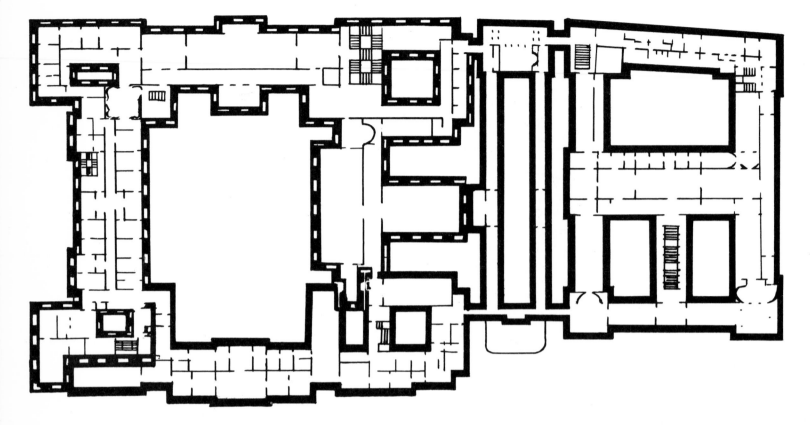

63. Plan of the Winter Palace and the Hermitage Museum, Leningrad. *In 1765, Catherine II started construction for an "ermitage" or pleasure pavilion on the banks of the Neva which she connected to the Winter Palace (built by Czarina Elizabeth) by means of a gallery. Here she put her collections which, however, became so extensive that she was obliged to construct in 1775, next to the pavilion, another building which today is known as the "Old Hermitage." Behind it Czar Nicholas I had the "New Hermitage" erected between 1840 and 1849 according to the designs of Leo von Klenze.*

Catherine's extravagant love for the wholesale collection of paintings and other art objects was not inherited by her son and successor, Paul I. Although he showed no interest in making new acquisitions, Paul did, at least, set up a commission formed of members of the Academy of Fine Arts to verify the inventory of paintings, drawings and engravings displayed and stored in the Hermitage. The commission's report showed that a staggering total of 3,996 paintings had been counted.

Chapter 7

The Cabinet and the Gallery

Under the *ancien régime* a principle of lavishness, bordering on excessiveness, governed the presentation of works of art. If our ancestors were to wander through our museums, with their great expanses of empty wall, they would find them poor and in bad taste. Visiting Roman *palazzi* from the end of 1739 to the beginning of 1740, Charles de Brosses noted: "The entire decoration of a room consists in covering its four walls, from ceiling to floor, with paintings, in such profusion and with so little space between them that, in truth, the eye is often as fatigued as amused. In addition there is hardly any expenditure for frames, the majority being old, black and shabby, with a great number of mediocre things among the beautiful." President de Brosses ought to have been pleased by the ornately framed pictures in the *galleria Palatina* in Florence's Pitti Palace which he visited on the same trip, but he seems to have been disappointed there as well.

Beginning in the sixteenth century, works of art or curiosities were kept in two sorts of places whose different purposes were not always clearly defined; the "gallery" and the "cabinet." Physically, the gallery was a long, grand hall; more restrained, the cabinet was a square-shaped room. The gallery designated a sumptuous, luxuriously appointed *salon* where works of art formed an integral part of the decor; in the cabinet, the greatest possible number of objects were crowded together, unencumbered by decorative trappings. It gradually happened, however, that a succession of splendid reception rooms became known as a gallery, like the *galleria Palatina* in the Pitti Palace, and that galleries per se assumed a purely utilitarian character. By the end of the sixteenth century, the English word "gallery" connoted exhibition areas for painting or sculpture, while "cabinet" designated both collections of curiosities, natural and otherwise, and places where small *objets d'art* were conserved—medallions, glyphs, metalwork and bronze statuettes. "Cabinet" came into English usage through the French language, which had adapted it from the Italian *gabinetto*; meaning at first a place or a piece of furniture for the safekeeping of personal papers and valuables, by the end of the eighteenth century it was used in a museological sense.

Since the word "gallery" also derives from Italian, it is surprising that the gallery itself originated in France. As explained in an as-yet-unpublished thesis by Mlle. Litoux

64. **Madonna della Sedia, by Raphael.** *Palatine Gallery, Pitti Palace, Florence. The grand dukes of Tuscany, after the end of the XVIth century, surrounded the paintings which were displayed in the reception halls of the Pitti palace with sumptuous borders which, in keeping with the baroque decor of the XVIIth century, at times almost rivaled the works themselves.*

of the Ecole du Louvre, the gallery, insofar as it is an elegant salon, derives from the *grande salle* of medieval châteaux. Italian palaces and villas in the fifteenth century and even in the beginning of the sixteenth do not have them, unless one considers as such the large, two-story *salone* in the villa built by Lorenzo the Magnificent at Poggio a Caiano; but, too wide and too high, it has not the format of a gallery. The first two *gallerie* in Italy were those designed by Bramante to connect the Belvedere of Innocent VIII to the Vatican; nearly a quarter of a mile long, they are more immense corridors for traffic than galleries in the modern sense. The vogue for the gallery in Renaissance France was, then, indigenous in origin. The royal château at Fontainebleau had no fewer than five galleries dating from the 1500's; the famous gallery said to have been built by Francis I or the Reformers and decorated by Rosso was unique in its time. However, by the end of the *cinquecento* the Italians had adapted the gallery to the presentation of works of art; such is the case in the *casino del giardino* at Sabbioneta or in the *antiquarium* in the Residenz at Munich; the former is today empty, but in the latter, antiquities complete a decor of delicate pastoral grotesques evoking Bavarian cities and villages.

An authoritative Italian architect acknowledged the French origins of the gallery. Vincenzo Scamozzi, in his *Idea dell'architettura universale* (1615), wrote: "Today in Rome, Genoa and other Italian cities, the structure known as the gallery enjoys wide use; possibly first introduced in France to serve as a passageway for the men at court, the gallery approaches in proportions our *loggia* but is somewhat less open. This type of construction was in some degree known to the ancients... In this city [Venice] the gallery is not used so much for the exterior of public places as in France, Spain and elsewhere; for some time, following Roman example, it has been introduced into the houses of many senators, gentlemen and collectors of antique marbles and bronzes, medallions, bas reliefs and paintings by the most celebrated and prestigious masters who have ever lived."

After a period of evolution in Italy, the gallery returned to France, having as its inimitable model the Hercules Gallery, painted by the Carracci for the Farnese Palace, Rome. In the seventeenth century all the grand and noble *hôtels* of Paris had their galleries, richly decorated by stuccoers, cabinetmakers and contemporary painters (*hôtels* Lambert, Bretonvilliers, de Lignières, La Vrillière). Louis XIV was only imitating his subjects in his decorative commissions for the Apollo Gallery in the Louvre or the Hall of Mirrors at Versailles. The *Grande Galerie* of the Louvre, that is, the gallery running along the river, was conceived by an Italian, Queen Catherine de'Medici; at first, it was no more than a monumental passageway, like the Vatican galleries, connecting a château in the city (the Louvre) to a country residence (the Tuileries); the efforts of Louis XIII to turn it into a banquet hall and ballroom, with all the attendant decor, failed. Certain galleries were especially designed for exhibiting works of art, such as the two superposed galleries, preserved in the Bibliothèque Nationale, Paris, and designated as the *galerie mazarine,* that was erected by the cardinal in the former *hôtel* Tubeuf, owned by him and enlarged by Mansard. The lower level held antiquities; the upper, paintings, furniture and the most divers objects, displayed against hangings of red damask and crowded closely together, as described by the *Grande Mademoiselle*, Anne-Marie-Louise d'Orléans, in her *Mémoires*: "The gallery was a full as a stall at a fair except that there was no rubbish." The two-story gallery of Arundel House, London, known to us through the paintings of Daniel Mytens, dates from the same period; as in the *hôtel* Mazarin, the lower level was reserved for antiquities; the upper, for paintings, which were disposed between windows. Laid out during the same period, the *galleria Palatina* in Florence is a succession of luxurious apartments, decorated with magnificent ceilings painted by Pietro da Cortona for Grand Duke Ferdinand II de'Medici between 1637 and 1647; gildings, marbles, crystals and ceiling paintings added to the lavishness of these princely apartments that Ferdinand II, fulfilling a plan of Cosimo II, fitted as a *quadreria,* formed by a qualitative selection of paintings from the Medici collections. Crowded together frame to frame, these pictures constituted an essential element of the decor not only in themselves but also by virtue of their rich frames; some were made in the mannerist period, when woodworking arts were influenced by goldsmithery, while others were baroque; they were conceived as triumphant crowns for the most illustrious of paintings. Anna Maria Ciaranfi rightly remarked that the guiding principle behind the arrangement of the *quadreria* was "to surround beauty with beauty." Pillaged only once by the government of Revolutionary France, with restitutions made in 1815 and a subsequent re-opening in 1833, the *galleria Palatina* remains one of the rare European examples of the princely presentation of a museum. In Paris the gallery of the La Vrillière mansion is another example, but on a smaller scale and in closer correspondence with the original format of the gallery. Built by Phélippeaux de la Vrillière in 1640, it was refurbished to suit the taste of the day by Robert de Cotte between 1713 and 1719 for the count of Toulouse; it was sumptuously wainscoted by Vassé and from then on was called the *Galerie dorée.* Set into the panelwork were six paintings by great masters: Poussin, Pietro da Cortona, Carlo Maratta, Guercino, Alessandro Veronese, Guido Reni. This time one more step was taken to integrate the works with the whole, for the paintings were incorporated into the paneling and had to conform to its irregular contours ([1]). The practice of treating paintings as decorative elements often led to a modification of their dimensions, either through reduction or, more often, through enlargement, without respect for the original intentions of the artist. As late as 1778, when the museological spirit had insinuated itself everywhere, do we not find in France the Count d'Angiviller proposing that the court painter cut Poussin's beautiful, but too large, *Martyrdom of Saint Francis Xavier,* acquired for the king at the Jesuit sale in 1763? It was not done because the artist said that it would destroy the harmony of the composition.

In the *palazzo Colonna* at Rome, a large gallery was constructed toward the end of the seventeenth century to house the collection brought together by Cardinal Geronimo I Colonna. Opened in 1703, the gallery, some 230 feet long, 39 feet wide and 32 feet high, was modeled after the Hall of Mirrors at Versailles; like the latter, it terminates in two *salons* at each end; antiquities were presented in the gallery, paintings in the *salons.* Charles de Brosses found the complex "preferable to the one at Versailles and filled with exquisite paintings." Very famous, it attracted countless visitors to Rome in the eighteenth century, becoming the archetypal gallery, the ideal setting for a real or imaginary museum. In 1749 Giovanni Paolo Pannini disposed in a gallery inspired by the Galleria Colonna the collection amassed by Cardinal Silvio Valenti

Gonzaga in his villa near the Porta Pia (today, the Villa Bonaparte); the painting, the sketch of which is in Marseilles, is in the Wadsworth Atheneum, Hartford, Connecticut ([2]). For the duke of Choiseul, who wanted an imperishable souvenir of the beauty of Rome where he served as French ambassador from 1753 to 1757, Pannini executed four paintings. Two depict actual sites, the *Square before St. Peter's* ([3]) and the *Interior of St. Peter's* ([4]). For the other two, which were to evoke "antique Rome" and "modern Rome" ([5]), Pannini arranged sculptures and *vedute*, painted in his own style, in ideal galleries patterned after the Colonna setting. These two imaginary museums enjoyed immediate success; Pannini made a replica of them soon after, in collaboration with Hubert Robert, into whose collection they passed; these are the canvases now in the Metropolitan Museum of Art, New York ([6]). The Louvre is indebted to the Princess de Polignac for another version, of larger dimensions, doubtlessly commissioned by Claude François de Montboissier, abbot, then cardinal, of Canillac, who lived in Rome from 1753 until his death in 1763 ([7]). Today's amateurs have photographic records of their collections; in former times, the records themselves were works of art.

The seventeenth century saw the revival of the practice of hanging pictures against red backgrounds, particularly suited to works of the Renaissance and also to *seicento* paintings which, often somber, were even painted on gesso of this color in Italy and France. The paintings gallery of Cardinal Mazarin was fitted in crimson velours; was this simply because the shade was appropriate for a cardinal? It was rather because it had already been recognized that this color enhanced a picture. In fact, Boschini in his *Carta del Navegar pittoresco,* published in Venice in 1660, recommended dressing the walls of galleries in scarlet and purple velours and using very ornate, gilded frames. Fallen into disuse in the eighteenth century with its preference for stuccos in clear colors, red regained its popularity the following century because of the influence of Pompeiian red backgrounds and was used on the walls of nearly all painting and sculpture galleries.

Here and there across Europe one still finds intact picture galleries from the baroque period. One of the best preserved is that housed in the castle of Pommersfelden in Franconia, begun in 1711 by Johan Dietzenhofer for the archchancellor of the Empire, Lothar Franz von Schönborn; although a few of its masterpieces were sold in the nineteenth century, the gallery remains more or less in its original form.

Insofar as it is a room of small dimensions destined to receive works of art, the cabinet made its appearance in the sixteenth century in the form of a portrait collection. The wood-paneled cabinet of the château of Pibrac, near Toulouse, dates from the sixteenth century although the paintings in it are seventeenth-century works; the châteaux of Beauregard and Bussy-Rabutin (the former in a gallery format, the latter in the more restrained form of the cabinet) are examples of seventeenth-century French cabinets.

In the seventeenth century both the cabinet and the gallery were in vogue; they became veritable catchalls as paintings and all kinds of objects accumulated. The tendency to horde is peculiarly characteristic of northern Europeans, who found monumental galleries ill-suited to their more restrained style of dwelling; this utilitarian reason is not the only one: a concentration of *objets d'art* and curiosities in a small space appealed to the amateurs of the North, trained by the humanist vision of Bruegel

65. **Picture gallery in Pommersfelden Castle.** *(Germany.) Pommersfelden Castle, in Franconia, was started in 1711 by Johann Dietzenhofer for the Imperial Arch Chancellor, Lothar Franz von Schönborn; its collection of pictures, distributed in several cabinets and a long gallery, has been preserved almost in its entirety.*

to see a microcosm in a grain of sand, to see the Infinite hiding in the specific. Paintings representing an "amateur's cabinet" were the *succès fou* of seventeenth-century Flemish genre painting. Few works document actual collections; the majority are imaginary cabinets. From time to time, however, paintings inspired by one or another Antwerp collection particularly pleased buyers. It is through these that we know the arrangement of Ruben's cabinet, an admixture of paintings and medallions disposed in a large *salon* that was a sort of apse, inspired by the Pantheon in Rome and, like it, illumined by a central oculus; Rubens had had it built to hold the antique busts purchased from Sir Dudley Carleton; cabinet and collection together created an evocation of Rome for him.

In several of these "views of cabinets," painters delighted in dressing figures in costumes of the preceding century; heedless of anachronisms, one artist showed Alexander the Great visiting the studio of Apelles, an Apelles who collected Massys and Rubens! Jan Brueghel turned to the theme of the amateur's cabinet to illustrate his *Five Senses,* a series of paintings of galleries and cabinets overflowing with all kinds of natural and man-made articles; these well-wrought microcosms afforded the public of the period, particularly the entrenched Flemish *bourgeoisie,* an escape through time as well as space. The seventeenth-century collection we know best is that assembled by Archduke Leopold-Wilhelm, governor of the Netherlands from 1646 to 1656, at the Château of Coudenberg, Brussels. At the magistrate's order, David Teniers the Younger, his curator and court painter, executed "views" of various rooms of the collection; these paintings were given as souvenirs to illustrious visitors. For these reproductions in miniature of the *chefs d'œuvres* in the archducal gallery, Teniers used the two hundred forty-four "pastiches," or copies in a small format, he had previously made for engravings in the *Theatrum pictorium.*

The vogue for depicting the amateur's cabinet had disappeared by the beginning of the eighteenth century but, if the style was no longer *à la mode,* the conditions it represented persisted in galleries and cabinets throughout the *Ancien Régime.* We know Jean de Julienne's collection through gouache copies, made in 1756, of each of the three hundred twenty-four paintings hanging on the walls of his apartment; bound together in a sort of catalog, they inspired Storffer's guide to the Vienna gallery.

Some *Bildersäle* of abbeys and castles in central Europe have remained intact, their paintings almost frame to frame, separated by only a thin strip of molding. During the eighteenth century collectors were fond of this decoration *en tapisserie,* which covered the entire wall; the castles of Peterhof and Tsarskoye Selo near Leningrad were, until their destruction in World War II, remarkable examples of this practice.

In the seventeenth century the lighting of galleries and cabinets was lateral. The eighteenth century, in order to find a light more suited to pictures and to free wall space for hangings by avoiding fenestration, took to overhead lighting; thus was the presentation of the regent's collection in the Palais Royal, Paris. This mode of lighting was, however, the exception. In buildings constructed or laid out for use as pinakothekai in the 1700's (at Dresden and Munich, for example), one length of wall was usually opened with glassed-in arcades which allowed abundant light for the other three.

The tapestried effect in decor prevailed everywhere, being used also for *objets d'art,* porcelains, faïences and metalwork. Augustus the Strong, Elector of Saxony and

King of Poland, decorated an entire room in the royal residence at Dresden with Chinese porcelains, most of them rare specimens bought at inflated prices to satisfy a particular passion; the last war, which destroyed the different cabinets of Zwinger, happily spared it. Augustus dreamed of outdoing the Dresden project by erecting a veritable temple of porcelain in his palace in Holland, an undertaking never brought to completion. Charlottenburg, near Berlin, has kept its *Porzellankabinett,* laid out in 1705 and 1706, and doubtlessly the model for the Dresden one. A unique ensemble is the cabinet devoted to objects in glass in Copenhagen's Rosenborg; built by Christian IV in 1606, this castle, where all sorts of marvels were accumulated throughout the seventeenth and eighteenth centuries, is a kind of palace of a thousand and one nights, with extraordinary silver furniture made at Augsburg and Copenhagen in the 1700's; the dynastic piety of the Danish royal family has kept it intact. Among its treasures the rarest, if not the most valuable, are those in the cabinet of glassware, planned by Frederick IV in 1714 for the second floor of the palace; crystal plates and vases gathered from all over Europe by the king glitter like stalactites in this gilded "cave." Part of the collection was an important gift of Murano glassware from the Venetian Doge in 1708. Rosenborg also boasts a *Porzellankabinett* and a *Buffetkabinett,* a small *salon* for the display of gold and silver services, a custom much in vogue in central Europe in the eighteenth century.

If superabundance was pleasing to our ancestors and seemed to them the most effective way to enhance the value of works of art, all the more reason why they were lured by cabinets of curiosities, where profusion symbolized the inexhaustible richness of nature's creations and the ingeniousness of means used by man to penetrate their mysteries. In the eighteenth century scientific progress turned physical and chemical experimentation into a subject for the *salon;* many an *hôtel* had its *cabinet de physique,* without which its proprietor could hardly be considered a *curieux* or a savant.

Curios and instruments were usually displayed in elegant, glass-paned armoires, a style of furniture which appeared at this time. One can still see in Paris in the former abbey of Sainte Geneviève (today the Lycée Henri IV), admirable Louis XVth show-cases for curiosities and archeological artifacts (now emptied of their contents). All has been left untouched—paneling, furniture, showcases, objects—in the natural history cabinet in the monastery at Seitenstetten, Austria, and in that conceived by Clement Lafaille in 1766 for his *hôtel* at La Rochelle; the latter, a cabinet of conchology, has passed out of the hands of the Academy, to which it was originally bequeathed, to the museum where it can be seen today. These science cabinets were sometimes given as sumptuous a decor as the art galleries. The most extraordinary was, without doubt, that of Jacques Bonnier de la Mosson. Having inherited from his father an enormous fortune, he squandered it on debaucheries and on collections. Of a sensual temperament, this man was passionately interested in the technical applications of science. Seven rooms on the ground floor of his Paris mansion housed his art collection; the science cabinet was on the first floor, presented in an extravagantly paneled setting that we know through very exact drawings made by Courtonne in 1739 and 1740, probably with the intention of having them engraved. After the *cabinet de tour,* a small mechanic's workshop, came the cabinet of pharmaceutics, then that of physics and chemistry with laboratory, kiln and retorts; this was followed by an array of mechanical objects and

67. **Museum of the Abbey of Heiligenkreuz** *in Austria. The great baroque abbeys of central Europe had a museum or* Bildersaal *where both old and new paintings were grouped together. At Heiligenkreuz it is in the* Kaisersaal *or ceremonial apartments, decorated with XVIIth-century stucco and with walls covered with the display of paintings.*

divers instruments and, finally, the natural history collection displaying animals in a naturalistic decor. This magnificent cabinet lasted but a short while for Bonnier de la Mosson died at forty-two, a ruined man. His collections, with all the paneling, were sold at auction.

No matter what was to be exhibited—paintings, sculptures or curiosities—and whether or not one sought luxury in decor and presentation, the principle of accumulation was always in operation. The Museo Pio-Clementino in the Vatican offers us an intact example of those museums of antiquities where, embarking on discovery, "antiquarians" delighted in losing themselves in a forest of marble and bronze, impatient to recognize rare pieces on their own without any help, for guidebooks were nonexistent. The gallery of busts was in every way comparable to the portrait gallery; busts were aligned on rows upon rows of shelves, similar to the stratified arrangement of paintings in the *museum jovianum*. Today we feel somewhat lost in these immense rooms, these interminable galleries peopled with sarcophagi, busts, statues of men and animals; but we must keep in mind that this universe was familiar to cultivated men of the time who were not confronted, as we are, by so ramified a field of knowledge, in a period when a gentleman could presume to embrace within his lifespan all human learning.

68. **Cabinet of Glassware** *in Rosenborg Castle, Copenhagen. The royal château of Rosenborg has preserved intact a cabinet of porcelain and its unique cabinet of glassware. The latter was created in 1714 by King Frederic IV after a visit to Venice in 1708 and contains extremely rare pieces from various European manufacturies. The glass and crystal are displayed as if in a sideboard.*

PRÆMIA
HONORARIA.

EX VNO OMNIA

Chapter

8

The Age of Enlightenment

Simultaneously with the aggrandizement of the royal collections, destined to enter public museums sooner or later, here and there in Europe corporate bodies began to accumulate works of art; the municipal organization found itself particularly suited to this activity. Thus in 1629 the city of Zürich established a library and gallery devoted to the fine arts in the Wasserkirche. This cultural complex had been created with allocations of manuscripts and antiquities from ecclesiastical goods confiscated by the Reform. In Italy, where municipal life had always been very active, certain men early showed devotion to the public cause; in 1523 Cardinal Domenico Grimani, in a move to beautify the seat of government and to further scholarship, bequeathed to the Venetian Republic the collection of antiquities and curiosities he had amassed while in Rome; his gift formed the nucleus of the present archeological museum. Sixty years later, the same museum profited from the bequest of his nephew Giovanni, patriarch of Aquileia. The latter was responsible for the Biblioteca Marciana's acquisition of the famous Flemish *Breviary* which bears his name. The Grimanis were a decidedly great family of benefactors; Marino, dying in the same year as his brother, Cardinal Domenico, also enriched the republic with a portion of his collection of antiquities. In 1680 Manfredo Settale bequeathed his museum to Milan's Biblioteca Ambrosiana. Such gifts became a frequent practice in the eighteenth century; in 1780 Annibale Olivieri gave to the city of Pesaro his cabinet of intaglios and coins.

From the sixteenth to the eighteenth century, the convents in the Provençal city of Arles built up collections of Roman antiquities found in local excavations; about 1785 Father Dumont assembled the various collections of antiquities in the Minim Convent, where they were consolidated into a public museum; to this end, he had entered into an agreement with the city council on December 7, 1784. Moreover, this body of municipal magistrates had amassed during the course of the two preceding centuries an art collection of its own in the *Hôtel de Ville*. In 1745 Monsignor d'Inguinbert who, having been the librarian of Cardinal Lorenzo Corsini (later Pope Clement XII), had acquired in Rome a taste for the arts, left "to the public" of the city of Carpentras, whose bishop he was, his library and his collections. The oldest public museum in France is doubtlessly that of Besançon; in 1694 J. B. Bloizot, head abbot of Saint Vincent de Besançon, bequeathed to his abbey his books, antique paintings and medallions "with the stipulation that the whole form a public collection." The museum was installed forthwith and opened to the public on Wednesdays and Saturdays of each week from 8:00 to 10:00 in the morning and from 2:00 to 4:00 in the afternoon.

In the eighteenth century art was taught and lectured about rather than learned from practice in a master's studio. The prototype for this kind of artistic instruction can be found in the sixteenth century but it was not to enjoy a widespread acceptance until the Age of Enlightenment when every city of some importance had its academy or art school. Such establishments owned collections of art works that served as models for the students; these often became more or less public museums. A case in point is the Accademia Carrara in Bergamo, a school of art founded in 1780 by Count Carrara, who at his death in 1796 left it his fifteen hundred paintings. In order to facilitate their studies, the Duke of Richmond opened to artists in 1760 his rich gallery of sculpture at Whitehall in London. Between 1748 and 1785 a score of drawing academies sprang up all over France, out of which many present-day city museums grew. Dijon's was created by François Devosges, who in 1783 persuaded the municipality to vote a loan for the construction of an eastern wing on the Palais des Etats, with the view "of establishing therein a museum for the progress of Art and the benefit of students." In Rheims, Antoine Ferrand de Monthelon (†1742), a mediocre painter but a man of taste, who had brought back from his trips works of art of all kinds, founded in his city a drawing academy that he furnished with the best pieces from his collections, among them, Lucas Cranach's astonishing portraits of Saxon and Pomeranian princes that his father had come upon in Germany in 1687; he willed them to the Académie de Rheims. Saint Quentin's drawing school was established in 1777 by a native of the city, the great portraitist Maurice Quentin de la Tour; the school received part of his atelier as a gift from the artist's brother in 1806. Science cabinets shared the same destiny. Clément Lafaille bequeathed to the Académie of La Rochelle his natural history cabinet, today in the city museum; its original *boiseries* are still intact.

During the course of the eighteenth century, the progress of archeological studies encouraged the establishment of learned societies that organized excavations and founded museums to contain the unearthed objects. The Etruscan Academy at Cortona was founded along such lines in 1726; most appropriately, its president was given the title of *Lucumo,* the name of ancient Etruscan nobles. Comprising one hundred forty members, it organized meetings—*Notti Coritane*—and opened a gallery for art lovers, its *Galleria del publico.* In 1774 this museum received one of the most "amiable" of false antique paintings, the famous *Muse* executed on slate; the picture arrived at the gallery after many an adventure; it had been venerated as a Madonna by a peasant who, when he realized his error, used it as a shutter for a window near his oven. That it was a neoclassical pastiche was not recognized until the present generation. In Volterra, another Etruscan city in Tuscany, Monsignor Mario Guarnacci, after his return from a long stay in Rome, devoted himself to financing excavations and buying Etruscan objects; he built up an important collection which he bequeathed "*al publico volterrano*" in 1781. The Accademia Filarmonica in Verona received the cabinet of the famous scholar Francesco Scipione di Maffei. In the Sicilian province of Catania, the pompous

70. **Portrait presumed to be that of Prince Wolfgang d'Anhalt, by Lucas Cranach.** *Rheims Museum. This painting is part of the famous series of portraits of Saxon and Pomeranian princes which were willed by Antoine Ferrand de Monthelon to the city of Rheims where he had founded a school of drawing with, as an annex, a museum formed from his collection.*

Ignacio Paterno Costello, Prince Biscari, erected a magnificent palace, one wing of which he reserved for use as a museum and filled with vases, bronzes and antique terra cottas excavated locally or bought at Naples, Florence or Rome. This museum, open to amateurs and students, was solemnly inaugurated in 1758. It was to become one of the most celebrated collections in Sicily; the Biscari family retained it until 1927, when the tenth prince of the house, willing his portion of the inheritance to the province, encouraged his co-heirs to do likewise; a few followed suit; the others sold their shares. After the last World War, the Biscari collection and that of the Benedictines went to Castello Ursino.

As an institution allied with the advancement of human learning, the museum found a ready niche for itself within the university complex. The oldest university museum is doubtlessly the one at Basel. In 1661 the Amerbach cabinet, which boasted some magnificent Holbeins, was put up for sale; it had been formed by that well-known family of publishers who had counted Erasmus among its intimates. The collection was going to be sold in Holland, when the city, objecting to its removal, acquired it at its own expense. The cabinet was exhibited from 1671 to 1849 in the university library, housed at the "Sign of the Fly" *(zu Mücke)*. In the course of the seventeenth century, it was enriched by new gifts. In 1712 Count Marsigli established an Academy of Sciences and a museum at the University of Bologna; in 1743 it was joined by the collections previously left to the city by the scholar Ulisse Aldrovandi and the Marchese Cospi. The benefactor of Verona, the erudite Scipione Maffei, was handsomely generous to the University of Turin, endowing it with a museum of epigraphy and archeology. In 1758 the municipality of Ferrara bought the collection of medallions, coins and statuary assembled by the archeologist Vincenzo Bellini; it joined the lapidary collection that had been formed at the university in 1735. The museum of antiquities founded at Parma in 1770 by Don Philip, Duke of Bourbon, to compensate for the loss of the *Museo borbonico* removed to Naples by his brother Don Carlo, owes a major portion of its collection to the excavations zealously conducted at the site of Volterra.

To Oxford befell the honor of having the first great museum organized as a public institution with a pedagogical purpose. The Ashmolean Museum at Oxford began with the collection assembled by two generations of a family of travelers, explorers and adventurers. John Tradescant the Elder (†1638) had fought against Algerian privateers; in 1618 he journeyed to Russia in quest of rare plants; after Russia, America saw this indefatigable traveler, sent by the Duke of Buckingham to study native animals, birds, plants and stones. Tradescant exhibited his collection of curiosities, scientific and archeological instruments and natural phenomena in a house and garden at South Lambeth, near London; open to the public, this museum and botanical garden were known as "Tradescant's Ark." The entire collection was the subject of a sumptuous publication appearing in 1656—*Musaeum Tradescantianum*. After the death of his only son, John Tradescant the Younger made a gift of the collection to the antiquarian Elias Ashmole but, two years later, he retracted, offering the collection to his wife, stipulating that she will it to either Oxford or Cambridge University. After Tradescant's death, Ashmole brought suit against Mrs. Tradescant for the return of the collections and won his case. In 1677, realizing Tradescant's hopes, he bequeathed

INSTITUTA ASHMOLEANA.

PRIMO, *MUSEI ASHMOLEANI Curatores* (quos ipse CLARISSIMUS ASHMOLUS *Decreto Anno* MDCLXXXVI. *scripto, designavit*) sunt D. Vice-Cancellarius, D. Decanus Ædis Christi, D. Principalis Collegii Ænei Nasi, D. Professor Regius in Medicina, & Academiæ Procurator uterque, vel eorum Deputati.

II. Semel quolibet anno, nempe die Lunæ Dominicam SS. Trinitatis proxime subsequente, ad horam octavam dictum Museum Curatores lustrabunt; vel saltem ibidem conventi, Lustrationem in alium diem differant. Hoc autem tempore Cimeliarchæ fidelitatem & industriam perpendent; videantq; quænam eo anno cujuscunque generis accesserint Cimelia.

III. Omnia quæ vel jam dicto Museo data sunt, vel olim donabuntur, Cimelia sub variis Classibus distribuentur; adjecta singulis sua tessera, *vel numero*; qui & iisdem adjiciendus erit in Musei Catalogo, quam citissime summa diligentia conscribendo.

IV. Pro Curatorum numero, dictum Catalogum in sex partes dividi volumus; quo citius nempe lustrationem absolvant; quolibet Curatore suam partem cum ejusdem Catalogo conferente; ne quid forte vel desideretur, vel per nimiam Cimeliarchæ incuriam, corruptelam patiatur.

V. Si plura in Museo inveniantur ejusdem speciei Cimelia, liceat Cimeliarchæ unum cum duobus aliis quibuscunque Curatoribus, unum aut plura Exemplaria, vel iis pro desiderato quodam commutare, vel etiam alicui honoris ergo gratis conferre.

VI. Præ nimia vetustate Cimelio quolibet pereunte; liceat Cimeliarchæ à suo loco in conclave quoddam dicti Musei, idem subducere.

VII. Museum Ashmoleanum iisdem horis pateat, quibus Bibliotheca Bodleiana; atque aliis insuper prout Cimeliarchæ eidem adesse per privata sua negotia licuerit.

VIII. Cimelium aliquod, vel Bibliothecarum Librum, extra Scholam Historiæ Naturalis nemini fas est deportare; nisi ut instauretur, vel saltem delineandi gratia, aut scalpturæ.

IX. Vacante loco Cimeliarchæ, successorem designare esto penes Curatores, (vel saltem eorum majorem Partem) eorumque Successores in perpetuum; quibus Procimeliarchæ nulla habenda est ratio, siquem alium magis idoneum judicaverint.

X. Procimeliarcham & Sublibrarium quod attinet; Cimeliarchæ ejusque Successorum in perpetuum est, eos ad libitum eligere, & loco amovere.

XI. Cimeliarcha quolibet mense quo Academia aberit, decem Nummos antiquos Museo reddet; vel saltem totidem alia Antiquitatis Cimelia, aut Mineralium, Plantarum, Animaliumve Exemplaria ibidem desiderata; sub pœna mulctæ decem Solidorum, in usum Bibliothecarum hujus Musei lustrationis tempore, pro quolibet mense quo anno elapso defecerit solvendæ: perinde autem est utrum hæc Cimelia antequam debentur, an postea, conferat.

XII. Museum intrare nemini concessum est, antequam Cimeliarchæ, Procimeliarchæ, aut Sublibrario Præmium mox dicendum persolvat.

XIII. Siquis seorsim Cimelia perlustrare velit, sex Denarios ad minimum persolvat, quo facto, Cimeliarcha, vel Procimeliarcha per horam integram ei adesse teneatur, quæcunque spectare cupit (sive ea in Scriniis, sive alibi conserventur) designans.

XIV. Si Duo simul intrare voluerint, unusquisque sex Denarios ad minimum persolvat; ministretque eis Cimeliarcha, vel is, quem deputaverit, per sesquihoram si id rogabunt.

XV. Si Tres eodem tempore aderint, quatuor Denarios ad minimum unicuique solvendum est; perque unius horæ spatium commorari poterunt.

XVI. Si Quatuor aut plures, tres Denarios ad minimum quilibet persolvat; atque idem tempus (si iis videbitur) permaneant.

XVII. Siquis per duas horas in Museo commoratus fuerit, Præmium duplex Cimeliarchæ reddat.

XVIII. In qualibet insuper Musei Visitatione Cimeliarcha veram & completam Curatoribus reddet rationem omnium præmiorum & emolumentorum, quæ præcedente Anno, Cimelia monstrando collegerit. Computus autem hic annuus ad Festum S. Michaelis proxime ante Visitationem elapsum terminabitur.

XIX. Academicorum nemini præterquam Graduatis librorum quorumcunque ad hoc Museum spectantium concessa est copia.

XX. Librorum autem usum quamdiu in Academia manfurus est siquis Graduatus cupit, Cimeliarchæ quinque Solidos, & Sublibrario unum (cum nomen suum libello in hunc finem destinato inseruerit) reddat: sin vero breviori tempore eosdem consulere voluerit, vel sex Denarios qualibet Septimana, vel duodecim per mensem solvat.

XXI. Siquis è Manuscripto quopiam aliquid exscribendum cupiat, id ei Sublibrarius exscribat, pro qualibet Scheda duodecim Denarios accipiens; quod si ipse exscribere, vel proprium Amanuensem eligere malit, id libere faciat, modo Sublibrario pro quolibet Codice quo usus fuerit, tres Denarios per diem solvat.

XXII. Penes Cimeliarcham est Manuscriptorum usum quibuscunque prohibere, uti & Cimelium quodvis delineandi copiam denegare, donec is qui alterutrum rogaverit, Syngraphum Mandatorium, cui major pars Curatorum manu propria subscripserint, protulerit.

XXIII. In ipsis Musei Bibliothecis Studiis vacare nemini concessum est, nisi Cimeliarchæ Syngraphum adferat, Curatorum omnium Chirographis signatum: Studiis siquidem loca constituta sunt Schola Historiæ Naturalis, & Procestrium Bibliothecæ Ashmoleanæ continuum.

XXIV. Absente Cimeliarcha, Procimeliarchæ eadem plane potestas & auctoritas.

In pleno Curatorum Conventu decimo tertio die Decembris Anno Domini MDCCXIV. *ratum est & statutum, ut hæc Decreta Typis mandentur, eorumque posthac Exemplaria in Museo Ashmoleano, Schola Historiæ Naturalis, & in utraque Bibliotheca Ashmoleana & Wodiana semper palam prostituentur.*

Bernardus Gardiner *Vice-Cancell.*
Geo. Bristol. *Dec. Æd Christi.*
Rob. Shippen *Coll. Æn. Nas. Princ.*
C. Tadlow *Reg. Med. Profess. Dep.*
Cha. Gardiner *Procurator Sen.*
Sam. Newte *Procurator Jun.*

71. Regulations of the Ashmolean Museum, Oxford. *1714. Written in Latin, the regulations provided for the administration of the museum, the editing of the catalog, security measures, the hours of admission and visiting privileges. Entrance fees were charged according to the time spent in the museum but there were special rates which depended on the number of visitors in a group.*

---

them to Oxford, together with his own collection of antiquities, charging the university to construct an appropriate building to receive them. Work on the building was finished in 1683 and the museum was formally opened to the public on May 21st of that year in the presence of the Duke of York, later James II, and his duchess, the future Queen Anne. The university annexed to the museum a chemistry laboratory and a library and appointed a conservator to prepare a catalog for it in Latin. Also drawn up in Latin is a memorandum dated December 13, 1713—still posted to this day in the museum—which painstakingly detailed the administration of the museum, the editing of the catalog and its inventories, and the duties of the *cimeliarchus,* more a guardian than a curator; the curatorial tasks fell to the *curatores,* chosen from the various Oxford colleges, who divided up the care of the collection according to their areas of specialization. There was a charge to enter the museum; the admission rate decreased according to the number of visitors in a group but was in proportion to the length of time spent; the visit consisted of a guided tour given by the *cimeliarchus* or his assistant, the *procimeliarchus.* The museum was enriched by many generous gifts. Bequests of a scientific or archeological nature fostered other museological centers at Oxford; some, like the Sheldonian Theatre (1669), predated the Ashmolean while others, such as the Old Philosophy School and the Old Logic School, came later.

Less than a century after the opening of the Ashmolean to the public, England established the first national museum whose origins were not rooted in a royal collection. In 1753 Parliament voted to acquire the collections and library of Sir Hans Sloane (1660-1753), with the view of establishing a public museum. Sir Hans, who had traveled to the West Indies, was physician to the royal family, president of the Royal College of Physicians and president of the Royal Society for Improving Natural Knowledge, the citadel of rationalism in England. In 1696 he inherited the collections of another savant, his friend William Charleton (or Courten), and during the next half

ICTA LICET FACIES VI
VAE NON CEDO SED INSTAR
VM DOMINI IVSTIS NO
BILE LINEOLIS
OCTO IS DVM PERAGIT
PIETH SIC GNAVITER IN ME
D QVOD NATVRAE EST,
XPRIMIT ARTIS OPVS.

BON AMORBACCHIVM
IO HOLBEIN DEPINGEBAT
A M D XIX PRID EID OCT BR

▲
73. **Polyhymnia the Muse.** *Etruscan Academy, Palazzo Pretorio, Cortona. This encaustic painting on slate was discovered in 1732 by a peasant. Marquis Tommasi acquired it in 1735 and bequeathed it in 1755 to the* Etruscan Academy *at Cortona. It has been attributed in turn to a master of the Renaissance and to an imitator of the 18th century. However, the* Etruscan Academy *still exhibits it as an antique work. The discovery of antique paintings in towns buried by Vesuvius led to forgeries which brought fame to the Neapolitan, Guerra. Raphael Mengs produced an imitation antique fresco which deceived Winckelmann himself.*

◄ 72. **Portrait of Bonifacius Amerbach, 1519, by Hans Holbein the Elder.** *Detail. Kunstmuseum, Basel. This portrait of the famous Renaissance humanist and printer was in the Amerbach cabinet which was bought in 1661 by the city of Basel to prevent its removal to Holland; the collection was placed on exhibition in the university library.*

century, he concentrated his fortune on building a library and amassing a scientific collection, which at his death numbered 80,000 pieces. In his will he offered the lot to the State for the sum of £20,000 which was to be paid to his two daughters and was far less than its actual value. However, King George II maintained that there was not enough money in the Royal Treasury to meet the offer. The acquisition was realized by Parliament through funds raised in a public lottery and amounting to £95,000. At the same time Parliament purchased for £10,000 the library of Robert Harley, Earl of Oxford.

These two collections and the library bequeathed to the nation by Sir Robert Bruce Cotton(1571-1631) were consolidated to form a public repository—the British Museum. The "Statutes and Rules Relating to the Inspection and Use of the British Museum" describe it as a "national establishment founded by Authority of Parliament, chiefly designed for the use of learned and studious men, both natives and foreigners in their researches into the several parts of knowledge." The institution had an important board of trustees which included six members from the Cotton, Harley and Sloane families, the Archbishop of Canterbury, the Lord Chancellor, the Speaker of the House of Commons, the President of the College of Physicians, the Lord Chief Justice of England, other high officials and fifteen elected members. The administrative council has always played an essential role in Anglo-Saxon museology.

On Monday, January 15, 1759, the institution, comprising three departments—Printed Books, Manuscripts and Medals, Natural and Artificial Productions—opened in Montague House in Bloomsbury, not far from Sir Hans Sloane's houses on Bloomsbury Place. The library had a reading room but the museum could be seen only on written request for a guided tour. With library and collection at the disposal of scholars, the British Museum was then, as it is today, an institution for the advancement of knowledge. As prestigious as they are, all its archeological collections were admitted as "curiosities." The institu-

74. **Towneley's Library on Park Street,** *in 1782, by Johann Zoffany. Towneley Hall Art Gallery and Museum, Burnley (England). In the library of Sir Charles Towneley, Zoffany depicts London's principal antiquarians in conversation with the famous amateur, whose collection was purchased by the British Museum after his death in 1805.*

148

75. **The So-called Bust of Clytie,** *First-century Roman art. British Museum, London. The best-known piece in the Towneley collection was a bust of a young Roman girl who is identified by some as the water nymph, Clytie, and by others as Isis. It can be seen next to Sir Charles in the Zoffany painting.*

tion's approach to art is from the standpoint of archeology. The first great archeological collection acquired by the Department of Natural and Artificial Productions was that of antique vases and marbles assembled by William Hamilton during his ambassadorship to Naples; it entered the museum in 1772. The celebrated collection of marbles brought together by Charles Towneley, a trustee of the museum, was bought after his death in 1805. The purchase of the Elgin marbles in 1816 and the acquisition of the Towneley collection transformed the British Museum into a museum of art. A curious picture by Johann Zoffany, painted in 1782, preserves for us a record of the library on Park Street, overcrowded with the marbles of the famous collector, Towneley, who is shown in conversation with three fellow antiquarians. Undoubtedly the essentially scientific and educational flavor of the British Museum led Parliament to reject a proposal in 1778 to annex to it a pinakotheke, which would have been formed by the purchase of the Walpole collection; this fine cabinet eventually passed into Russian hands.

Cambridge University had to wait much longer than did Oxford for its museum. It was the bequest of Richard, Viscount Fitzwilliam, who died in 1816, which established it, but its creation can be attributed to the same intellectual renaissance which engendered the British Museum: the Age of Enlightenment. Viscount Fitzwilliam was graduated from Trinity Hall, Cambridge, in 1764; a fanatic melomane, he built up a remarkable music library. The legacy to his alma mater included 10,000 volumes, among them, some admirable illuminated manuscripts, and 144 paintings, some of which had come from the collection of the Duc d'Orléans.

By the time the doors of the British Museum opened, the French public had been enjoying for some years an assemblage of masterpieces which, although not "national property," was reasonably accessible to all. One could admire at the Palais du Luxembourg the twenty-two Rubens paintings in the Medici gallery and one hundred ten paintings and some drawings in the apartments of the Queen of Spain across the court. The realization of this exhibition attested to a peculiarly eighteenth-century outlook that encouraged the participation of a larger public in the benefits of culture. In France, where there was widespread censorship by the state, freedom of speech found its sole outlet in treatises and pamphlets published abroad and secretly distributed at home; this was the only form of the press under the *Ancien Régime*.

In the first half of the eighteenth century, the *chefs d'œuvre* belonging to the Crown had become virtually inaccessible. At the time of Louis XIV, who lived in the public eye, visible to all, Versailles, the official residence of the monarchy, belonged to the whole of France; permission to visit it was easily obtained; in order to be present when the king dined, it sufficed to have a sword and a plumed hat—which could be rented from the palace concierge. The gardens also were public and Louis XIV himself had written a notice giving pointers on how best to visit them. Under Louis XV, Versailles became the home of the king. Tiring of the grandiose apartments, he had other, smaller ones installed, following the example of the Sun King who by the end of his reign was seeking refuge from so much pomp in the intimate surroundings of Le Trianon, Marly or even in the paneled apartments he had had laid out at Versailles in 1684. There was no place for the large-scale classical or baroque paintings acquired in the seventeenth century in the mirrored, paneled salons. The older works were put aside in other quarters by the *Direction des Bâtiments* and the king's indifference to the matter was so great that he thought nothing of lending them to private individuals to ornament their houses; thus, the Duc d'Autun had in his gallery from 1715 to 1736 Raphael's *Baldassare Castiglione*, Annibale Carracci's *Fishing* and *Hunting* and Titian's *Pardo Venus*, *Madonna of the Rabbit* and *Portrait of a Man*. Artists could hardly find any Old Masters to admire and study, with the exception of those in the celebrated *galerie d'Orléans*, generously put at their disposal. An old servant of the regent, acting as custodian for the collection toward the end of the *Ancien Régime*, contributed to the gallery's success among visitors with his countless anecdotes. Formerly a jockey for the prince, he refused tips. "Monseigneur pays his people," he would say with pride, "and old Laplace has been eating the bread of the house of Orléans since he came into the world."

The monarchy's insolvency provoked strong criticism and on November 23, 1744, Orry, the *Directeur des Bâtiments,* found on his desk an anonymous memorandum deploring the dispersion and inaccessibility of the royal collections and demanding that they be exhibited in the Galerie des Ambassadeurs in the Tuileries; Bachaumont is occasionally suggested as its author. It produced no results and three years later was followed by a pamphlet edited and printed by Lafont de Saint Yenne and entitled *Reflexions sur quelques causes présent de la peinture en France*. The author lamented the decline in painting, attributing it to the fact that artists were deprived of seeing examples "by the great European masters and although no expense was spared in the forming of his Majesty's cabinet, today the paintings are hidden away in badly lighted rooms at Versailles, unknown or unexciting to strangers, owing to the impossibility of seeing them." One of the reasons he gives for resurrecting them from oblivion is "the inevitable decay caused by lack of air and light" and he invokes the precedent of the Bibliothèque Nationale "installed in new quarters that scholars find accomodating."

The *Direction des Bâtiments* seemingly paid no attention and two years later, Lafont de Saint Yenne repeated his plea, publishing *L'Ombre du Grand Colbert, le Louvre et la Ville de Paris* in 1749. This complicated treatise was conceived in the form of a "dialogue among the dead," with Colbert, the city of Paris and the Louvre meeting on the Champs Elysées to manifest their anger over the artistic situation in France. The Louvre declared to Colbert that the *chefs d'œuvre* he procured for the royal collection "have not seen the light and have relinquished the places of honor they occupied in their owner's cabinets for an obscure cell at Versailles where they have been decaying for the last fifty years."

This time officialdom was provoked to action and in a move to satisfy the public, the royal administration of the Louvre ordered an exhibition of 110 paintings at the Palais du Luxembourg to begin the fourteenth of October, 1750; it could be visited from October through April on Wednesday and Saturday mornings and in the afternoon of the same days in August and September. The choice of paintings was eclectic and included works by masters of various schools; it was particularly strong in masterpieces from the Italian Renaissance, the forte of the royal cabinet. There were also a few drawings which, as Bailly, keeper of the king's paintings, noted "were left unnumbered and unlabeled in order to give enlightened amateurs the privilege of deciding on authorship." A strange way to educate the public! The exhibition was obviously

152

77. **Count d'Angiviller at 49, by Joseph Siffrein Duples-
sis.** *Versailles Museum. Directeur Général des Bâtiments under
Louis XVI, Count d'Angiviller is shown holding the plan of the
Grande Galerie of the Louvre where the paintings from the collections
of the Crown would be exhibited to the public.*

◀ 76. **Jacob Ruisdael: Le Coup de Soleil.** *Louvre Museum,
Paris. Though the efforts of Count d'Angiviller, Director of public
Buildings, to bring the Crown collections before the public in the Main
Gallery of the Louvre came to nothing, nevertheless, in preparing for
this event, he can be credited with introducing a methodical policy for
acquiring works with a view to completing collections in schools where
gaps existed. He was the real initiator of the move to acquire the collections of Dutch paintings in the Louvre. This masterpiece by Ruisdael
was bought in 1785 at a sale held by Count de Vaudreuil.*

addressed to the connoisseur. About the same time,
the conservation of art works became an important
concern; the techniques of relining, transfer and
restoration were practiced. A *Catalogue raisonné* of
the collections of the Crown was published in 1752,
edited by the keeper of paintings, the artist
Lépicié.

The partisans for the exhibition of paintings
belonging to the monarchy soon had the backing
of Diderot. In 1765, in the article *Louvre* for his
Encyclopédie, Volume IX, the writer outlined a project for turning the Louvre into something which
would approximate the Mouseion of Alexander the
Great. The palace was to house not only the collections but scholarly societies as well, that is to
say, various academies. Already installed in the
Louvre, but only on the chance that unused space
was available, they were to be accomodated according to a rational plan and the academicians themselves were to be given lodging; the sculpture
collection would be disposed on the ground floor
of the palace, paintings, in the gallery along the
Seine (then containing relief maps of fortified cities
in the kingdom, which were to be removed to a
north hall Diderot proposed constructing). Scholarly organizations in other parts of Paris were to
be regrouped at the Louvre, destined to become
the Temple of Arts and Sciences: the Cabinet of
Medals, the Royal Library and the Natural History
Cabinet.

Inspired by these ideas, the Marquis of Marigny,
Directeur des Bâtiments, submitted to the king as
early as 1768 a plan for carrying them out, but
without success. However, the notion of opening
a "museum" in the Louvre received fresh stimulus
under Louis XVI. One is wrong to attribute to
this king a certain indifference toward affairs of
state; the victim of an inherent lassitude which
kept him from making decisions, he was much
more open to new ideas concerning the national
and public well-being than was his predecessor,
Louis XV, who remained ensconced in monarchical traditions current since Louis XIV. Louis XVI
took care to avail himself of advice, perhaps too

much so; in short, what this unfortunate monarch failed to do was to chart a direction for the state. The history of the museum can be instructive on this point. In 1774, the first year of his reign, Louis XVI named as *Directeur Général des Bâtiments* Count d'Angiviller, who was to prove an intelligent and zealous administrator who instituted a veritable fine arts policy. Posterity has not condoned his numerous commissions to contemporary artists, too immersed in an academic, sentimental and moralizing aesthetic, but he is given credit for the efforts he made with regard to the opening of the museum. At the outset he took stock of the royal collections, perceiving that while rich in certain areas, in others they presented considerable lacunae, the result of an indifference to changes in taste on the part of Louis XVth's government. During the course of the eighteenth century, amateurs placed the Flemish and Dutch schools on an equal footing with the Italian, precisely the areas in which the royal cabinet was weakest. D'Angiviller decided to change this situation and henceforth the king was represented at public sales and agents combed Europe for paintings. Masterpieces of northern art joined those from Italy in the storehouse: *Helena Fourment and her Two Children, The Martyrdom of Saint Lievin, The Four Evangelists* by Rubens; Van Dyck's *Charles the First*; Ruisdael's *Burst of Sunlight*; Rembrandt's *Hendrickje Stoffels, The Philosopher, Supper at Emmaus* and *Man with a Gold Chain*. Nor were paintings by minor Dutch and Flemish masters neglected. Conforming to the neoclassic aesthetic of the period, d'Angiviller showed a marked preference for the history painting of the preceding century and bought two important series by Eustache Le Sueur (1617-1655). The king of France was represented at the sale of Jesuit treasures in Belgium, but his agent found himself competing against a serious contingent from the Austrian government which, also in the process of establishing a public museum (in the Belvedere, Vienna), had schemed to appropriate the most beautiful pieces: thus Austria carried off Caravaggio's *Madonna of the Rosary* and Rubens's *Miracles of St. Francis Xavier*. To compensate for having been outwitted, d'Angiviller, always eager for paintings by northern artists, sent agents to French Flanders to seduce with words the Superiors of its various convents, hoping, but in vain, to wrest from them their painted altarpieces.

As early as 1777, d'Angiviller had the relief maps of the fortified cities removed from the Grande Galerie to the Hotel des Invalides, where they remain to this day. With a view to their eventual exhibition in the Louvre, he began a methodical restoration of the paintings in the royal collection and had his new acquisitions made ready for hanging. The frames executed by Buteux were well suited to the museum setting —sober, uniform and with a cartouche for the artist's name and the title of the painting. In 1784 the painter, Hubert Robert, who had already collaborated on studies undertaken to plan the future museum, was named keeper of the royal collection.

When one consults the thick dossiers on the museum project preserved in the National Archives, one cannot say that preparation was lightly undertaken. The theory and technique of modern museology began with these works. In 1779 or 1778 d'Angiviller appointed a commission of nine to study the divers problems posed by the transformation of the Grande Galerie into a museum; the question of lighting was the most difficult to solve. Soufflot proposed a system of lighting from above but the commission rejected it as too inconvenient and costly; however, the project appealed to the board of directors who continued to support it even after Soufflot's death in

154

78. Page of the illustrated inventory of the paintings gallery of Emperor Charles VI in Vienna. *Ordered by Count Althann, this inventory was made in the form of a three-volume album of miniatures painted by Ferdinand Storffer.*

79. The Hall of the Italians at the Düsseldorf Gallery. *This detail from an old engraving shows how the collection of the Elector Charles Theodore was arranged. Established in 1756, the Düsseldorf Gallery presented a remarkable, early attempt at museologic rationalization. Although the paintings were crowded together, almost frame to frame, on the walls, they were grouped according to the individual artists and schools of painting.*

1780. Seeking to avoid delays, d'Angiviller asked the Académie d'Architecture for an opinion. The study panel appointed elaborated six basic principles treating the lighting, the adaptability of the area and measures of fire prevention. The Academy proved very progressive on these issues, stipulating as early as 1786 that the wooden framework be resheathed in noncombustible materials and that iron be substituted for wood wherever possible. As for the lighting, it recommended an overhead method. With the commission still hesitant, having been impressed by the opinion of certain artists that overhead lighting was unsuited for pictures, d'Angiviller decided to try an experiment. On November 2, 1788, he submitted to the king a project limited to an expenditure of 80,000 livres, which would attempt to realize the overhead lighting of the Salon Carré in time for the August 1789 exhibition of the Academy of Painting and Sculpture. Since the public attending these exhibitions had always protested about the difficulty of seeing the paintings in this location, the experiment would be decisive. The king accepted the proposal; at the same time the *salon* opened with its new lighting, the brick fireproofing of the framework of the Grande Galerie was completed.

Despite all the investigations, or perhaps on account of them, the situation grew worse for the public. In 1779 the gallery in the Palais du Luxembourg, bestowed as an appanage upon the Count of Provence (later Louis XVIII), was ordered closed. The warehouses of the Department of Buildings were filled with paintings removed from the Luxembourg, including the wonderful works by Rubens from the Medici Gallery, which had been withheld from the gift made to the brother of Louis XVI, indicating that the individual worth of a painting superseded its decorative function.

D'Angiviller intended to carry out his plans quickly for the remodeling of the Grande Galerie after 1789 but was prevented by the Revolution. When one examines the causes for this failure, one perceives that it was due less to the financial crisis sustained at the end of the *Ancien Régime* than to the scruples plaguing the Director of the Department of Buildings. D'Angiviller himself conceded this point in a journal entry for November 2, 1788: "Plans for creating the museum were abandoned, owing not so much to the difficulties of the time as to the diversity of opinions—not on the question of overhead lighting (the advisability of which was not doubted by informed people) but on the different methods that ought or could be employed to obtain it." The problem was certainly thoroughly studied, but a little more empiricism would have been preferred to this excess of theoretical speculation to which French rationalism too easily succumbs. D'Angiviller was convinced of the worth of Soufflot's scheme, which in truth was excellent. Why did he not have it carried out? He would have provided the gallery with good lighting, thereby avoiding Lefuel's destructions with their mediocre results less than a century later. He could have resolved the issue had he not been so respectful of "authorized" opinions and the counsels of the various commissions. The king, represented by his *Directeur des Bâtiments,* cannot be reproached for exercising absolutism in this affair, only for failing to act decisively. On this subject, an historical comparison of the project for the Grande Galerie with that of the Colonnade of the Louvre is instructive. Louis XIV and Colbert, like Louis XVI and d'Angiviller, wished to consult the maximum number of authorities, with Louis XVI going so far as to give his inquiry international scope. The differences of opinion on the subject of the proposed colonnade would have resulted in an anarchy similar to the one precipitated by the projects suggested for the Grande Galerie had not the personal influence of Louis XIV, firmly backed by Colbert, intervened. D'Angiviller conducted himself like a minister responsible to a parliament and to opinion.

Although deprived of the collection of the Crown, the Parisian public could visit a few cabinets. In the Couvent des Grands Augustins, the seat of the Order of the Holy Ghost, hung portraits of the knights of the order; it constituted a sort of historical museum open to the public on weekends. In 1778 the *Garde Meuble,* located in the present-day Hôtel de la Marine on the Place de la Concorde, was open on the second Tuesday of each month from 9:00 to 1:00 between Quasimodo and Saint Martin's Day (the first Sunday after Lent until November 11); displayed there were the jewels belonging to the Crown, suits of armor worn by the kings of France, a few antique marble statues and some bronzes.

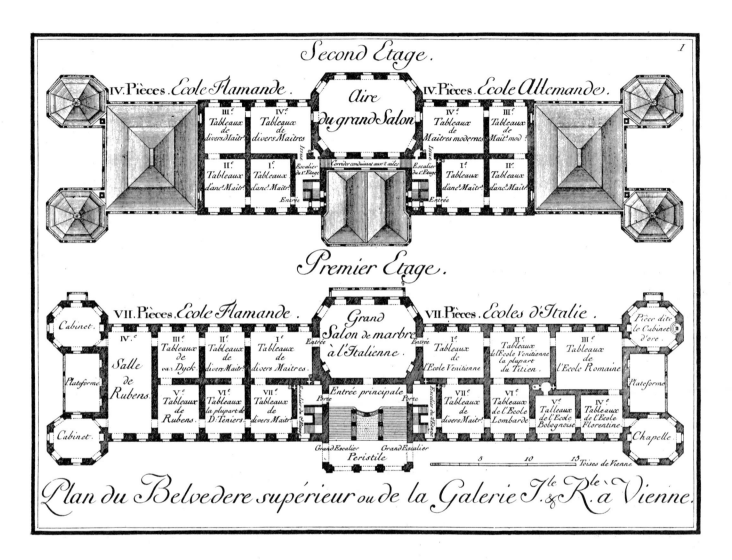

80. **Plan of the Paintings Gallery installed in Schloss Belvedere, Vienna.** *This plan of the installation realized by Mechel in 1778, under the orders of Chancellor Kaunitz, shows that the gallery of paintings belonging to the Crown were given a logical arrangement; the works were grouped chronologically and by school.*

Private individuals organized museums also. In 1778 Pavin de la Blancherie, author of *Nouvelles de la République des Lettres et des Arts,* opened to the public his collection of art works, natural curiosities and scientific instruments in his quarters on the Rue de Tournon; the museum was the rendezvous of amateurs and scholars until its closing in 1785. Beginning in 1781, one could visit in the Palais Royal the museum of Pilatre de Rozier, opened with the government's approval and the personal sanction of the king and queen; in addition to the scientific cabinet, provision had been made to give courses in mathematics, anatomy, chemistry, modern languages and art; anyone could attend upon payment of the enrollment fees. Jacques Bonnier de la Mosson

(1702-1744) welcomed visitors to his scientific cabinet, the most beautiful in Paris and among the richest and best catalogued in Europe; it was liberally opened to the public by the owner who liked to greet his guests himself.

Museums became the vogue. In his *Tableau de Paris,* published in Amsterdam in 1783, L. S. Mercier gave his definition of the current rage: "New establishments that various individuals are trying to force on us. They will have difficulty in succeeding because there is too little liberty in our government to permit the sure development of private views and, besides, the capital cultivates tastes and fancies rather than a real and constant love for the arts and sciences."

Vienna's picture gallery furnishes us with a particularly representative example of the metamorphosis of a royal collection into a public museum during the course of the eighteenth century.

The artistic policy of Emperor Charles VI (reigned 1711-1740) ushered in the Age of the Baroque in Austria; he encouraged architecture and collecting on a truly imperial scale. The emperor found in Count Althann, whom he named his chief architect, great resources and staunch support. The count's chief task was to realize a new presentation of the royal collection of paintings, most of which had come from Rudolf II and Archduke Leopold-Wilhelm; the cabinet was to be housed in the remodeled Stallburg, a former arsenal. This installation, which involved the execution of a decor of paneling and the fashioning of new frames, took eight years: 1720-1728. Every facet of the project is known to us through two iconographical documents, one a unique piece of museology—the inventory drawn up by Count Althann, illustrated on parchment by the painter Ferdinand Storffer with miniatures of all the pictures; this pictorial inventory comprises three volumes, realized in 1720, 1730 and 1733. As to the disposition of the collection through the various rooms, it is reproduced in a volume of etchings by Frans van Stampart and Anton von Prenner published in 1735 under the title *Prodomus Theatrum artis pictoriae*. Given black frames embellished with gilt *rocaille,* the paintings were treated as simple decorative elements; all the schools were mixed; format and subject, not quality, determined the choice. Some masterpieces were omitted, others hung beside astonishingly mediocre paintings; baroque compositions predominated; to achieve an overall symmetry, there was no hesitation in cutting down or, as was more often the case, in enlarging the pictures. In the principal *salon* hung a vast painting by Francesco Solimena, *Count Althann presenting Emperor Charles VI with the Inventory of the Picture Gallery,* somewhat of a misconstruction of this museological effort, all the more surprising since it was not conceived as a suite of *salons* for entertaining but, from the first, as a museum.

One is led to believe that this baroque conception of miscellanea with regard to the exhibition of paintings expressed a particular *Zeitgeist* that forty years later, when a more logical installation of the museum was undertaken, provoked lively criticism. One readily distinguishes in this re-installation project the talent for organization that was the forte of Joseph II; ruling with his mother, Maria Theresa, since 1765, he had a hand in the shaping of the State from that time on. A regrouping of the paintings in the various royal households was ordered; "modern" paintings as well as those expressive of a different aesthetic, for instance, works by the early German School, were affected. Between 1776 and 1778 the painter Rosa worked on re-installing the royal collection in more appropriate quarters—in Schloss Belvedere, formerly the summer palace of Prince Eugene of Savoy. Rosa was reproached for his insufficiency of knowledge and in 1778 Chancellor Kaunitz entrusted the commission to the Basel expert, Chrétien de Mechel; despite some quarrels with his rival, Rosa, Mechel successfully acquitted himself of the task and the finished catalog, written in French, appeared in Basel in 1784. The exact date of the museum's opening is not known; the public was admitted three times a week. The reform had been radical; paintings which had been enlarged were reduced to their original dimensions; they were stripped of the sumptuous frames given them at Stallburg and received new ones in a simpler, uniform, neoclassical style; for these frames alone the considerable sum of 70,000 florins was expended. In the preface to the catalog, Mechel extolled the advantages of a methodical presentation: the paintings were grouped according to schools, within which works by the same master were kept together; progress from room to room was according to chronological order "so that one learns at a brief glance infinitely more than one could if the same paintings were hung without regard to the period which had made them… It must interest artists and amateurs the world over to know there actually exists a Repository where the history of art is made visible."

Mechel left no doubt as to the pedagogical character of his new installation: "A great public collection of this type [is] more for one's instruction than delight." There existed, however, a whole faction of Viennese who preferred to have their senses delighted; they insisted that "an exhibition is more impressive when all kinds of paintings are presented together" and they cherished the "effects of contrast." In 1785 von Rittershausen published an indictment of the situation in his *Betrachtungen über die Kaiserlich-Königliche Bildergalerie zu Wien*. He went so far as to say, "One who desires to write an art history can enter [the museum] but the sensitive man is kept away." The purpose of a gallery is not to divulge historical knowledge but "to develop taste and awaken the noblest instincts of the heart. This is why it must be founded on aesthetic principles." Von Rittershausen proposed a redivision of the collection into four groups according to matters of drawing, color, composition and spiritual content and, within each group, a further redivision by subject. A "Holy of Holies" category would receive the greatest masterpieces.

Mechel's methodical presentation, corresponding to a taste for logic endemic to the Age of Reason, was "neoclassical" in spirit; von Rittershausen's plan, reflecting an attitude that still championed the aging painter Maulbertsch, was governed by a baroque aesthetic that liked variety and fantasy and was plunged into an imaginary world beyond the reaches of time. This polemic at the very dawn of modern museology commands our attention, for it re-occurs each time a major transformation is about to upend the museological institution. Attuned to changes in taste, the public museum often finds itself caught between the divergent aesthetics of an old and a new generation. The choice of which to follow rests with the curator.

Vienna debated the merits of the rational presentation of paintings, but the gallery at Düsseldorf went ahead, thirty years earlier, in 1756, and realized such an installation. Elector Charles Theodore (†1799) had the collection disposed in a building constructed for that purpose in 1710 by his predecessor, Johann Wilhelm. Extant engravings inform us of the arrangement eventually decided upon by the Düsseldorf painter Lambert

Krahe; paintings still covered all available wall space but at least they were classed according to master and school; very simple, "functional" borders enframed them. A rational presentation and absence of ornament likewise governed the installation of the Hofgartengalerie, a public museum established by the Bavarian Charles Theodore. In 1780 and 1781 the collection was installed in a specially designed area under the existing arcades of a garden court; the space was lighted laterally by lofty windows. At Kassel the landgrave of Hesse opened his gallery to the public in 1760. That at Dresden could be visited on request. Its fame spread with the appearance in 1753-1754 of two volumes of reproductions with accompanying text in French by its curator Heinecken; a French guide to the collection was published in 1765 and one in German in 1771. In a celebrated passage in *Dichtung und Wahrheit*. Goethe described his excitement upon visiting the gallery for the first time in 1768: "The impatiently awaited hour of opening arrived and my admiration exceeded all my expectations. That *salon* turning in on itself, magnificent and so well-kept, the freshly gilded frames, the well-waxed parquetry, the profound silence that reigned, created a solemn and unique impression, akin to the emotion experienced upon entering a House of God, and it deepened as one looked at the ornaments on exhibition which, as much as the temple that housed them, were objects of adoration in that place consecrated to the holy ends of art." Looking at art in terms of a religious experience began a new chapter in museology. No longer existing solely for the delectation of refined amateurs, the museum, as it evolved into a public institution, simultaneously metamorphosed into a temple to human genius. As either artists or aristocrats, the early connoisseurs felt at home with art. On the other hand, the "general public" experienced a sense of admiration that eluded expression when it was exposed to the fruits of genius; out of this confrontation arose the notion of art's transcendant worth. This opinion rapidly gained ground in the nineteenth century, as did the more or less express view that an incurable sterility had stilled the wellsprings of modern art, exiling the creative act itself to a sort of golden world.

P. J. Grosley, a Frenchman who had traveled in Italy, recounted in his *Observations sur l'Italie et les Italiens* a visit he paid to the Paduan Faccioli, an ecclesiastic and professor at the local university, who had built up "a collection as scholarly as it was singular. His series of pictures constituted a history of painting since its rebirth in Europe. It began with Greek icons, on the imitation of which the first painters of Italy had trained their artistic sensibilities. The earliest Italian works were tasteless, servile copies of Madonnas, as dryly and as flatly executed as these crudely colored woodcuts that decorate the cottages of our peasants. Art gradually matured in the succeeding masters. Giotto, Mantegna, the Bellinis prepared the way for Raphael and Titian…"

Faccioli's *galleria progressiva,* already formed by 1758, might have its prototype in another, quite similar cabinet assembled during the first half of the *settecento* by Father Lodoli, a Venetian monk who was one of the theorists of neoclassicism. With scant financial resources at his disposal, this curate managed to bring together a collection of paintings by Venetian masters that began with "a few scraps of Greek paintings" and ended with Bellinis and Mantegnas; he also added a few examples from the Florentine, Bolognese, German and Flemish schools.

This essentially pedagogical concept of a gallery devoted to tracing the history of painting since its origins was formulated as early as 1550 by Vasari in the first edition

81. **Galileo's Lens.** *Museo Nazionale di Storia della Scienza, in the Palazzo Castellani, Florence. In 1677 this lens (broken), with which Galileo observed the satellites of Jupiter, was mounted like a valuable relic in a magnificent ivory frame, made by Vittorio Croster; it was one of the most beautiful ornaments in the grand dukes' scientific cabinets (which had been started by Cosimo I). In 1775 Grand Duke Leopold I installed the museum near the astronomic observatory. When Florence was flooded on November 4, 1966, this exhibit was one of the three hurriedly removed from the museum by the curator, Mme. Bonelli, to save them from the rising waters.*

160

of his *Vite*; the principles had been set forth but were not put to use until the eighteenth century. A Vasarian system was adopted in 1770 by Luigi Lanzi for the *Gabinetto di Antichi Quadri* in the Uffizi. Lanzi gave a theoretical exposition of his methods in his *Storia pittorica dell'Italia del Risorgimento delle belle arti presso al fino del XVIII secolo,* which appeared in 1789. In this treatise he fitted the various schools of painting into a grid that was to govern the arrangement of European pinakothekai until the present generation.

The Uffizi, like all the Medici collections, were turned over to the state by the last princess of the house, Anna Maria Ludovica, daughter of Cosimo III; widowed at twenty-six by the death of the Palatinate Elector Johann Wilhelm of Neuburg-Wittelsbach, she returned to Florence to live out her days under the reign of her brother, Giovanni Gastone de'Medici, last of the Medici grand dukes. He was succeeded in 1737 by Francis of Lorraine (later Emperor Francis I). Anna Maria Ludovica lived in a wing of the Pitti Palace until her brother's death in 1737 when, seeking to avoid frequent contact with the Austrian grand duke, she withdrew to a convent. Her piety and charity endeared her to the people who venerated her as the last descendant of the family that had brought grandeur to Florence. She received a good education from her great-uncle Cardinal Leopoldo de'Medici, himself a collector of artists' self-portraits and drawings; the latter, catalogued by the Florentine scholar Baldinucci, was to form the nucleus of the Uffizi's drawings cabinet. Anna Maria Ludovica assembled a pinakotheke of her own that concentrated on the German and Flemish schools she had come to love during her long residence in the north of Europe. She also spent enormous sums for dresses and jewels. She died in 1743, having stipulated in a will drawn up in 1737 that Florence was to receive the Medicean collections. According to the terms of the bequest, all her family's treasures in Florence, Rome and elsewhere became the property of Tuscany, in the custody of the grand duke and his successors under the double condition that the collections forever remain in Florence and that they be made available to the Tuscan people and the public of all nations. These conditions have been respected almost without exception, which explains why the Medici collections are the only princely assemblage Italy has kept intact to the present day.

Grand Duke Leopold I succeeded his father Francis when the latter was elected emperor in 1745 and was himself forced to relinquish the duchy in 1790 upon the death of his brother, Joseph II, whom he replaced as emperor. Leopold governed the modest territory of Tuscany with ability and foresight, proving to be one of the most enlightened heads of state in eighteenth-century Europe; he completely re-organized the government along resolutely modern lines and instituted a remarkable museological policy. He appointed a director for the Uffizi who was responsible to the Minister of Finance; his task was to overhaul the picture gallery with the help of Luigi Lanzi, who was given the title *assistante antiquario*; Lanzi re-arranged the paintings by schools and in 1782 published a guide for the visitor's use. As for the antiquities, a comprehensive inventory listing all pieces in the various palaces, villas and gardens of the Medici was drawn up in 1781, with the express purpose of consolidating them under one roof—the Uffizi. In 1775 the celebrated group of *Niobids* was sent from Rome and a beautiful long gallery in neoclassical style was laid out to receive them. Grand Duke Ferdinand III, ascending the throne of Tuscany in 1791, continued his predecessor's museological policies. He had cartouches made for all the paintings and in 1798 he negotiated an exchange with the gallery in Vienna whereby Dürer's *Adoration of the Magi* and Titian's *Flora* entered the Uffizi. The prelate Lanzi, originally an Etruscologist, condensed his vast knowledge of the history of painting into his book *Storia pittorica dell'Italia,* which appeared in 1795/96; in this work he set up the geographical categories which museums in the nineteenth century were to follow. The finest antique and Renaissance works were installed in the *Tribuna* by Buontalenti—a presentation that was marked with success. A rather whimsical painting by Zoffany, exhibited at the Royal Academy in London in 1780, shows a group of amateurs, with the best-known English residents of Florence among them, meeting in the *Tribuna.*

In his consolidation and re-organization of the Medici collections, Grand Duke Leopold I took care not to neglect science. He put the prelate Fontane at the head of a museum for physics and natural history, installed in 1775 in quarters adjoining the *Specola,* an old Florentine observatory. The grand duke evinced great personal interest in chemistry and the cabinet he devoted to it has been kept intact with its original cabinets and all his instruments and beakers. Florence's Museo Nazionale di Storia Della Scienza, today housed in the Palazzo Castellani, contains all the scientific objects and instruments amassed since the sixteenth century by the grand dukes; the beautifully executed and elaborate mountings given these instruments make it as much an art as a science museum.

During the course of the eighteenth century Naples emerged as one of Europe's great museological centers. The first accretion of treasures was realized with the transfer of the Farnese collections in Parma and Rome to the Neopolitan city. The last of the Farneses, wife of Philip V of Spain, celebrated for her matchmaking triumphs —she managed to marry each of her children to a kingdom—bequeathed her collection to her son, Charles of Bourbon, crowned king of the Two Sicilies in 1735. Started by Pope Paul III and added to throughout the sixteenth century, it numbered among the finest collections of the Renaissance. Upon their arrival in Naples, the medallions and paintings were installed for better or worse in the old *Reggia.* It was there that Charles de Brosses could, in 1739/40, admire the medallions, extol the worth of the library (still unshelved) and contemplate the paintings "*accumulés sur un escalier borgne où tout le monde allait pisser.*" He thought the paintings had sustained great injuries in their hasty removal during a time of war. As the marine air was causing further damage to them, housed as they were in a palace not far from the bay, it was decided to remove the entire *quadreria borbonica* to the Palazzo Reale di Capodimonte on a hill overlooking the city; the large rooms of this new palace (construction had begun only a few years earlier, in September 1738) were remodeled to receive the cabinet but the alterations took a painfully long time. The antiquities from the Palazzo Farnese in Rome, many of which had come from the Baths of Caracalla, were likewise installed in Capodimonte. The excavations at Herculaneum and Pompeii so enriched the store of antiquities at Naples that the city suddenly found itself the rival of Rome. Emmanuel de Lorraine, Prince of Elbœuf, had discovered Herculaneum in 1709; excavation of the site was vigorously renewed by Charles IV of Bourbon as early as 1738, the first year of his reign. Although it had been discovered in the seventeenth century (by the architect, Fontana), digging commenced at Pompeii only in 1748 by Charles who was passionately interested in

82. **Transport of Antiques from the Portici Museum to the Naples Museum,** *by Jean-Louis Desprez. Water color. Wildenstein Collection, New York. In a triumphant procession the antiquities from Herculaneum—until then kept in the royal villa at Portici, near Vesuvius—were moved to a university building which was remodeled as a museum and where the treasures would be protected from the danger of a volcanic eruption.*

these excavations; even after he became king of Spain, he kept *au courant* about the discoveries, growing impatient with his son Ferdinand for his near abandonment of the projects. To receive the superabundance of antiquities recovered from the two cities, the king had a museum installed in a wing of his royal villa at Portici, the former port of Herculaneum. Bronzes, marbles, medallions, intaglios, furniture, papyri and all manner of utensils filled the ground floor; paintings, the second. Still visible today is the inscription *Herculanense Museum* over one of the gateways to Portici. This windfall of antiquities was cloaked in mystery; aware of the growing curiosity among an international public, the king commissioned a publication on the excavations from a learned society which was to spend years on the task. In the interim, the museum was only halfheartedly open to the public—drawing and note-taking were forbidden. The son of a shoemaker in Stendal, the autodidact Johann Joachim Winckelmann, who was to become the greatest antiquary of his time and the first modern art historian, was graciously received at the palace. He was, however, suspected of being a spy sent to pilfer the works of the Royal Academy and was made to wait a long time for permission to visit the museum and, once admitted, was subject to the same interdicts as the other visitors. In truth an emissary of the Elector of Saxony, whose daughter was the queen of Naples, Winckelmann had arrived in 1756, with the charge to gather data on the excavations. Despite the difficulties he encountered, he succeeded in publishing reports on Herculaneum but the affair ended with a revocation of his rights to visit the kingdom of the Two Sicilies.

83

84

83 and 84. **Medallion struck for Clement XII** *on the occasion of the opening of the Capitoline Museum in Rome which was founded by the pope in 1734. The medallion is in a building constructed in the XVIIth century facing the Palazzo dei Conservatori where Clement XII installed an important museum of antiques, a large part of which came through the purchase of the collection of Cardinal Alessandro Albani.*

The excitement over discoveries, particularly over paintings, stimulated the forgery industry; the engraver Francesco Giuseppe Casanova and the painter Giuseppe Guerra made forgeries their specialty. Even artists of great repute, like Raphael Mengs, were quick to capitalize on deceit; Mengs made a pastiche in fresco of Jupiter and Ganymede which Winckelmann celebrated as "one of the most beautiful pieces bequeathed us by Antiquity."

The state of affairs in the archeological museum eventually improved. After an eruption of Vesuvius on August 8, 1779 threatened the royal villa at Portici, the newly founded Academy of Sciences and Fine Arts asked Ferdinand I to transfer the cabinet of antiquities from the villa to Naples. He complied and they chose to install it in a building originally intended as stables at the time of its completion in 1586 by Domenico Fontana; then, in 1615, it was remodeled as a *Palazzo degli Studi* (university); today it houses the Museo Nazionale of Naples. The transport of the statuary, columns and objects stored at Portici was effected with great pomp—the wagons, transformed into triumphal chariots, passed before an elegant audience that sat in shaded reviewing stands along the route; a drawing by the Frenchman Desprez, then in Naples where he was working on illustrations for Vivant-Denon's *Voyage pittoresque de Naples et de la Sicile,* preserves for us a record of the day. The following century another story was added to the Museo Nazionale in order to accommodate the *pinacoteca* from Capodimonte; when the present renovations are completed, the museum will once again be devoted exclusively to antiquities; after World War II, the paintings collection was removed to its original location in the Palazzo Reale di Capodimonte, now the Galleria Nazionale di Capodimonte.

The more or less fortuitous growth of the museum in Naples was a much more ordered process in Rome. At that time Rome was the antiquarian's paradise; intellectuals, artists and scholars found ready patrons and protectors in the cardinals. Hordes of foreigners visited the city and the outlying *campagna*; excavations progressed under

165

85. **Pope Pius VI visiting the Vatican's Pio-Clementino Museum with Gustavus III of Sweden, by Gagneraux, 1784.** *Prague Château. Named for the two popes Clement XIV and Pius VI, the Pio-Clementino Museum was installed at the Vatican near the Belvedere according to plans drawn up by the architect Simonetti in a neoclassical style inspired by ancient Roman architecture.*

the watchful eye of Winckelmann. The English cornered the art market (the unscrupulous Thomas Jenkins, the painter Gavin Hamilton, Nollekens). Despite controls on the exportation of works of art, Rome lost many of her collections; in 1720, 1,300 pieces of sculpture passed from the Giustiniani collection into the hands of the Earl of Pembroke; the Odescalchi, Chigi, Massimo and Mattei collections were swallowed up by Frederick II of Prussia, Catherine the Great and the Duke d'Orléans. The Medici treasures were carted off to Florence and those in the Palazzo Farnese, to Naples. On the other hand, Cardinals Neri, Corsini, Borgia, Valenti and Albani amassed collections; the popes, after a century of indifference to amateurism, resumed a vigorous patronage of the arts, conscious of their "cultural" commitments as heads of the pontifical state.

To relieve the overcrowded conditions in the Palazzo dei Conservatori, the popes conceived the idea of building a palace facing it on the other side of the Piazza di Campidoglio, following a suggestion of Michelangelo; begun in 1603 by Girolamo Rainaldi, the palace was completed in 1655. After some interior renovations, Pope Clement XII turned it over to the public as a museum in 1734, the now-famous Museo Capitolino. Benedict XIV had the fragments of an early city plan of Rome (the *forma urbis* realized under Emperor Septimius Severus) removed from the Palazzo Farnese, where it had fallen into decay, to the new museum. Hoping to turn the Capitoline Hill into a museological center for Rome, Benedict XIV installed a pinakotheke in the Palazzo dei Conservatori in 1749; his idea was to further the artistic education of the students at the *Accademia del Nudo*. The picture gallery was formed with the purchase of the Sachetti cabinet and with requisitions from the collection of Cardinal Carlo Pio of Savoy before its exportation. Clement XIII, succeeding Benedict XIV, appointed Winckelmann, a convert to Catholicism, his Prefect of Antiquities. Clement XIV undertook a reorganization of the Vatican's collection of antiquities, withdrawing pieces from the gardens to relocate them in rooms in the Palazzo Belvedere, which had been constructed by Jacopo di Pietrasanti for Innocent VIII about 1487. Pius VI erected an entire complex of buildings to house the collection; this museum bears the name Museo Pio-Clementino. Michelangelo Simonetti conceived the idea of presenting the statuary in settings similar to those for which they had been created; the vast halls of baths, the galleries of imperial palaces and the cubicula of private homes furnished the architect with basic layouts which he decorated in a sober, neoclassical style; the curator Giovanni Battista Visconti realized the installation of the statues with the assistance of his son Ennio Quirino, who later immigrated to France at the time of the Revolution.

The neoclassical architecture of the Museo Pio-Clementino, opened in 1772, furnished the canon for museums of antiquities for more than half a century. The museum itself has not changed since its founding; the works pillaged by the French during the Revolution were later returned. With its thousands of unlabeled statues, busts and fragments on exhibition, this museum constitutes a sort of labyrinth where specialists delight to wander but where the general public gets lost on its quest for known masterpieces. This multitude of very often mediocre statues provokes an incommensurable ennui; if it is the charm of an eighteenth-century humanist's foyer that one seeks, one must go to the Villa Albani. About 1760 Cardinal Alessandro Albani commissioned the architect Carlo Marchionni to build a villa on the Via Salaria; here the cardinal installed his collection of choice antiquities, which boasted a few Greek pieces—a rarity for Rome. The museum expressed the neoclassical ideals of Winckelmann and Raphael Mengs, who painted his famous *Parnassus* fresco for the villa; countless of Winckelmann's letters, dated 1757 and 1758, attest to his enthusiasm for the project. In the peace of its solitude (visit is by request only) the uninhabited Villa Albani (now the Villa Torlonia) seems consecrated to the memory of the great archeologist who built it; his bust is as much honored there as are those of antique heroes. Under the beautifully proportioned, semi-circular portico of the *Canopo o caffè* still hovers the memory of those humanists for whom, like Winckelmann, life lived to its fullest meant life lived *agli antichi*.

Another beautiful expression of the neoclassical taste is found in the extreme north of Europe. With the view of creating a public museum, Gustavus III of Sweden amassed a collection of antiquities numbering 182 pieces. Assassinated at a theatre in 1792, the king himself did not live to see his project completed; however, in a decree dated June 2, 1792, the Regent, Charles, Duke of Sodermanland, ordered that the work be started again. The museum was installed in a neoclassical gallery built below the library, which occupied a wing of the royal palace. In 1866 the collection had grown so large that it had to be installed elsewhere; in 1956 Parliament ordered a reconstitution of the gallery, the original layout of which had been preserved in a water color.

Chapter 9

Revolution

The movement which was to transform the great sovereign collections of Europe into museums for the public was distinctly outlined by the end of the eighteenth century. The French Revolution precipitated a tidal wave of activity when, suddenly, a considerable number of works which, the eve before, had belonged to the king, the church or private individuals, were handed over to the nation. Beginning in France, then spreading to the countries under French jurisdiction from 1793 to 1814, the flood coursed through a Europe which at first resisted but then saw itself constrained to adopt certain ideas propagated by the Revolution. The museum became one of the fundamental institutions of the modern State.

It could be said that the Revolution confined itself to realizing the museological projects of the *Ancien Régime* but, if this is the case, it did so on a vaster scale than had been intended. The passion for logic that dominated men's minds in this period of great political speculation transformed into regulated institutions the organisms that hitherto had had a fortuitous existence. Diderot's *Muséum central des Arts et des Sciences* was still an ever-present dream but this project of consolidation was not to be realized at the Louvre. Between 1792 and 1795, several museums received various sections intended for the proposed central unit: the Muséum National (temporarily housing the art museum destined for the Louvre); the Musée des Monuments Français (the history cabinet destined for the Couvent des Petits Augustins); the Muséum d'Histoire Naturelle (the science museum eventually established in the Jardin des Plantes); the Musée des Arts et Métiers (the scientific and technical museum later installed in the Couvent de Saint Martin des Champs).

The French Revolution affected the fate of enormous numbers of works of art; earlier, the currents that had set art in motion had been commercial in character; works remained where they had been created and only an evolution in taste occasionally menaced their fortune. With the advent of the Revolution, works of art by the thousands became available, the freed property of physical or moral bodies which had lost their existence—the king, the Church, the emigrating aristocracy. What fate awaited them? Not all were requisitioned for public use; many, like the furnishings of Versailles or the

86. **Bonaparte showing the Apollo Belvedere to his Deputies.** *From an old engraving. The* Apollo Belvedere *and the* Laöcoon *were the two most precious works among the masterpieces of antique statuary which the pope ceded to France and which remained in Paris from 1798 to 1815.*

169

87. First page of the Instructions prepared on the order of the National Convention for the preservation of cultural objects. *Bibliothèque Nationale, Paris. These instructions, prepared in 1794, were distributed throughout France. The first page shows a preamble imprinted with the revolutionary ideology.*

goods left behind by *emigrés* to satisfy their creditors, were auctioned off but not before special agents could make appropriations for the museums then taking shape.

In compliance with a decree of the Convention, works confiscated over the whole of France were sent to a few key warehouses; newly secularized convents, now but vast, empty spaces, were often utilized for this purpose. In Paris the major storage areas were the Convents of the Petits Augustins, the Capucins, the Grands Jésuites, the Cordeliers and the Hôtel de Nesles. Special deputies worked on cataloguing the art; unfortunately, not all were qualified scholars—some had been purely political appointments. In the end, a great many works in some way marked with feudal, religious or royal devices forbidden by law, were set aside to be destroyed and were broken, melted down or burned.

At no other time in history was the instinct of preservation so closely allied with the act of destruction; like a defective compass, the Convention continually contradicted itself; at one time it upheld laws prescribing the destruction of seditious emblems; at another, alarmed by the wave of vandalism it had helped to promote, it voted for severe penalties against all those who defaced monuments belonging to the nation. The Legislative Assembly established on October 14, 1791 a "Committee for Public Instruction," entrusted with the surveillance and upkeep of monuments; in legislation dated September 28, 1793 it was replaced by a "temporary commission on the Arts" which drew up museological instructions for all directors of art depots; the text was approved by the Assembly on November 25, 1794 and the information was disseminated in a brochure done on the presses of the Imprimerie Nationale with the lengthy title of *Instructions on Methods for Conserving in every Sector of the Republic all Objects of any Service to the Arts, Sciences and Education, Proposed by the Temporary Commission on the Arts and Adopted by the Committee for Public Instruction of the National Convention.* Finally, in order to combat acts of depredation done out of passion, the Commission was obliged to denounce them as "counter-revolutionary plots," an accusation which led to the scaffold.

The bill of May 26, 1791 establishing the king's *liste civile* appropriated the Palais du Louvre for art and science monuments. The bill of November 19, 1792 ordered that all art objects confiscated in the royal households be sent to the Louvre; this was an act of official possession for the profit of the nation. However, the public was not admitted to see the art until after the king's execution. On July 27, 1793 the Convention ruled that the "museum of the Republic" would open on the tenth of August, the anniversary of the downfall of the monarchy. The *vernissage* took place as scheduled on the very same day as the opening of the exhibition devoted to living artists, held as usual in the Salon Carré; however, urgent repairs necessitated closing the museum from the end of September to November eighth, when it re-opened. Five hundred thirty-seven paintings lined the wall spaces between windows in the Grande Galerie and one hundred eighty-four *objets d'art,* including three astronomical clocks, were arranged on tables in the center of the hall. Since by that time the Revolutionary calendar with its decadary system had replaced the seven-day week, the admission schedule was arranged so that the first five days were reserved for artists, the following two for cleaning and the last three for the public. It was for the artists, who had the museum to themselves five days out of ten, that it had been created. One recalls that fifty years earlier Lafont de Saint Yenne had already appealed for the opening of the royal collections for the benefit of artists. This proclivity for artistic pedagogy is peculiar to French museology, unlike its more scientific character in England. Beginning then and continuing until the time of Cézanne and Matisse, the Louvre was the great laboratory where modern art was developed. From the start, copyists abounded; their number had to be limited to one hundred and the term of their permits to six months.

The museum enjoyed such success that the crowds at its doors attracted a wave of prostitutes in search of clients, which caused great consternation in the local police precinct and in the Ministry of the Interior; the latter ordered "the severe punishment of any crime against morality, without the maintenance of which there can be no Republic." Plied with intensity during the hours of admission, this "infamous trade" continued into the night, to such a degree that it became necessary to install street lights to illumine the approaches.

The paintings were hung in the gallery according to schools, but within these general categories the old baroque principle of miscellanea governed the arrangement. When one remembers the violent criticism aroused by the rational installation of the pinakotheke in Vienna's Belvedere, one is not surprised to find a return to a method which pretended to bring out by contrast rather than by analogy the particular value of each work of art. The Board of the Museum explained its intentions in this way: "The arrangement we have adopted is one of a flower bed composed of an infinite variety of blooms. If by a different disposition we had shown art in its infancy, in its developing stages and in its present state... we might have pleased a few erudites but we would have feared the well-founded reproach... of having impeded the studies of the young." Thus it was always the artist and not the connoisseur who was kept in mind. However, this installation displeased the Parisian public, all the more so because there were no labels to come to their aid in this labyrinth where all periods and all genres were mixed, where one came upon, for example, "very imperfect works by Raphael long after one had admired his great ones." The Louvre was far from the *galleria progressiva* proposed in an article appearing in the *Décade philosophique* for the tenth Pluviôse, Year III. The Grande Galerie seemed too narrow and poorly illuminated by reason of the incorrect lighting coming from two rows of windows opposite each other; sunlight streaming in "somethimes falls on the paintings themselves, which will not take long to bleach and spoil them if the situation is not quickly remedied."

The museum was managed according to the principle of collectivity dear to the Revolution; the commissions and the conservatories changed as often as the government. Hubert Robert, released after a brief imprisonment in the Tuileries, was a member of most of these commissions; he followed the progress of the museum until its closing by decree of the Consulate in 1802 and illustrated the life of the gallery in several paintings, many of which today hang in the Louvre.

Because the museum had been opened in a delapidated building, it became necessary to close it for repairs in May 1796. For the next three years, only a portion of the paintings was exhibited in the Salon Carré. In the Salon of 1796 Hubert Robert entered a painting entitled *Project for Lighting the Gallery of the Museum by means of a Vault and for Dividing it without Obstructing the long View*. Here was a visualization of the proposals made by the Academy of Architecture in 1786. The artist created a strange companion piece for this work: his *Louvre in Ruins*; not content to show the gallery as it ought to look in the near future, the painter-poet spanned the coming centuries to picture it as it might look after some disaster in history. In Hubert Robert's aesthetics, the condition of ruin was the noble state par excellence, the state of the monuments of antiquity. These two paintings had a curious fate; formerly in the imperial palace of Tsarskoye Selo near Leningrad, they were sold by the Soviets and today are in a private collection in Buenos Aires. The preliminary sketches are now in the Louvre; that of the first work was given by a certain Fenaille; as for the second, I had the good fortune to discover it one day in an obscure sale, where the subject had not been recognized, which enabled me to buy it at a good price for the Louvre.

The shortcomings of the 1793 installation had been rectified by the time the gallery re-opened in 1799. Paintings were arranged by schools and an attempt was made to relieve the monotony of the long gallery by putting here and there high marble columns to support cippi and busts. Six hundred forty-three paintings were on exhibition.

Emptied of its masterpieces, Versailles was filling up with an anomalous stock of confiscated goods as it was the storehouse for the Department of Seine et Oise. Over the protests of the city, which suddenly saw itself reduced from a royal capital to a simple municipality, it was decided in legislation dated March 16, 1797, to create at the palace "a special museum for the French School," thus avoiding clashes of interest with the museum in the Louvre, consecrated to the chefs d'œuvre of foreign schools. It became, so to speak, a purgatory to which were consigned the condemned works of artists whose *fêtes galantes* and *pastorales* had delighted the old aristocracy. The paintings were arranged in the royal apartments, the Hall of Mirrors and on the first floor of the north wing, on the garden side.

In Paris itself, meanwhile, one of the depositories for art works slowly evolved, thanks to the tenacity of its director, into a museum that was to have considerable influence on the Romantic generation in France. In the Convent of the Petits Augustins, located across the Seine from the Louvre, a depot was set up on October 15, 1790, to receive works confiscated from churches in Paris. The painter Alexandre Lenoir was given the directorship; discovering in himself a talent for archeology, he set about acquiring all the medieval and Renaissance artifacts he could find in an effort to prevent "the disfigurement and complete destruction of masterpieces that formerly decorated the temples of fanatics, the palaces of tyrants and the houses of their accomplices." The Abbey of Saint Denis, where he witnessed the profanation of the royal tombs, yielded him a veritable mine of treasures. This enterprising man was so successful in his intrigues that he managed to obtain from the Convention, five days before its dissolution (that is, on October 21, 1795), the decision to create a *Muséum des monuments français* with the artifacts stored in the Convent of the Petits Augustins; this move on the part of the Convention is surprising when one remembers that this was a matter of honoring the monuments of the old monarchical, feudal and religious France. Moreover, during the brief restoration of monarchy under Louis XVIII, the institution bore the name *musée de la monarchie française*. In his installation Lenoir followed the principle of the *galleria progressiva,* worked out some fifty years earlier in Italy for pinakothekai; Lenoir went even further—not content to show the evolution of styles, he endeavored to define the qualities peculiar to each historical epoch. "The Musée des monuments français," he explained, "is the only place where one can study the birth, evolution and eventual florescence of the arts within a context… The advances in art follow those of civilization; they sometimes provoke glorious associations and often bring to mind personalities who hastened art's development either through their genius or through their patronage."

The layout of a convent, with its succession of vast rooms, was particularly suited to this idea. The Chapel, where the principal monuments were grouped, served as a point of confluence where the "observer" was transported "from the infancy of art among the Gauls to its decay toward the end of the seventeenth century." Each of the succeeding rooms was devoted to a century that had witnessed progress in the "arts of drawing": the thirteenth, fourteenth, fifteenth, sixteenth and finally the seventeenth century "when one thought art could dispense with study and that inspiration sufficed." A true precursor, Lenoir was already imbued with the prejudice still current in France of the superiority of anything that emanated from the Middle Ages. In order to create atmosphere, the curator of the Musée des Monuments Français fashioned artificial monuments from all manner of debris and provided each room with a suitable period decor. To complete this historical evocation, Lenoir conceived the idea of creating an "Elysian Field" peopled with monuments—both empty cenotaphs and real tombs—to the memory of great men: Dagobert, Descartes, Turenne, Louis II de Bourbon (the Great Condé), Molière, La Fontaine, Boileau, Mabillon, Montfaucon and Du Guesclin were honored there. Hordes of idlers visited this pantheon where the most touching monument was the one Lenoir had consecrated to Héloise and Abélard, made with pieces from their original tombs supplemented with debris from other edifices, chiefly those ornamental arcades torn from the lower walls of the Eglise de Saint Denis, of which he availed himself at every opportunity. This is the sole monument still intact from the Elysium; when the museum was dismantled, the statuary was transported to the cemetery of Père La Chaise. In my youth it was the custom for students in love to go there in the springtime to throw bouquets of violets; it seems to me that in today's era of the twist, the monkey and the jerk students no longer bother with such sentimental preliminaries. This is, no doubt, the reason why some serious advocates of pure archeology have proposed destroying the monument to Héloise and Abélard; this would be a new act of vandalism comparable to the one out of which it was created in the first place since this vestige of Lenoir's museum is revered for the touching admiration it evoked for several generations. "An Elysium," remarked Lenoir, "seemed to me to fit the character I had given my establishment." Cypresses, tombs, funerary reliefs, statues, votive columns—all conspired "to imbue this place of happiness with the sweet melancholy that speaks to the sensitive soul." During its ten years of existence, thousands of visitors frequented Lenoir's museum; among the many sensitive souls were some, like Delacroix and Michelet, who experienced there a sense of history. "It was there and no other place I felt a keen intuition of history," wrote Michelet in his old age; he was among those who regretted the destruction of the museum in 1815. Returning from a visit to the Convent of the Petits Augustins, children would dream, not without some fright, about the plantoms they had gone in search of, "ardent, curious, fearful, from one room to the next, from one age to the next."

By the time the Grande Galerie of the Louvre re-opened (in part in 1799, in its entirety on July 14, 1800), it had been enriched by a number of masterpieces taken from various countries in Europe by special commissions that had followed the victorious French armies. In 1794 and 1795 the first convoys returned with Flemish pictures pillaged in Belgium which, for a time, became French territory. In the wake of the Italian army, commanded by General Bonaparte, a commission comprising the mathematician Gaspard Monge, the chemist Claude Louis Berthollet, the botanist Thouin, the painters Barthélemy and Antoine Gros, the sculptor Moitte and the archeologist Wicar, appropriated "goods of artistic and scientific nature" which, as stipulated by the treaty, were to be remitted to France by the conquered states, including the Vatican. In a heteroclite assemblage of books, celebrated paintings, exotic animals, scientific instruments, typefaces and all manner of natural curiosities, the most appreciated trophy was a collection of antique statues taken from the Capitoline and Vatican museums; the interest was more than purely aesthetic as the revival of antique influence, sparked by neoclassicism, had assumed a moral aspect during the Revolution. The commissions did not want the "precious ruins" of Rome and Italy to arrive in Paris like "shipments of coal or cases of soap." Their entry turned into a triumphal procession *à la romaine,* with military detachments, members of the Institut de France, administrators of the Muséum Central des Arts, professors at the Academy of Painting and Sculpture and typesetters among those marching; the latter were present to receive the typefaces from the pontifical presses, dispatched in the hope of "putting into the hands of the government powerful means for furthering the principles of philosophy, the creations of science, the discoveries of genius and for accelerating the development of reason and happiness among men." Arriving in the Champ de Mars, the wagons hauling all these trophies formed a circle three lines deep around a monument to Liberty. The solemn presentation to the Directors took place on the following day, July 27, 1798, the fourth anniversary of the fall of Robespierre.

88. **Madonna with a Candle, by Carlo Crivelli.** *Pinacoteca di Brera, Milan. This painting was taken in 1811 from the Dominican convent of Camerino to be sent to Milan, at that time the capital of the kingdom of Italy, where the museological policy of the French Empire created a great museum with works plundered from all of Northern Italy, from the Emilia and from the Veneto.*

The removal to France of paintings and antiquities seized in Italy was both condoned and vehemently opposed. A petition signed by great lovers of Rome (the aesthetician Quatremère de Quincy, the architects Pierre Fontaine and Charles Percier, the painters Pierre-Henri de Valenciennes and Jacques-Louis David) was sent to the Directory to protest the seizure of antiquities. A counterpetition answered it. The notion of deflecting the "principal monuments of art and science" to Paris originated in the messianism of the French Revolution, expressed in countless official or journalistic texts. Paris was to be the art capital of Europe and masterpieces would find in France their true home, for whatever creations of genius might be found in the "countries where the victorious armies of the French Republic had routed hordes of slaves who were the mercenaries of tyrants... their true resting place for the honor and progress of the arts is in the home of and under the hand of free men" (decree of the Convention dated Messidor, Year II). Napoleon as Emperor adapted this policy of the Revolution to the design of empire that motivated him. Wherever his triumphal armies passed—through Germany, through Austria, through Poland—works of art were requisitioned for France.

The Administration of the Musée Central des Arts (¹) was burdened with processing all the paintings, antiquities and *objets d'art* sent to it and with seeing to their repair. A workshop at the Louvre effected restorations of paintings which were often in a state of decay, never having been attended to since their creation; the repair work on these pictures, since returned to their original museums, is still admired. An example is the transfer of Raphael's *Foligno Madonna* in the Vatican on to a new canvas, the restoration still being in good condition after many years.

During the last years of the Revolution, lack of funds severely limited the life of the museum. The situation was ameliorated under the Consulate and the administration of the museum was overhauled. The Ecole des Beaux Arts underwent re-organization. A bill passed on November 19, 1802 regrouped several museums and artistic services under a single director, naming to the post the Chevalier de Non, later Baron Dominique Vivant Denon under the Empire. A former gentleman of the Privy Chamber under Louis XV, an ambassador's secretary under Louis XVI, he had been one of the most active members of the Egyptian campaign, where Bonaparte had remarked his knowledge and bravery. Here was a fine and cultivated mind, a draftsman of talent, an author of *contes galants* who adapted himself with ease to the successive regimes he lived through; at fifty-eight Denon brought to his new position broad experience, "having obtained," as Anatole France put it, "the favors of Madame de Pompadour and Louis XV... having visited Frederick the Great at Potsdam and formed a liaison with Voltaire at Ferney; having sparkled in the drawing rooms at Versailles and at the court of Catherine II; having visited by turn Germany, Italy, Switzerland and Spain, manifesting everywhere an artist's curiosity; having lived without inconvenience under the government of the Terror and accepted Robespierre; more than fifty years old, having welcomed like a young man the adventurous Egyptian campaign... having obtained the confidence of Napoleon, sometimes even on matters other than the arts; having accompanied the great commander on his campaigns to Germany and Spain; having fought in fierce skirmishes and great battles... happy from the day he was born to the day he died: *voilà, en résumé, la destinée de Denon.*" He who had been a brilliant wit at court, who, according to Anatole France, looked as though "he had just stepped out of a fête

89. **Portrait of Baron Vivant-Denon,** *by Pierre Paul Prud'hon. Louvre Museum, Paris. He became the Louvre's director in 1802.*

90. **Drawing showing the arrival of the first visitors to the Koninklijk Museum on September 15, 1808.** *Drawings Cabinet, Rijksmuseum, Amsterdam. This very naïve drawing shows the eagerness of the visitors at the opening of the museum founded by Louis Bonaparte which later became the Rijksmuseum.*

by Watteau," became a great administrator and a paragon of the "museum man," as we say today. He explored on a grand scale the multifarious problems of conservation and all the technical questions relevant to museum architecture. On this last point, Denon met with his greatest difficulties: tension built up between the conservators and the maintenance personnel, a problem which still plagues museums today.

The curator of paintings at the Louvre was the former administrator, Dufourny; that of antiquities, Ennio Quirino Visconti, who changed his given names to the more French Ennius Quirinus. Visconti had already realized the installation of the *antiquarium* in the former summer apartments of Anne of Austria, opened the 18th Brumaire, 1800. He knew these antiquities better than anyone else since he had catalogued them before in the Capitoline and Vatican museums. A champion of the ideals of the Revolution, he had been chosen one of the five consuls of the ephemeral Roman republic of 1798; he defected to the French army when its occupation of Italy ended.

Upon the recommendation of the consul Jean Jacques Regis de Cambacéres, the Musée Central des Arts became the Musée Napoleon in 1803, a name it kept until 1814. It enjoyed enormous success in France and was acclaimed throughout Europe, with foreign visitors, especially the English, flocking to see it during periods of peace. This era witnessed a veritable efflorescence of studies and works; it was a great age for museology. Denon, who aspired to have an architect under his authority, was in reality subordinate to the government's architect Fontaine, with whom he conflicted violently at times. The Archives Nationales preserve for us the story of the latrines razed by the architect without notifying the director. Denon was constrained to summon Fontaine to re-install them "as promptly as possible, in order to avoid evacuation in the courtyards, on the stairways and perhaps even in the gallery of the museum, which would surely happen if the guards appointed to safeguard and maintain the propriety of this monument had no place to which to direct those

177

in need." These controversies caused, as they do today, many delays and compromised the realization of projects. Denon was unable to carry out for the Grande Galerie the plan of Raymond, which was inspired by the one studied with such care by the *Ancien Régime* and which is known to us through the painting by Hubert Robert for the Salon of 1796; modified against the will of Denon, the project was finished, after many delays, in 1810 and the gallery opened for the marriage of Napoleon to Marie Louise of Austria, which took place in the Salon Carré; the elegant cortege passed from the Tuileries to the Salon, borrowing for its triumphal way the gallery along the Seine, laden with the masterpieces of Europe. The director was happier with the enlargement of the antiquities museum, another of Raymond's designs effected at the expense of the apartment once reserved for queen mothers; this *antiquarium,* with its red-and-white marble revetment after the fashion of the Roman baths, strongly resembled the Museo Pio-Clementino in the Vatican—a creation of Visconti, backed by Denon.

Paris was not alone in its interest in the museological uproar. Storehouses were set up all over France, primarily in convents, to receive confiscated art. Local initiative often turned these repositories into museums. A case in point is the Couvent des Grands Augustins in Toulouse, established by order of the council of the Department of Haute Garonne on December 12, 1793 as a *Muséum du Midi de la République.* The museum was opened in the vast church, paintings graced the walls, *objets d'art* were disposed on tables but stone artifacts from destroyed monuments (later esteemed the museum's most prized holdings) were left in storage. At the other end of France, Lille, which had founded a commission on the Arts in 1792, requested the painter Louis Watteau to inventory its confiscated goods and open a museum in 1795. Caen's commission on the Arts, formed in 1793, operated along the same lines but its museum did not open until 1809. At Angers, the Ecole Centrale, installed in 1796, was the prelude to the establishment of a museum. At Le Mans, two rooms in the former Couvent de la Couture were laid out as a museum in 1799.

In five university towns in France the Directory worked out a project for founding adjunct museums for the schools of art; to safeguard these collections and to explain the works they contained, a curator and a lecturer were appointed; the latter is the origin of what is known today in museum parlance as "educational services." The Consulate gave this project an even greater scope. Finding the Louvre somewhat congested with works of art, Jean Antoine Chaptal, minister of the interior, decided the provinces should benefit from this abundance and to this end he submitted a report to the consuls on September 1, 1800; he envisioned the distribution of—not just a sampling from—the collections "to places where education has prepared the public to appreciate them and where a large population and native dispositions will presage success in the formation of students." Each museum was to have a complete range of works by masters of the different schools—a small "central museum" at the provincial level. One recognizes in Chaptal's proposal the encyclopedic approach indigenous to the Revolution, heir of the Age of Enlightenment. The bill signed by Bonaparte on the 14th of Fructidor, Year IX, listed fifteen cities in the territory of the Republic slated to receive art: Bordeaux, Caen, Dijon, Lille, Lyons, Marseilles, Nancy, Nantes, Rennes, Rouen, Strasbourg, Toulouse, Brussels, Mainz and Geneva. Six hundred fifty-six paintings were distributed among

◄

91. Hubert Robert. Plan for arranging the Main Gallery of the Louvre as a museum. *Louvre Museum, Paris. The painter Hubert Robert was associated with the life of the Louvre Museum in several different capacities under the old regime and during the Revolution. In 1778 he was appointed by the Director of Public Buildings to a commission charged with preparing the future museum; in 1784 he was named Keeper of the King's Pictures. He painted a number of pictures illustrating his plans for the Main Gallery and views of its opening in 1793. This plan seems to have preceded the one he showed at the 1796 Exhibition which was partly carried out under the Empire but was not finally completed until 1949.*

◄

92. Hubert Robert. The Main Gallery of the Louvre during restoration before its reopening in 1799. *Hubert Robert was actively associated with the Louvre Museum for more than 25 years and his paintings represent a veritable chronicle of the life of the museum. The museum was opened in 1793 by the Convention, was then closed for repairs in 1796, and was reopened in 1799. In this picture Robert shows painting in progress ready for this reopening.*

them, to which others were added during the course of the following years; other cities, such as Montpellier, Tours, Grenoble, brought to twenty-two the number of municipalities benefited by the distribution; eventually 1,508 paintings were in circulation. The galleries were slow in opening as construction and installation were the responsibility of the individual cities. The museums in Marseilles and Bordeaux opened in 1804, that of Lyons in 1806 and those of Rouen and Caen in 1809.

In the conquered territories under her rule France provoked the opening of museums, either by direct action or by the shock of restitution; Italy became the theatre of particularly intense museological activity.

The confiscation of ecclesiastical goods following the suppression of the convents necessitated the formation of depots for works of art, installed as in France in secularized convents—at Milan in Santa Maria di Brera, at Genoa in the Oratorio di San Filippo, at Venice in Santa Maria della Carità.

By the Treaty of Pressburg (December 26, 1805), Venice, which had been ceded to Austria in 1797, was restored to the kingdom of Italy, the capital of which was then Milan. A decree dated February 12, 1807, established a Venetian Accademia delle Belle Arti which adopted the by-laws drafted in September 1803 by the Academies of Bologna and Milan. To the Academy was annexed a hall for sculpture and a pinakotheke, under the curatorship of Pietro Edwards, the head of the restoration works in San Zanipolo; since 1797 Edwards had been obliged to put himself at the disposal of the French government to effect requisitions on behalf of Paris. Legislation passed on April 26, 1806 ordered the collection of all art works in the kingdom of Italy, designating special officials for the task; the decree of August 4, 1807, restricted the conservation of monuments to official art. In the *pinacoteca* in Venice, around the paintings from the old Accademia, which had been founded in 1756 and of which Tiepolo had been president, were regrouped pictures confiscated from the city's convents, abundantly rich in art. This wealth attracted the covetousness of the kingdom and in April 1808 the exodus of masterpieces to Milan commenced—continuing, to the great despair of Venetians, for the duration of the Empire.

The formation of the Pinacoteca di Brera in Milan illustrates Napoleon's museological policy on the transcontinental level. Just as Paris, the capital of Napoleonic Europe, used art to accent its position, so Milan sought to confirm in the same manner its role as capital of the kingdom of Italy. The glorious "galleria di Brera" has retained the name of the old Gothic church that served as its depot, even though the cabinet has been transferred to the beautiful seventeenth-century palace built by the Jesuits which Empress Maria Theresa turned into a cultural center in 1772. The empress installed a public library, an observatory, a Lombard Institute of Sciences and Letters and an Academy of Fine Arts. The gallery opened on August 15, 1809. Throughout the kingdom—in Lombardy, the Veneto and the Emilia—the Brera effected requisitions; it amassed the richest collection in all Italy of Venetian *quattrocento* works, to which the officials seemed particularly drawn. Napoleon's stepson, Viceroy Eugène de Beauharnais, was very attached to this museum and lavished it with personal gifts, such as Piero della Francesca's *Madonna da Montefeltro* and Giovanni Bellini's *Pietà*. In 1806 the government of the viceroy acquired a prestigious work for the museum, Raphael's

Sposalizio or *Marriage of the Virgin* (1504); in 1798 the painting had been given by the city of Milan to General Lechi, who sold it to a convent three years later.

The Palazzo e Pinacoteca di Brera remains an intact example of the *musée révolutionnaire,* formed from requisitions and confiscations—"pillages," if you will—made throughout all of northern Italy.

The political ideology of revolutionary and Napoleonic France was encyclopedic and European in its aims; if Paris, capital of the one hundred thirty departments of the Empire, was to be a faithful reflection of European art, so also, on a lesser scale, should be each city that had been chosen to support a regional museum. Thus the museum at Brussels received 31 paintings, including three Tintorettos, one Bonifazio de'Pitati, one Barocci, one Guercino, one Veronese and even a Rubens, his *Martyrdom of Saint Lievin,* bought by the Crown under Louis XVI. After expropriating the Rubens paintings in Antwerp, the French government sent one to Brussels which had had none. Once the institutions were established, exchanges between museums were proposed on an international basis. In 1812/1813, Denon effected an exchange with the Brera; the latter was lent paintings by the Northern School (Rubens, van Dyck, Jordaens, Rembrandt) to offset a weakness in its permanent collection, while the Louvre received Italian works by Carpaccio, Boltraffio, Moretto da Brescia and Marco d'Oggiono. If the imperial government had lasted, had it been able to profit from a peacetime exploitation of its conquests, Denon's genius for organization would certainly have accomplished, by exchange or apportionment and in a spirit of internationalism, a regrouping of national collections.

Not all the museums proposed by the imperial government in Italy were realized; such was the case with Genoa and Treviso; on the other hand, some institutions seemed to spring up spontaneously, sparked by efforts to avoid French requisitions. Thus in 1796 the Senate of Bologna created an Accademia delle Belle Arti ostensibly to receive works of art expropriated from convents, in truth to foil the designs of the Brera's officials. At the other end of Europe the city of Antwerp was dismayed by the loss of some of its masterpieces; its executive council decreed the founding of a special school for painting, sculpture and architecture with an adjoining museum which would benefit, in its turn, from the generosities of Paris. Heading the executive branch of the municipal government was a Frenchman established in Antwerp, Simon Pierre Dragonne; despite his devotion to the French cause, he instituted proceedings to obtain the return of artistic treasures but was successful in restoring only two Rubens paintings to the city on the Scheldt. When the Directory was succeeded by the Consulate, d'Herbouville, French prefect for the Deux-Nethes, supported the interests of his district and tried continually, but with little success, to interest the imperial administration in the artistic plight of Antwerp. This failure, in contrast to the favors bestowed upon the recently founded Brussels museum, shed light on the museological policy of the Revolution and of the Empire. The French governments quite often removed works of art from their places of creation to other, more preferred, locations. Brussels was designated the great center of culture in Belgium; Antwerp, a marginal city which was considered nothing more than a military outpost of Napoleon's empire, mattered little. Later, when Antwerp's art treasures were restored in 1815, Brussels thought she had been wronged and sought to plunder the city in her own behalf.

93. **The Night Watch, by Rembrandt.** *Rijksmuseum, Amsterdam. Since 1808 this work has been in the museum which was opened in Amsterdam's town hall by Louis Bonaparte, King of Holland. It was turned over to the museum by the city of Amsterdam.*

Napoleon's relatives, given kingdoms by the emperor, immediately occupied themselves with founding museums in their respective capitals. Louis, king of Holland from 1806 to 1810, so concerned himself with the problems of his new country that he risked violent conflict with his brother, a stand which won him the devotion of his subjects but cost him his crown. A day after his arrival in Amsterdam, on April 21, 1808, he signed a bill to found the Koninklijk Museum (the basis for today's Rijksmuseum), the establishment of which he had promised two years earlier when he organized by decree a general commission on the arts and sciences (November 20, 1806). At that time the progressive Dutch already had a museum. When the French armies conquered Holland in 1795, the collections of the stadholder William V were confiscated for Paris, an action which aroused no protest since the Batavian Republic itself sold whatever remained. However, the Minister of Finance, Gogel, who was something of a Francophile, took the initiative to organize at Huis ten Bosch (formerly a summer residence of the House of Orange), a rather heteroclite museum of an historical nature. Opened on May 30, 1800, the establishment was closed when Louis, who dreamed on a grander scale, ascended the throne of Holland. When he resolved to move the seat of government to Amsterdam, Louis installed himself in its town hall, which was transformed into a royal palace with rooms reserved for a gallery. The museum was opened with paintings belonging to the municipality, from a collection which had always been in the town hall, and with others already purchased for the royal cabinet. On August 15, 1808, the city turned over to the gallery seven large paintings, among them Rembrandt's *Night Watch* and *Syndics of the Drapers' Guild*. The museum was enormously successful. A former diplomat, Cornelis Apostol, was appointed its director on August 25, 1808; he nobly acquitted himself of his task, acquiring important paintings and publishing in 1809 the first catalog of the collection, which contained 459 pieces. Louis Bonaparte's forced abdication in 1810 put an end to this vigorous activity; annexed to France, Holland lost all the advantages of personal rule and no longer had the same financial resources at her command. The museum fell into a lethargy in which it remained until the second half of the nineteenth century.

At Kassel, despite its having been stripped of its chefs-d'œuvre by French agents, Jerome Bonaparte, king of Westphalia, commissioned Grandjean de Montigny to complete the museum begun by Simon Louis du Ry. In Madrid Joseph Bonaparte schemed to hide from his brother's covetousness the paintings destined for Spain's national museum which had been formed with works expropriated from the royal collections and from convents. The particulars of the writ of foundation (December 20, 1809) are worth noting: they proclaimed "the intention of resurrecting for the sake of art a considerable number of paintings buried in cloisters, of restoring to honor the Spanish school which is little known in neighboring countries, of assuring a just tribute of glory to the immortal names of Velázquez, Rubens, Murillo, Ribalta, Navarete, Juan San Vincente and others." One article decreed the establishment of a museum at Madrid (to be installed in the Buena Vista Palace and to be called the "Josefina" gallery) and another, the formation of a "general" collection of works by the great Spanish painters "to be offered to our august brother, the Emperor of the French, and thereby make known to him our desire to see it placed in the rooms of the Musée Napoléon." One of the members of the selections committee set up for this purpose was Goya. Despite all the beautiful words, more than three years elapsed before shipment was made, and then it was a collection of mediocre paintings which disappointed Denon. Paralyzed by the civil war, King Joseph, who despite his real talents for governing was unable to rule effectively, did not succeed in opening the museum. Work was resumed by King Ferdinand VII who inaugurated the picture gallery on November 19, 1819; its 311 paintings were installed in the Prado, a building constructed by the architect Juan de Villanueva at the end of the eighteenth century to house the Academy and Museum of Science.

Of all the museological projects of the *Napoléonides,* the only one fully realized, then, was the Pinacoteca di Brera at Milan.

Before his brief tenure as king of Spain, Joseph had been king of Naples for an even shorter period (two years) but had managed to infuse new life into the Pompeiian excavations, which had already attracted the French general Jean Etienne Championnet, founder of the short-lived Parthenopean Republic in January 1799. Joseph immediately asked Michele Arditi, director of the royal museum, to draft plans for a methodical excavation. Pompeii was the site of feverish activity under King Joachim Murat, Joseph's successor; nearly 400 workers were employed; planning additional excavations, Murat bought up acres of fields which were resold by Ferdinand II, who became king of the Two Sicilies in 1830. Murat's wife, Napoleon's sister Caroline, was intensely interested in the diggings and moved to Portici so she could oversee them, occasionally spending several days at the site itself. In the spring of 1815, in the days preceding the downfall of the kingdom and the execution of her husband, Murat, Caroline withdrew to Pompeii to forget her anguish. The Museo Nazionale of Naples owes much to Joseph, Murat and Caroline whose efforts greatly enriched the archeological collections.

After the wholesale movement of art during the twenty-five years of Revolution and Empire, there followed another *bouleversement* in 1815. The 1814 Treaty of Paris more or less respected the Musée Napoléon and its loans to various museums; only Prussia and the German principalities obtained restitution of a number of their works; it is true that Napoleon had inherited the Revolution's hatred for these states which had given asylum to French *emigrés* and, therefore, he had strongly mistreated them. With Italy the problem was nonexistent since the consignment of art works had been largely arranged in agreements not affected by the Treaty of Paris. In the few reparations made, care was taken to conduct the business in a part of the Louvre unexposed to the public; the foreign sovereigns who re-instated a Bourbon on the throne of France were eager to see that Louis XVIII did not present a figure of defeat; for this reason, they found it important that he be allowed to keep the Louvre collections. The monarch announced to the House of Deputies on June 4, 1814: "The chefs d'œuvre of the arts are ours a priori by laws more lasting than those of victory." The allied sovereigns who visited the Louvre congratulated Denon on the good appearance of his museum; the director was, after all, well known and esteemed in Europe; had he not served as adviser to Czar Alexander I, acquiring for him some beautiful paintings for the Hermitage, among them Caravaggio's *Lute Player?*

The situation was reversed in 1815. At the time of the first Treaty of Paris, foreign rulers persuaded themselves that they had restored to France the beloved monarchy overthrown by the Revolution; they were, however, undeceived when the French people rallied behind Napoleon upon his return from Elba in 1815. After the Hundred Days, the despoiled countries sent agents to Paris to retrieve their art works; restitution was effected somewhat "illegally" (in the case of Italy, in particular) because it was done in secret; this action had not been agreed upon at the Congress of Vienna and, in addition, a tax had been levied in 1814 to cover war losses. These reparations were made in haste during the period of occupation; the Ministry of Foreign Affairs and the Ministry of the Interior willfully left Denon without instructions, even disavowing the need for them. An appreciable number of works remained in the Louvre by consent of the agents, thanks to the energy, influence and diplomatic *savoir-faire* of Denon. The greediest claimant was the sculptor Antonio Canova, on whom Napoleon had once lavished favors; he worked as an agent for Austria to whom Venice had been given by Napoleon in 1797. Canova called himself "*Monsieur l'ambassadeur*" but the caustic Talleyrand preferred "*Monsieur l'emballeur.*" The restitutions did not affect works on permanent loan from the Louvre to the provinces; certain foreign cities (Geneva, Mainz and especially Brussels) retained what had been sent them. Other works changed owners. For example, a group of paintings once in the collection of the Landgrave of Hesse was given to Empress Josephine by Napoleon at the time of their divorce; they were in her possession (after the capture of Kassel and Jena in 1806) until her heirs sold them, with the Malmaison gallery, to Czar Alexander I in 1815. Despite his entreaties to the Czar, the Landgrave of Hesse was not able to regain his property, which had included four paintings by Claude Lorrain, among the most beautiful works now in the Hermitage.

Once returned to their rightful cities, many of the art works were not replaced in the churches or private cabinets from which they had come. Instead, they were used to form public museums, thus realizing, in their transition from private to public domain, a basic principle of the Revolution that had uprooted them. Such was the case in Parma where a pinakotheke was built up around the former ducal *quadreria* created by Don Philip of Bourbon in 1752; several Correggios, a few Carraccis and a Cima da Conegliano, were placed in the museum instead of being restored to the churches from which they had come. The Accademia in Venice, impoverished by requisitions for Milan's Brera, found compensation in the return of masterpieces from France; Count Leopoldo Cicognara, who became president of the Accademia in 1818, obtained permission from the Austrian government to accept these paintings, rather than restoring them to their original churches. Cicognara even succeeded in removing from convents some beautiful altarpieces they had been able to keep until then; one of the most important was Titian's *Assumption of the Virgin,* the glory of the Church of the Frari. A chief attraction in the Accademia until 1917, this painting was evacuated during the war and later was returned to the church for which it had been painted. On August 10, 1817 the gallery of the refurbished Accademia opened—in its original quarters, the old convent of Santa Maria della Carità, whose beautiful Gothic church had unfortunately been ruined in 1811 by the addition of flooring to divide it into two stories; in the hall of the nearby *Albergo* hung Titian's *Presentation in the Temple*; in an adjoining room was Veronese's *Feast in the House of Levi,* which had not been re-installed in San Zanipolo after being returned by France.

186

94. **Arrival in Antwerp of paintings returned by France, drawing by Louis Titz** *from the original work by Ferdinand de Brackeleer in the Bibliothèque Royale de Belgique, Cabinet des Estampes, Brussels. The arrival in Antwerp of a convoy of works of art restored to the city by France prompted a display of pageantry in the style of the "triumphal entries" of princes and rulers in the XVIth and XVIIth centuries.*

Everywhere in Europe where revolutionary principles had been imposed, old and new museums alike benefited from confiscations made at the expense of ecclesiastical institutions, often never re-established. Munich's Pinakothek enriched itself with art yielded in the secularization of Bavaria's convents in 1803. The phenomenon seemed particularly widespread in Italy where it affected the cities of Bologna, Pisa, Arezzo and Verona. After the suppression of religious confraternities in Florence, works of art were concentrated in the Convento di San Marco during a three-year period from 1806 to 1809; under consideration was a plan to construct a new building for the famous Accademia del Disegno and to provide it with a large *pinacoteca* formed from the San Marco holdings, with medieval art its forte; the idea was not realized until 1841.

The return of art works to their original places was sometimes solemnly celebrated. In 1815, to receive her beloved paintings, the city of Antwerp revived the tradition of "triumphal entries" which had been reserved in former times for princes and governors, with allegorical pageants, bell ringings, gun salutes, banqueting and drinking that continued far into the night. The people of Antwerp had, in truth, feared a second loss of their masterpieces. The convoy hauling art to be returned to Belgium and the Netherlands arrived in Brussels on the twentieth of November; city officials there prevented the departure of the four wagons en route to Antwerp, alleging it was their duty to requisition paintings from suppressed convents for the capital's museum. A deputation from Antwerp was obliged to journey to The Hague to obtain permission from the king of Holland for the release of the convoy. Imagine the commission's anger when they returned with the royal consent only to find that the municipality had already had the cases unloaded at the museum under the pretext of safeguarding the works from Prussian troops who were expected to pass through Brussels! This episode of petty quarrels typical of Belgian cities at the time also illustrates the impatience of French-speaking Brussels to shake the Netherlandish yoke, an ambition realized some fifteen years later when Belgian independence was declared.

In an effort to avoid art raids by French agents, the occupied states of central Europe either hid or evacuated their treasures. For example, the paintings collection of the Elector of Bavaria was cached in the castle at Ansbach; after the battle at Jena in 1806 when Napoleon defeated the Prussians, forty-eight paintings belonging to the landgrave of Hesse were discovered in a gamekeeper's cottage in the middle of a forest. As for the *objets d'art* of the Duke of Brunswick, Denon and Pierre Antoine Daru had no difficulties in shipping them to France because they were found already crated, ready to be sent to England. The largest "operation evacuation" realized during the wars of the Revolution and Empire was the one methodically carried out by the House of Austria; it had far-reaching museological consequences because it effected a complete regrouping of art treasures in Vienna.

To protect them from the victorious troops of Marshal Jourdan, Emperor Leopold II ordered the evacuation of the coronation regalia of the German-Roman emperors of the Holy Roman Empire from Austrian territories and possessions; the imperial relics in Nuremburg were sent to Vienna in 1794 and those in Aix-la-Chapelle in 1796; also in 1794 the precious emblems of the Order of the Golden Fleece, until then kept in Brussels, were sent to Vienna for safekeeping. In 1806 these treasures were hidden from Napoleon during his occupation of Vienna. The collections at Schloss Ambras had already gone to Vienna in 1805, before the French emperor's victory at Austerlitz.

None of these treasures was restored to its rightful city; the imperial treasures remained in Vienna despite the dissolution of the Holy Roman Empire in 1806. As for the treasure of the Order of the Golden Fleece, Belgium tried, during the drafting of the Treaty of Saint-Germain (signed September 10, 1919) to have it returned, but it remained in the possession of Austria on hereditary grounds—it had passed into the hands of the Hapsburgs after the marriage of Maximilian I to Mary of Burgundy in 1477. The diplomatic agents who negotiated the treaty decided that dynastic history should be given preference over artistic history and so the emblems of the Order are still in Vienna. The *Schatzkammer* in Vienna's Hofburg has a prodigious ensemble of precious objects: the crown of Charlemagne and that of the kings of Hungary; the crown and scepter of Rudolf II which had been used by the Austrian emperors; the coronation robe of Roger II of Sicily; the astonishing, embroidered liturgical vestments of the Order of the Golden Fleece. In a dismantled Europe possibly on the verge of putting itself together again, this wealth of marvels attested to the mystical significance of the Holy Roman Empire which had united so many divers peoples.

The artistic collections of Austria were much admired by the plenipotentiaries at the Congress of Vienna, just as those of France, amassed at the Louvre, had been by the allies in 1814 and 1815. These two great museological centers, then the most important in Europe, had a profound influence, provoking the emulation of all nations.

Another dispersal of works of art was caused by the Peninsular War (1808-1814) in Spain. Although the delays and subterfuges of King Joseph Bonaparte (who was thinking about his proposed museum for Madrid) kept the Louvre from acquiring masterpieces of the Spanish School, the French generals of the Army of Spain looted

95. **The Water Carrier of Seville, by Diego Veláz-quez.** *Wellington Museum, Apsley House, London. This painting was part of the booty captured from the French army by the Duke of Wellington in the battle at Vitoria on June 21, 1813. The duke offered to restore the paintings to the Spanish government but instead the government made a gift of them to him.*

188

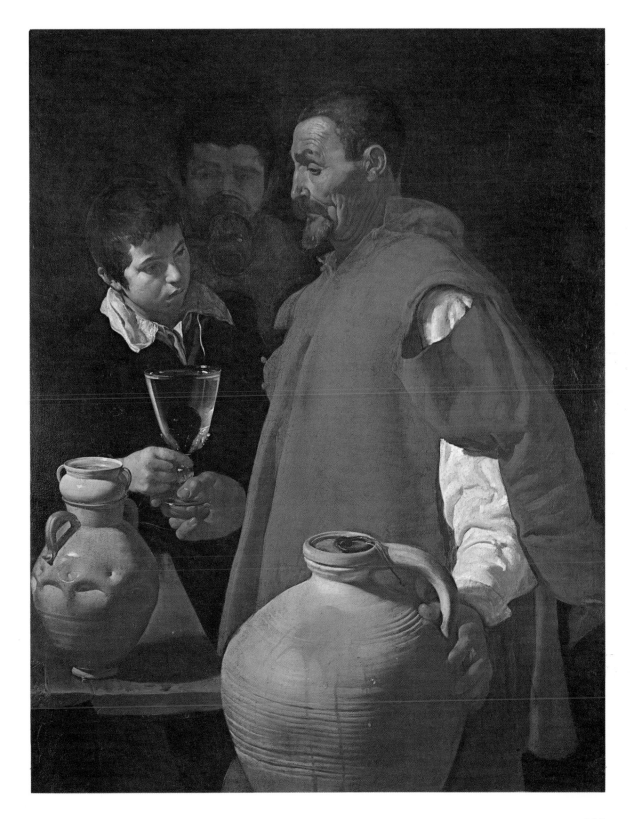

in their own interests; one of the most rapacious was Marshal Nicolas Soult. When King Joseph was forced to leave Spain, he took with him a whole convoy of paintings; it was seized, along with all the baggage of the French army, by Wellington in the decisive battle at Vitoria on June 21, 1813. The English general hastened to propose their restitution to the Spanish government. The capture of works of art as war booty was such a common practice that this was an astounding proposition to which Spain answered, "His Majesty, moved by your consideration, does not wish to deprive you of what has come into your possession by such just and honorable means." Thus, one hundred sixty-five Spanish paintings went to England where they still remain. Recently, London's Apsley House, once the Duke of Wellington's residence where the paintings were installed, was given to the State and transformed into a public museum, the National Wellington Museum. This scattering of Spanish paintings across Europe helped to bring to the public's attention painters who were little known and appreciated; the exception was Murillo whose success began in the eighteenth century with the first exodus of his masterpieces from Spain.

In this general disorder, some curious *chassés-croisés* occurred. After the death of Anna Maria Ludovica de' Medici and despite the terms of her will, many pieces of *oreficeria* from the Medicean treasury were removed to Vienna by the Lorraine; more than a thousand gold medals, jewels and art objects were sold, given away or stolen. The 1919 Treaty of Saint-Germain stipulated their restitution to Florence but only eighty-three pieces were returned, the jewels of Anna Maria Ludovica having been carried off by the last emperor of Austria, Charles I. In revenge, the Museo degli Argenti in the Pitti Palace in Florence exhibited a remarkable collection of eighty-five pieces of German metalwork, among them some masterpieces from the Nuremburg and Augsburg ateliers. Grand Duke Ferdinand II of Tuscany, deposed in 1803, received as compensation the principality of Salzburg. In 1805 when the principality was re-awarded to Austria, he carred off in his baggage the entire *Silberkammer* of the bishops of Salzburg, first to Wurtzburg, then to Florence, to which he returned in 1814. This "pillage" at Salzburg's expense was in addition to the one effected in 1806 by the imperial administration, which removed the city's art works to Vienna.

Napoleon's name remains associated with the requisitioning of art works over the whole of Europe and one continues to impute to him a personal responsibility. In reality, if his victories permitted it, the initiative came from the Directory. It is, without a doubt, only proper to judge this policy according to the standards of that time and not those of today. Perhaps some future age will find immoral that which we think entirely natural. Is not the power of money as much an instrument of domination as military strength? Which is more moral—to conquer works of art with dollars or by men fallen "on the field of honor"? All depends on motives and circumstances. For a revolutionary France attacked by Europe and turned conqueror under the menace of invasion, the capture of works of art was the prerogative of the victor, a noble means of seeking indemnity for losses sustained in men and arms at the hands of the enemy. "How beautiful it is to capture the productions of genius. It is the only conquest worthy of a people friendly to the arts," wrote an editor of the *Décade* in 1794. Soon, following the victories of Bonaparte, with the revolutionary ideology less on the defense and becoming more expansive, it seemed normal that Paris be the "capital of the arts" of this new Europe, delivered by France from the rule of tyrants, and tribute paid in art seemed somehow the price of liberty. In this domain as in many others, Napoleon was the heir of the Revolution. If he lavished such attention on the enrichment of his museums, it was because of the impassioned interest this statesman and militarist, son of the Age of Enlightenment, evinced for science and the arts, for what we would call today "culture." Illuminating in this respect is his conduct during the Egyptian campaign.

The intellectual aims of the expedition were almost as important as its political aims, which rested, moreover, on chimeras. It was a question of opening the mind to the mystery of the East, which hid the secret of an antiquity more profound than that of the Greeks and Romans. The ships conveying Bonaparte and his staff officers also quartered members of the "commission on the sciences and the arts." There were more than one hundred sixty-five persons: astronomers, botanists, surgeons and physicians, pharmacists, composers, writers, economists, printers, orientalists. After his entry into Cairo, Bonaparte established, in imitation of the one at Paris, an Institut d'Egypte; installed in a complex of palaces abandoned by the Mamelukes after the battle of the Pyramids (July 1798), the institute housed chemistry and physics laboratories, an Arabic press, conference halls, a library and a museum—the first Egyptological museum—with a collection that included the famous Rosetta stone discovered by French troops, which later would reveal to Champollion the secret of hieroglyphics. With the surrender of General Menou on January 4, 1800, this embryonic museum was confiscated by the English and removed to the British Museum. Thus the flood tide of museology precipitated by the French Revolution reached as far as Cairo.

Museums were scattered over the whole of Europe and beyond. Art treasures were made available to the masses which hitherto had been accessible only to an elite group of connoisseurs and artists; these assemblages of objects were to foster the study of past artistic civilizations. Some aestheticians deplored the situation. The same Quatre-mère de Quincy who had protested against the transfer of Roman statuary to Paris stigmatized in his *Considérations morales sur la destination des ouvrages d'art* (1815) "the strange system which has prevailed for some time in Europe. The public has become persuaded that the secret to making the Arts flourish lies in the virtue of these assemblages of works known as *collections, cabinets, museums*. All the nations, in emulation of one another, have made such a singular thing of them that one has not yet thought of noticing that masterpieces or models, brought together at great expense, all existed before there were collections and that since one has made Museums to create Masterpieces, there are no longer any Masterpieces to fill the Museums."

Chapter 10

The Museum Age

The early part of the nineteenth century was the golden age of collectors, of true amateurs whose instincts led them to make good purchases for little money. Such a practice was possible then and prevailed, with regard to certain categories of objects, until the beginning of the war in 1914. Before 1860, when an older attitude was revived, the work of art ceased to be an object of speculation as it had been at the end of the seventeenth century and all through the eighteenth. In creating rapid accumulations of fortune and, therefore, readily available assets, an economic vigor based on the upsurge of industry gave new impetus to the art market, while in the first part of the century the constant revenues from wealth dependent on the exploitation of land little favored this kind of speculation. In 1801 Baron Vivant-Denon, not yet director of the Musée Napoléon, bought for 150 to 300 gold francs an "unstylish" painting no one wanted, Watteau's *Gilles* (today in the Louvre). It had been displayed for a long time, it seems, in the shop window of a dealer on the Place du Carrousel with a large placard bearing this bit of doggerel:

Que Pierrot serait content
S'il avait l'art de vous plaire.

96. **French Art. 1739. Marquetry Commode, by Antoine Gaudreau,** *with gilded bronzes signed by Caffieri. From the royal apartments at Versailles. Wallace Collection, Hertford House, London. One of the most beautiful pieces of furniture in the Wallace Collection, this piece belonged to Lord Hertford as early as 1865 when he lent it for exhibition at the* Musée Rétrospectif *held that year at Paris.*

As late as 1839 the Louvre was able to buy two Chardin pastels (a self-portrait and a portrait of his wife) for 196 gold francs; in 1834 the same museum acquired Simone Martini's *Christ Carrying the Cross* for 200 gold francs and Baron Taylor, sent by Louis Philippe to Spain to profit from the opportunities offered by the Carlist War, brought back a fabulous collection of 553 pictures at the cost of 1,327,000 gold francs, an average of 2,489 gold francs each. Prices were even lower for Medieval and Renaissance *objets d'art* and furniture which were considered practically worthless, secondhand goods—a curious attitude in view of the passion the romantic period felt for these eras but which doubtlessly can be explained by the fact that the industrial arts had not yet lost all faculty of invention. Despite a certain taste for the Gothic, furniture and the decorative arts perpetuated a degenerate neoclassicism ("*Louis-philippard*" in France, the Biedermeier style in Germany and Austria). Thus Charles

Sauvageot, with the modest salaries of a customs official and first violinist at the Paris Opera, accumulated medieval and Renaissance treasures which were to enrich the Louvre at his death. He was one of the characters who inspired Balzac's *Le Cousin Pons* (1847): "Pons... subscribed to the axiom of Chenavard, the learned collector of precious pictures, who pretended one could not enjoy looking at a Ruisdael, a Hobbema, a Sebastiano del Piombo, a Giorgione or a Dürer unless the painting had cost only fifty francs. Pons permitted himself no acquisition over a hundred francs and for him to pay fifty francs, an object had to be worth three thousand. If the most beautiful thing in the world cost three hundred francs, it did not exist for him. Opportunities were rare but he possessed the three ingredients for success: the legs of a deer, the time of an idler and the patience of an Israelite." Later, Chocquet, an official in the Ministry of Finance, succeeded in bringing together an astonishing collection of pictures by Delacroix and Cézanne. Having inherited a fortune, he bought himself an *hôtel* and stopped buying paintings; to a surprised friend, he remarked, "It no longer interests me; I can afford them." The mentality of nineteenth-century collectors was in some measure the inverse of that of today's amateurs, for whom the priceless has its place.

It is not to our purpose here to trace the history of the great nineteenth-century amateurs, as we have done in preceding chapters where private collections are shown to have constituted veritable museums, liberally open and, to a certain extent, "public." Let us cite, however, a last example of this type, the gallery of the Regent, Philippe, Duc d'Orléans. The motive behind authorization to print a *Description of the Paintings in the Palais Royal* in 1727 was given thus: "The public in general is well acquainted with the range and interest of this prodigious collection which contains some of the rarest and most beautiful of paintings, but it was useful to present it with a detailed account." In the nineteenth century an ever-growing number of museums was organized in the public interest; private collections were closed, accessible only to friends or the "initiated," that is, provided the owners were not so jealous as to hide them from everyone—sometimes, especially from scholars, like misers concealing their treasures. The contemporary art world does not have to a comparable degree annuals like those so frequent under the *Ancien Régime* which provided tourists with a list by city of noteworthy private collections or catalogues like the *Description of the Paintings in the Palais Royal,* offered to the public at pocketbook size and price.

The term *museum* must henceforth be reserved for official institutions in the public interest. Since the beginning of the century, museums had become so much a part of everyday life that they were closely linked with politics and answerable to a new factor in public life in the age of democracy: opinion. The creation of the Musée Napoléon and the overall museological program of revolutionary and imperial France were an integral part of the international political designs of these regimes. Throughout the nineteenth century, monarchs and governments in power took care not to neglect so efficacious a means to influence public opinion, almost to the point of brainwashing. Opposition to this attitude also served to engender museums. Thus, in 1818, responding to the Germanic nationalism developing in Austria under Metternich in opposition to the European inclination towards an empire, the Czechs also became conscious of their own identity and founded at Prague a museum to serve as a center of study for Czech and Slavic civilizations. Later, the creation of a museum at Oslo, the Norsk

Folkemuseum, was sparked by struggles against Sweden which led to Norwegian independence in 1905. The museum was established in 1895, its founder proclaiming it was to be "a monument erected to the evolution of our race, to the development of national thought and culture..." So strong was the nationalistic tradition of this Norsk Folkemuseum that as late as 1932 its director could write, "Museums help to dam up foreign influences, subdue them and transform them into forces to profit national life." Throughout the nineteenth century officialdom tended to view the museum as a foyer for this nationalism then the dominating political form in Europe.

The nineteenth century saw the extension of the museum to encompass all the creations of human life, even the most humble; it professed to be a compendium of all knowledge like the *Speculum Majus,* the thirteenth-century encyclopedic treatise by Vincent de Beauvais. The resultant enlargement was violently attacked by certain thinkers who sought to limit the museum to its original purpose. In the nineteenth century, Germany more than France emerged as the theatre for this kind of academic discussion of the museum; toward 1830 controversy erupted between partisans of the intensive museum, limited to art, and champions of the extensible form, broadly scientific in scope. Adherents of the first group rallied around Wilhelm von Humboldt; they believed the museum should contain the masterpieces of antiquity and of the great European schools; the others found a leader in Leopold von Ledebur, curator at the museum of ethnography, who defended the universality of the museum, which should present the culture and history of all peoples of all time, particularly the German people.

The best way to understand this principle of extension is to study the formation and development of one of the great museological complexes. The dispersion of museums in London poorly illustrates the phenomenon; at Paris, the housing of several collections in one incommodious historical building produced a certain confusion. On the other hand, in Berlin each species of museological collection had its own building and the tendency to group these edifices in one place gives a clear insight into this principle of growth.

It was doubtlessly the sight of the wonderful Louvre of Napoleon that gave King Frederick William III the desire to create for Berlin a museum comparable to the one in Paris; in 1814 and 1815, in fact, he had greatly admired Denon's well-ordered galleries. The Prussian king's advisers began by enriching his collections with various acquisitions. A special building was constructed (1824-1828) by the neoclassical Berlin architect, Karl Friedrich Schinkel. In keeping with the tastes of the time, the Schinkelbau (known today as the Altes Museum) had a peristyle (Ionic order) around its exterior while on the interior, rooms radiated off a rotunda inspired by the Pantheon. The first floor of the museum was devoted to an *antiquarium,* the second, to medieval and Renaissance treasures with 378 paintings, a print cabinet and ethnographic elements from the former treasury or curiosities cabinet of the Hohenzollern. The building stood on a peninsula (Museuminsel) formed by the juncture of a stream, the Küpfergraben, with the Spree. The very day of its opening, in August 1830, the museum appeared too small and from 1843 to 1855 Stüler was charged with constructing another (known as the Neues Museum). Built to the side of the earlier one, it was connected to it by a corridor; thus began the excellent system of separate buildings linked by passageways. Opened in 1859, the Neues Museum housed the Egyptian collection, antique ceramics, the print cabinet and an important ethnographic collection, nucleus of the future Museum für Völkerkunde, as well as an ensemble of national antiquities, embryo of the future Museum für Vor- und Frühgeschichte (museum of pre- and protohistory); the latter had formerly been installed in Monbijou where it constituted the Museum Vaterländischer Altertümer, a museum of national antiquities. In 1876, in another of Stüler's buildings, a veritable pastiche of a Corinthian temple designed for other purposes, a museum of contemporary art was established, the Nationalgalerie. It was for this museum, intended for modern German art, that the famous Hugo von Tschudi bought French impressionnists, a policy that resulted in his banishment by Kaiser William II; von Tschudi, however, continued his activities in Munich.

The accumulation of all manner of works by different sections of the museum eventually required limiting the Museumsinsel to the conservation of artistic and archeological collections. The ethnography cabinet was therefore re-installed in a special building constructed (1880-1886) by Ende on Saarlandstrasse. Shortly before, a museum devoted to the decorative arts, the Kunstgewerbemuseum, was set up in a new (1877-1881) building on Prinz-Albert-Strasse.

Toward the end of the century construction on the Museumsinsel resumed with the marked encouragement of an expanded buying policy and archeological excavations, by Dr. Wilhelm von Bode in particular. Several associations, the Kaiser-Friedrich Museum Verein, the Deutsches Orient Comité and the Deutsche Orient Gesellschaft, furnished the means for carrying out this policy on a vast scale in Europe, along the Mediterranean and in the Near East; entire structures, like the Altar of Pergamum, the Gate of Ishtar from Babylon, the market place of Miletus, the frieze from the façade of Arabian palace at Mshatta (given by Sultan Abdu-l-hamid II to William II), made Berlin, in competition with Paris and London, one of the great centers for archeological study. A specialist in the Renaissance, Dr. von Bode, after heading the Christian antiquities and paintings departments, was director general of the royal museums from 1906 to 1920; he completely re-organized the collections and proposed new buildings to receive them. At the end of the island, Ihnes built (construction lasted from 1897 to 1903) in German baroque style, the Kaiser-Friedrich-Museum to house the medieval, Renaissance and contemporary collections; it is now called the Bode-Museum. Installation was according to the principle of historical totality, which mixed the different objects created by one period in order to evoke its unique style; this was an innovation of Bode as collections had been exhibited according to technique since the beginning of the nineteenth century—painting, sculpture, *objets d'art*—a division kept by most of the great museums until the present time. In 1907 Dr. von Bode conceived the design for a great museological compound to fill the space between the Kaiser-Friedrich-Museum and the Neues Museum. It comprised three U-shaped wings around a central plaza (Museumsforum). The central part contained the Altar of Pergamum; the right wing, the Near Eastern collections (Vorderasiastisches Museum) and the left, German art from the barbarian invasions to the rococo style (Deutsches Museum). The building, constructed by Alfred Messel, was not completed until 1930; doubtlessly its purpose determined Messel's choice of the neoclassical style for the exterior.

The old residence of the Hohenzollern, laid out in 1698-1706 by Andreas Schlüter at the neck of the peninsula, was turned into a museum for the decorative arts (Schloss-

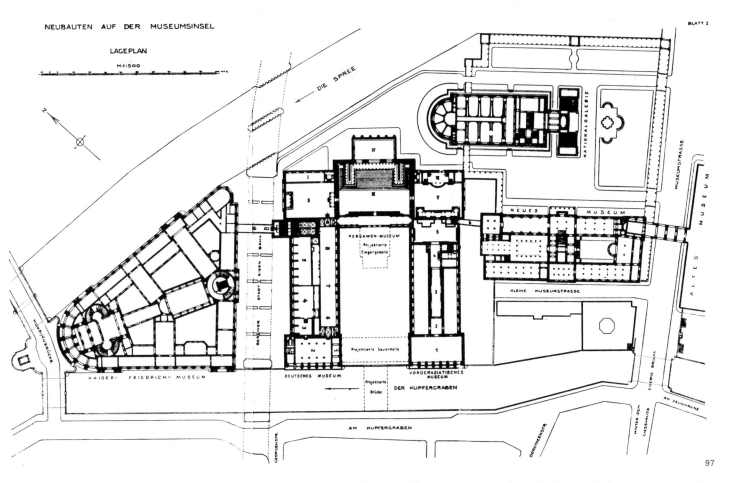

Museum) in 1921. The industrial art collections completed the artistic group on the Museuminsel. The last museological center created in Berlin before World War II was a museum devoted to German folklore (Kunstgewerbe- und Völkerkunde-Museum) installed in 1937 in Schloss Bellevue in the Tiergarten.

Berlin's collections were dispersed following the war. Almost all of the pinakotheke is preserved in West Berlin, installed in the Museum Dahlem the former quarters of the ethnology museum. Seized, then restored by the Soviets to the government of East Germany, the archeological collections are being slowly regrouped in the various museums, either restored or undergoing restoration, on the Museuminsel; only the Schloss-Museum has disappeared, the East German government having demolished, for symbolic reasons, what remained of the Hohenzollern residence after it was burned during the war.

Over the whole of Europe museums sprang up. More or less until mid-century, and even later in the Anglo-Saxon countries, their architecture reflected the neo-antique style of the first museological installations. In the Vatican, parallel to the great hall of the library, the Braccio Nuovo (the new wing constructed from 1817 to 1822 by Raffaele Stern to display the most beautiful statues from the Museo Chiaramonti)

197

reproduced the neo-Roman style created by Michelangelo Simonetti for the Museo Pio-Clementino (built in 1775-1882) and adopted by Percier and Fontaine for the *antiquarium* in the Louvre, based on a design of Raymond and laid out from 1802 to 1806. The section of the Louvre known as the Musée Charles X, realized (1827-1833) by Fontaine in the south wing of the *cour carrée,* received the new collections of antique ceramics and Egyptology; influenced by the taste current at the time of Louis Philippe for over-all decor (gilt stucco, bronzes, imitation cameos, historical and allegorical paintings), the style is not pure classical revival.

Exterior architecture adopted the austere façades of the Greek revival style. In the first half of the century, the museum took the form of a temple. Begun in 1823 by Sir Robert Smirke on the site of the former Montague House, the British Museum took shape as a majestic Ionic temple with two wings, the over-all design of which was inspired by the Parthenon of Athens. Similar in style was the new building erected in 1839 to house Oxford's Ashmolean Museum.

The construction of museums was integrated into general building programs. The European city in which the museum played the greatest role in the municipal fabric is unquestionably Munich. The city itself is a museum, inspired by the nostalgia for Italy and Greece that troubled the spirit of King Louis I of Bavaria, already enamored of antiquities and archeology when still a crown prince. The largest city in the south of Germany, Munich had always looked toward Italy; by the end of the sixteenth century, her princes, who had started a school for bronze workers there, were desirous of making Munich a "new Rome." Louis I looked even further to the south: "I will have no rest until Munich resembles Athens." He dreamed of the unity of Germany, in the interest of Bavaria but against Gothic barbarism. Louis contributed to the independence of Greece and managed to install one of his sons, Otto I, as the first king of the new nation. Munich was, then, rebuilt in a spirit of reaction against the baroque, the rococo and the Gothic; her new buildings reproduced both Greek and Italian edifices. Louis brought to the remaking of his city the mentality of a collector and his endeavors recall Emperor Hadrian's plans for a microcosm of the antique world at Tivoli. The new Residenz or Königsbau of Leo von Klenze was inspired by the Palazzo Pitti in Florence with the addition of the three-order program of the Palazzo Rucellai. Florence's Loggia dei Lanzi provided the model for the Feldherrnhalle (Hall of Marshals); a succession of Florentine *palazzi* lined the Ludwigstrasse, the main boulevard of the new city; the Staatsbibliothek was a pastiche of *quattrocento* buildings; the Siegestor reproduced Trajan's triumphal arch in Rome, another copy of which had been commissioned by Napoleon for the Cour du Carrousel of the Louvre. Munich's churches presented a compendium of old Christian architectural styles: the primitive basilica of All Saints, the Byzantine basilica of St. Boniface and the Romanesque church of St. Louis. Museums also had a part in this symphony of classicism; of these the oldest is the Glyptothek. Unsatisfied with the entries in an architectural competition, in 1816 Louis commissioned Leo von Klenze to design a building to house his antiquities, in particular the pediments from the Temple of Aphaia in Aegina. Completed in 1830, the quadrilateral building was lighted from above; the windowless exterior walls were rhythmically punctuated with niches provided with statues and the entrance was a pronaos surrounded by an Ionic peristyle. During his reign, Louis I had Ziebland build

(1846) an exhibition palace opposite the Glyptothek; this later became known as the Secession Palace, from the name of the avant-garde society (founded in 1892 by Stuck, Trübner and Uhde) which convened there. After his abdication, Louis completed the ensemble by commissioning from Leo von Klenze a pastiche of the Propylaea to fill the space between the two buildings, thereby creating a square (the Königsplatz) where the three Greek orders were commemorated: the Ionic, the Corinthian and the Doric.

Leo von Klenze was well suited to serve the neo-Greek tastes of the prince; they had met in Paris where von Klenze was studying with Napoleon's architect, Charles Percier. As early as 1815 the prince, already obsessed with Athens, entrusted von Klenze with building a copy of the Parthenon near Regensburg—the consecration of this temple to the gods of Valhalla must have made Pallas Athena tremble on Olympus! This act is expressive of the strange "antiquitizing" and Germanizing syncreticism that troubled the mind of the prince, who was profoundly inspired by Goethe. In Munich Louis I had von Klenze build still another Greek temple, the Doric-style Ruhmeshalle or Hall of Glory.

Munich needed a museum for exhibiting, in a rational fashion, the admirable collections of paintings which dynastic movements had precipitated upon the city and which the nineteenth century had swelled with works by Italian, Flemish and German primitives. Leo von Klenze was the innovating architect; he provided a building that combined the two systems developed for pinakothekai under the *Ancien Régime*: the gallery and the cabinet. In construction from 1826 to 1836, the Alte Pinakothek presents a succession of large rooms lighted from above which constitute a gallery; it is framed on one side by a series of laterally illuminated cabinets designed to receive small paintings and, on the other, by an open-air portico or loggia (which was ill suited to Munich's climate). Rejecting the neo-Greek style, this time Klenze adopted a Renaissance format that seemed to him more in keeping with the building's purpose.

Munich's museum for modern art is older than that in Berlin. One wonders why the architect Voits adopted the style of a pre-Romanesque Lombard church for this Neue Pinakothek (constructed 1846-1853). Formerly the exterior was decorated with large frescoes by Wilhelm von Kaulbach, depicting the history of modern painting and Louis I's patronage of the arts. Such "illustrations" were at that time requisite decoration for museums; for the Alte Pinakothek Peter von Cornelius traced the history of painting in twenty-four allegories. In Berlin's Neues Museum, the ground-floor rooms devoted to Nordic antiquities were decorated with paintings tracing the cycle of Teutonic myths. France had furnished the prototype in the Musée Charles X of the Louvre where a team of artists was mobilized by Count de Forbin, director of museums, to commemorate in ceiling decorations the history of the antique civilizations then known—quite mediocre paintings, except for Ingres' *Apotheosis of Homer* which was removed for the 1855 international exposition, later installed in the Palais du Luxembourg and, finally, given to the Louvre; a copy now replaces it on the ceiling of the Salle Clarac.

The first half of the nineteenth century was a great period for archeological museums. Museums were looked upon as temples which preserved the vestiges of human history, the origin of which was being pushed back further and farther into past millennia. For centuries Rome had eclipsed Greece in the Occidental world. Toward the end of the

eighteenth century scholars, diplomats and collectors discovered with wonder the pure creations of the country of light, viewed until then only through the bias of Rome. Museums vied with each other for masterpieces wrested from monuments or from the soil of Greece and the Orient. France, who at the moment possessed the most celebrated antiquities of Rome, let herself be outdistanced by England and Germany in the quest for things Greek. In 1811 Fauvel, French vice consul at Athens, informed the Louvre of the discovery of seventeen statues in Parian marble, found by two Germans and two Englishmen in a temple to Aphaia on Aegina. The marbles were to be auctioned off on Zante. The question of dating aroused lively controversy; the tendency was to place them later than the Parthenon sculptures. After studying crude sketches sent by the archeologist Chauvel, Ennius-Quirinus Visconti, curator of antiquities at the Louvre, recognized them as important fifth-century works, but Vivant-Denon was worried about the price; negotiations dragged; the statues were eventually sent to Malta on orders from the agent working for Louis, the Bavarian crown prince. After being restored (1815-1817) in Rome by the Swedish neoclassical sculptor Thorvaldsen (who "completed" them after the seventeenth-century custom), the Aeginetan marbles finally went to Munich in 1828 where they formed the nucleus of the Glyptothek.

The Louvre also failed to lay hands on the Parthenon marbles, with the exception of that which had already come into its possession following the revolutionary confiscations: a fragment of the Panathenaic frieze which vice consul Fauvel had appropriated in 1787 for the French ambassador to Constantinople, Count de Choiseul-Gouffier, who had taken it from Athens to Marseilles where it was seized by the revolutionary commission. The history of the Parthenon marbles is a veritable suspense story. Thomas Bruce, seventh Earl of Elgin and British ambassador to Constantinople, obtained from the Turkish government permission to sketch and to make casts of the sculptures on the Acropolis and, later, to remove a few examples; taking advantage of this privilege, he seized fifteen metopes and fifty-six additional pieces of the Parthenon, four sections of the frieze from the Temple of Athena Nike, a caryatid from the Erectheum and a hundred or so inscriptions. Recalled to London in 1803, the ambassador ordered his booty crated for shipment to England; there were two hundred cases. During the voyage home, Lord Elgin was captured by the French in 1805 and imprisoned for two years. As for the cases, after Turkey entered into war with England, the French seized them and were about to send them to Piraeus and thence to Paris when an opportune peace with Turkey reversed the situation and the crates left for England by ship; one of the ships sank with its precious cargo, which was later recovered. However, in 1807, the two hundred cases arrived in various ports all over England. Brought together, the marbles were exhibited from June 1807 to the summer of 1811 in an annex to the earl's house on Park Lane, where they formed Elgin's Museum. Scarcely had they been put on display when the marbles became the subject of a stormy dispute. Influenced by the academic conceptions of the *Dilettanti,* Payne Knight, a great collector of antiquities and an arbiter of taste in London, pronounced them workshop copies after Phidias and possibly even Hadrianic productions. Led by the American Benjamin West, the Anglo-Swiss Heinrich Füssli (Henry Fuseli) and the young enthusiast Benjamin Robert Haydon (who had made many drawings of the marbles), the artists of the Royal Academy considered them masterpieces by Phidias.

98. **Horse drawing the Chariot of Selene, by Phidias.** *From the Parthenon. British Museum, London.*

99. **Drawing of the Horse of Selene, by Benjamin Robert Haydon** *in 1809. British Museum, London.*

The comparison of the drawing with the original shows a neo-classic interpretation of the work which explains how the Parthenon marbles were, perhaps, considered by the Dilettanti as works from a later era. This suppleness of Greek art astonished the amateurs accustomed to the harshness of Roman copies.

100. Attic mixing bowl from the last quarter of the 5th century. Meeting of the gods. *Louvre Museum, Paris. This vase came into the possession of the Louvre Museum with the acquisition of the Durand collection in 1824. Following the purchase of the Tochon collection in 1818, this acquisition formed the nucleus of the famous collection of antique ceramics which constitutes one of the Louvre's richest sections.*

101. Egyptian Art. *IVth Dynasty. Louvre Museum, Paris. This work, one of the most beautiful of the Ancient Empire, was acquired in 1828 by the Santoni brothers of Leghorn in a group of 4,000 pieces from the collection formed in Egypt by the English consul, Henry Salt.*

The dispute lasted until 1814 when it ended violently with Lord Elgin being accused of vandalism and scorned as a "marble pedlar." About the same time Lord Byron lamented the loss sustained by Greece in his *Childe Harold* (Cantos I and II appeared in 1812). Elgin suffered a financial setback and found himself constrained to put the marbles up for sale. The opinion of the *Dilettanti* contributed to the British Museum's reluctance to buy them; moreover, the institution had just procured for itself the sculptures from the Temple of Apollo Epicurius at Phigalia. In 1814 the crown prince of Bavaria, who had already acquired the Aeginetan pediments, and the Louvre, represented by Visconti, figured among the interested buyers. The arrival of Canova in London and the opinion of the sculptor John Flaxman turned the tide against the *Dilettanti*. Lord Elgin's secretary, at that time Undersecretary of State for Foreign Affairs, doubtlessly favored the transaction, thus smoothing the way for their acquisition. Convening on February 29, 1816, the House of Commons voted to purchase the lot for the insignificant sum of £35,000, which did not even cover the expenses incurred by Lord Elgin. Haydon, the impassioned defender of the marbles, could then write that the British Museum was "the finest museum in Europe." In any case it became Europe's finest museum of Greek art as it continued to expand in this area throughout the century as a result of successful excavations by English archeologists in the Middle East; statues from the monument of the Nereids at Xanthus arrived in Bloomsbury in 1845. In addition to the Parthenon, London soon boasted the remains of two other marvels of the world: statues from the Mausoleum of Halicarnassus, acquired in 1855-1860, and a few artifacts from the temple of Artemis at Ephesus.

To receive the Parthenon marbles a Greek temple was needed; Robert Smirke, who had studied in Greece, undertook its construction in the Ionic style in 1823. At the advice of Canova, the statues from the Acropolis were allowed to remain in the condition in which they were found, unlike the Aeginetan marbles which Thorvaldsen had

"completed" earlier. An evolution in taste had engendered respect for the original artifact, whereas the earlier amateurs did not appreciate mutilated works and believed that the "idea" of their creators would be betrayed if they were not completed.

With regard to the major arts of Greece, France—lamenting the loss of the Vatican antiquities—found herself in an inferior position. However, she soon ranked first in another area, that of antique ceramics, owing to the purchase of the Tochon (1818) and Durand (1824) collections, followed by other acquisitions over the century. With the Durand collection, more than two thousand bronzes entered the Louvre. In 1820 an admirable statue of Venus was discovered in a wall by a peasant on the island of Melos (Latinized to Milo). The celebrated navigator Dumont d'Urville, then an ensign on the *Chevrette,* informed the Marquis de Rivière, French ambassador to Constantinople, of the discovery and the latter resolved to present it to Louis XVIII. He sent one of his secretaries, a certain de Marcellus, to procure it; the task was accomplished only after several dramatic episodes. The news of the discovery having quickly spread, the English and the Dutch arrived at Malta in the hope of carrying off the statue. First on the *Estafette,* then on the *Lionne,* the goddess toured the Mediterranean, arousing the admiration of numerous visitors at every port of call: Rhodes, Cyprus, Acre, Alexandria. At Piraeus she was paid homage by the aging Chauvel, one of the pioneers among French archeologists. The *Venus de Milo* entered the Louvre in 1821, becoming the most celebrated work in the *antiquarium.* She was soon joined by other Greek works. In 1829 the Greek senate, in recognition of aid offered by France in the War of Independence, presented the Louvre with two metopes from the Temple of Zeus at Olympia which had been discovered by the French expedition to the Peloponnesus. In 1863 another French diplomat, M. de Champoiseau, discovered on the island of Samothrace the celebrated *Nike* from the sanctuary of the Cabiri and removed it to the Louvre the same year.

The French expedition to Egypt first opened universal history to perspectives beyond the contemporary Greek revival trend. France did not profit immediately from the interest generated by Bonaparte's scientific mission which, however, did provoke wide-scale emulation in Europe. Nevertheless, the first museum of Egyptian antiquities was founded by France and was given its own curator in 1823; it was created by removing from the department of antiquities the few Egyptian objects it had contained. Thanks to Jean François Champollion this museum did not long remain purely theoretical. Since Napoleon, Egypt had been a theatre of intense activity, with excavations most often having a commercial end. Henry Salt, British consul general in Alexandria from 1815 to 1827, operated a veritable antiquities trade; maintaining agents, the most active of whom was Giovanni Battista Belzoni, Salt entered into competition with the Italian Bernardino Drovetti, who had been appointed by Napoleon as French consul general in Egypt. Their struggles occasionally assumed the dramatic character of a picaresque novel. France lost the Drovetti collection because Louis XVIII found the price too high; it went instead to Italy. Bought by Carlo Felice di Savoia in 1824 for 300,000 lire, the collection went to the small Egyptian cabinet in Turin which had been formed with pieces brought back from a scientific expedition to the Orient in 1763 by a professor at the local university, Vitaliano Donati. The adventures of one of the most precious pieces in this collection merit re-telling; they concern a papyrus

102. The Michaux Stone or Sumerian Kudurru.
Cabinet of Medallions, Bibliothèque Nationale, Paris. Brought from the Orient in 1786 by the French botanist André Michaux, this stone marker is the oldest Mesopotamian object known in Europe.

listing all the sovereigns of Egypt, giving their divinities and the duration of their reigns. This unique artifact, the first of its kind to be unearthed in Egypt, was found by Drovetti during the course of excavations of Theban tomb sites; the excavators were looking for treasures, not documents and Drovetti, attaching little importance to the discovery, inserted the papyrus into a phial he found in his saddlebag and returned to camp at a gallop; when he arrived, the document was in pieces. Champollion came upon the fragments in a box in the Turin museum and was the first to recognize their importance; unfortunately the famous royal list has many lacunae and Egyptologists ever since have deplored Drovetti's negligence. Champollion, who had proposed in vain that Louis XVIII purchase the Drovetti collection, was happier with the administration of Charles X and in 1826 succeeded in acquiring for the Louvre more than four thousand pieces from the collection of the British consul Salt that had been sold to the Santoni brothers in Leghorn. Thus, what had been intended for France enriched Italy while that which England coveted fell into the hands of France. The struggles between Drovetti and Salt had been in vain. In truth, Salt, whose collections seemed inexhaustible, also sold to the British Museum; he was, then, an early benefactor of two great Egyptian museums.

Champollion, on his research expedition to Egypt in 1828-1829, took with him an Italian team, headed by Ippolito Rossellini, which was working on behalf of Grand Duke Leopold II of Tuscany. The fruits of this mission were added to the Nizzoli collection (purchased in 1824) to form the Egyptian museum in Florence. In 1839 a second Egyptian museum opened in Italy—in the Lateran Palace in the Vatican, where Gregory XVI had it installed among other collections of antiquities. The rooms were decorated with Egyptian-style columns and paintings representing landscapes along the Nile; the collections were installed by Luigi Maria Ungarelli, a pupil of Champollion. France's cultural position in Egypt enabled her throughout the nineteenth century and well into

103. **Mexican Mask in Turquoise Mosaic.** *British Museum, London. This piece entered the British Museum in 1865 with the collection of Henry Christy. It was about this time when interest was aroused in pre-Columbian civilizations.*

104. **Arrival of a Winged Bull from Khorsabad at the Louvre.** *Anonymous engraving from the* Antiquities of Nineveh. *Bibliothèque Nationale, Paris. The transport of colossal pieces from the excavations at Khorsabad was an adventure filled with mishaps. The Assyrian Museum opened in Paris in May 1847.*

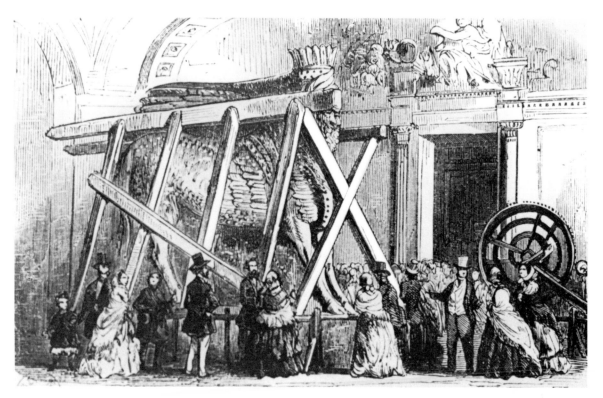

the twentieth, thanks to the talents of her archeologists and her buying campaigns, to amass at the Louvre the most important collection of Egyptian art outside Cairo and even there the museum was organized by French scholars to whom the khedives had entrusted the care of the antiquities of Egypt. Since agreements made with the Egyptian government had long granted excavators the right to half of the objects found, the culture of the land of the Pharaohs was thus carried to all parts of the world.

For a long time the only Mesopotamian object conserved in Europe was the *Michaux stone,* a *kudurru* or stone marker brought back in 1786 by the French botanist whose name it was given and sold by him to the Bibliothèque Nationale in Paris for the inflated sum of 4,200 francs. After that, British diplomats and officers retraced the steps of Herodotus to the site of Babylon, which, however, they only perfunctorily explored. As early as 1826 the British government, acting on behalf of the British Museum, bought for a thousand livres a small Mesopotamian collection brought back from the Orient by the Consul Claudius James Rich. A Frenchman, Paul Emile Botta, took the initiative in excavating for traces of the ancient Assyrian civilization. Sent as the French consular agent to Mosul, he began digging at his own expense on the site of Nineveh and discovered Sargon's palace at Khorsabad; he soon received a very modest subsidy from the French government and, after shutting down the works in 1844, proceeded to prepare for export a selection of the principal sculptures unearthed. They were sent

by sea to Paris where they arrived in February 1847; the following May first a two-room Assyrian Museum opened in the Louvre. Botta's success awakened the interest of the English; in 1845 a British traveler, Austen Henry Layard, who had met Botta at Mosul, resolved to undertake excavation at the site of Calah (Nimrud); at first he was befriended by the British chargé d'affaires in Constantinople, Sir Stratford Canning and was later financed by the British Museum. The fruits of his excavations arrived in London during the summer of 1847 where they provoked as much wonder as had Botta's in Paris. In the end the two museums found themselves rivals; they vied for the tells, or ancient mounds, of Mesopotamia—a competition not always civil; a Turkish archeologist and English agent who bore the name of a Mazdean god, Hormuzd Rassam, went so far as to dig clandestinely, at night, at the site of Kuyunjik, occupied by the Frenchman Victor Place, in order to remove some of the most beautiful pieces; thus the famous wounded lioness and the thousands of bricks from the library of King Ashurbanipal's palace went to London, not Paris. The magnificent yields of the second and third French missions, those of Victor Place and Fresnel, were unfortunately lost for the most part in transport on the Tigris, from Mosul to Basra, in 1856; the cases were loaded onto keleks (rafts made of reeds supported by inflated goatskins), a mode of navigation in use since the time of the ancient Mesopotamiams. Two keleks were attacked by Arabs and were sunk; a third ran aground at Basra. The few reliefs that were saved arrived in Paris in July 1856; there still remained something to astonish the Parisians for, although Botta had had to cut two of the colossal winged bulls that flanked the gates of Khorsabad, Place managed to transport two others intact; they weighed more than thirty-three tons each. One remained where it sank in the Tigris and the other, grounded at Basra was recovered with great difficulty and sent to Paris. A new room was laid out in the Louvre, under the Colonnade; the bulls flanked each side of the doors according to their position *in situ*; since one was missing, it was replaced by a cast of one of the other three. The talented French archeologists received from their country only those tokens of ingratitude that France, dominated by political intrigues and upsets, so often reserves for her most efficacious servants, pioneers and scholars; Botta died in disgrace, Fresnel in poverty, Place in exile. Their contemporaries, the English archeologists Austen Layard and Henry Rawlinson, were knighted.

Another European museum sought to acquire Mesopotamian antiquities. The king of Prussia subscribed, for 50,000 francs, to the Assyrian Excavation Fund, a society founded to 1853 to subsidize research in Babylonia; the excavations were disappointing and the association was dissolved; however, the Berlin museum did acquire several cases of antiquities.

With Ernest de Sarzec, the excavator of Tello, ends the great tradition of diplomat-archeologists that began in the seventeenth century. French consular agent to Basra in 1875, Sarzec chose for his field of action a deserted tell whose depths hid the secret of the origins of the Mesopotamian civilization. After eleven excavation campaigns, undertaken from 1877 to 1900, the third millenium B.C. revealed its story in the Sumerian city of Lagash, where the patesi, or priest-king, Gudea had reigned. The first lot of artifacts, arriving in Paris in 1881, was bought by the Louvre for 130,000 francs from Sarzec. In the end the diplomat received official subsidies. From this time on, Germans, Englishmen and Americans competed with each other in Mesopotamia, in

105. **The Reconciliation of Cephalus and Procris, by Claude Gelée, Le Lorrain.** *National Gallery, London. Included in the purchase of the Angerstein collection in 1824, this is one of the first paintings acquired by the National Gallery.*

209

106. **Interior View of the National Gallery, London.** *Private collection. The building designed to house the National Gallery was begun in 1833 at Trafalgar Square according to the plans of Wilkins and was opened to the public in 1838.*

Elam and in Iran. Now, however, the discoveries were the fruits of scientific missions, generously financed, organized by institutes and directed by specialists divided into various schools. One cannot help longing with some regret for the not-too-distant past when the search for buried history was a consul's pastime, when the author Mme Jeanne Dieulafoy astonished the world by dressing in men's clothes, like George Sand, to explore Susa with her husband, the engineer Marcel Auguste Dieulafoy, when a grocery boy from Mecklenburg with a gift for languages succeeded in making a fortune and, to satisfy a childhood dream, discovered Troy and Mycenae, defying the scholars who refused to believe in his windfalls. The treasures Heinrich Schliemann found at Troy and Mycenae enriched Berlin's Museum für Vor- und Frühgeschichte, newly installed in the building erected by Ende on Prinz Albertstrasse.

The Americas kept their secrets locked in the earth for a longer time. There was, however, a room called the *Musée Mexicain* which was opened in the Louvre in 1850; it contained pieces acquired from the Latour-Allard collection. The crowds of visitors were so large that "they fought to get in." The following year Peruvian artifacts were added and the name was changed to the *Musée Américain*. The British Museum had already bought Aztec sculptures in 1823 and in 1865 it acquired the great collection assembled by Henry Christy, a pioneer in the study of aboriginal cultures. Henceforth ethnography ranked as one of the numerous scientific interests of the British Museum and became an important theatre of activity. This world of archeology which makes up the British Museum attracted large crowds—in 1843 a census showed that half a million people had visited the beautiful new building designed by Robert Smirke.

A large share of the activity of European museums in the first half of the nineteenth century was of an archeological or historical nature; museum directors were less preoccupied with painting, which had been the object of passionate interest during the preceding period. It is true that

107. **The Rembrandt Room in the Hermitage Museum.**
Leningrad, middle of the 19th century. This engraving clearly shows how the rooms of the Hermitage which were annexes to the Imperial Palace were set out as living quarters. On the left is the Return of Tobias *by Rembrandt. Opposite, a large desk in walrus bone from the beginning of the 19th century, now in Pavlovsk Castle.*

all the capitals and great cities of Europe had their rich pinakothekai, either former princely collections turned over to the public or the creations of the great museological era during the years of Revolution and Empire. Only London remained without a picture gallery. In contrast to all other great European museums, the National Gallery does not owe its origins to a former sovereign collection transformed into a public museum; it was created under the aegis of the Royal Academy, planned over several decades of discussions and realized in 1824 by the British Institution, a society founded in 1805 to encourage the fine arts in the United Kingdom. The near loss of the collection of John Julius Angerstein, Russian-born philanthropist and so-called "father of the modern Lloyds of London" (†1823), provoked the decision. The celebrated cabinet of this friend of Lawrence, noted in particular for its admirable Claude Lorrains, was acquired in 1824 and installed in Number 52 Pall Mall, where the new museum opened. Two years later Sir George Beaumont bequeathed it his personal collection. The building designed by William Wilkins on Trafalgar Square expressly to house the National Gallery was opened to the public on April 9, 1838; it shared quarters with the Royal Academy until 1869 when this institution moved into the new Burlington House. For his picture gallery Wilkins abandoned the sober Greek revival style Smirke had used for the British Museum, preferring for the interior colored marble and the Corinthian style he found more suited to the polychrome pictures.

It is curious that strong prejudices were manifested on the part of certain artists against the foundation of a gallery devoted to the paintings of the past. As in the eighteenth century, they feared the unfair "competition" of their predecessors. Two years before the realization of the National Gallery John Constable went so far as to say in a letter of December 6, 1822, "Should there be a National Gallery (which is talked of), there will be an end of the art in poor old England, and she will become, in all that relates to painting, as much a nonenity as every other country that has one."

108. Water Color by Leo von Klenze for the large Hall of XVIth- and XVIIth-Century Italian works. *Drawings Cabinet, Hermitage, Leningrad. In the construction of the New Hermitage, which lasted from 1840 to 1849, Leo von Klenze decorated the museum as if it were a palace. Paintings were hung frame to frame, the ceiling was decorated with stucco, furniture was gilded, the lamps were bronze, there were malachite ornaments and the flooring was in marquetry.*

Decidedly, the English museum was for a long time confined to a purely scientific role, in which archeology figured, whereas in France artistic reasons motivated painters and critics, as early as 1750, to seek public display of the royal collections. London applauded each new enrichment of the British Museum but lamented the idea of opening a national picture gallery. Even Smirke, the architect of the British Museum, opposed the creation of a pinakotheke.

Contemporary English artistic taste greatly influenced the new museum. The National Gallery emerged from a Pre-Raphaelite ambience and the tastes of that time have persisted down to the present, which explains the predilection this museum's administration has always shown for the "Renaissance primitives." The first impetus came in the main from the painter Charles Locke Eastlake. Author of a famous treatise on pictorial technique which is still profitable reading today, Eastlake was first appointed keeper, then a trustee and, in 1855, became the director of the National Gallery; he remained in that post until his death in 1865. As early as 1836 a committee was formed to advise on the purchase of works anterior to Raphael; the 1854 report to the Treasury on the administration of museums sanctioned, supporting their position with solid arguments, the same policy of buying. The painter William Dyce, who had moved in Rome in the circle of the Nazarenes, German precursors of the Pre-Raphaelites, sent in the beginning of 1853 a letter to the prince consort in which he vehemently criticized

109. Water Color by Leo von Klenze for the Dutch Gallery at the Hermitage. *Drawings Cabinet, Hermitage, Leningrad. Notice the coffered ceiling, the marquetry floor and the rich furnishings in gilded wood, marble and semiprecious stones. Von Klenze himself designed even the smallest details.*

the National Gallery's policy of buying and recommended forming a national collection that would embrace the whole field of painting. After this the purchase of primitives was intensified; in 1857 the museum bought thirty paintings from the Lombardi-Baldi collection in Florence for the sum of £7,035; the *pièce de résistance* was Paolo Uccello's panel of *Niccolò da Tolentino at the Battle of San Romano*. Probably on the advice of William Dyce the Krüger collection of German primitives was purchased en bloc in 1854. It was only towards the end of the century that the museum's administration corrected the excesses of this tendency by acquiring more recent chefs d'œuvre, principally Flemish and Dutch works.

In a Germany under the influence of Romanticism, the northern primitives came into vogue. The poet Goethe, the architect and painter Karl Friedrich Schinkel, the museum director Waagen, collectors like the Boisseree brothers in Heidelberg and Barthold Suermondt in Aachen, and scholars like Ruhmor encouraged this new taste. The passion for the Middle Ages took for its rallying cry the completion of the Cologne Cathedral. The Prussian King Frederick William III, who had bought seventy-three Italian paintings from the Giustiniani collection in 1815, found some beautiful Flemish primitives in the important lot of works he acquired from the dealer Solly in 1821. The crown prince, the future Frederick William IV, brought to this policy all his romantic enthusiasm. At the other end of Germany, nostalgia for antiquity did not prevent

213

Louis I from passionately interesting himself in the primitives. From 1814 to 1816, King Maximilian I of Bavaria and his son Louis, the crown prince, combed Italy for Florentine primitives; nor did they neglect Flemish and German works. In 1827 Louis I put his hands on Germany's most important private collection of early northern masters, that of the Boisserée brothers.

Opened in 1823 in temporary quarters, moved in 1828 to the Schinkelbau, Berlin's pinakotheke was a triumph of the rational approach in museology; it benefited greatly from the long directorship of Gustav Waagen (1794-1868), a great scholar who introduced a new principle into art criticism, backing the connoisseur's instinct by the scholar's erudition. His work was continued by Dr. Bode.

So respected were Waagen's abilities that he was called to St. Petersburg in 1861 to reorganize the picture gallery and oversee the composition of a catalog, which appeared in 1863. The Hermitage was the last royal collection to open to the public. Nicholas I, czar from 1825 until 1855, was intensely interested in his museum, which he augmented with prestigious paintings. To give it a worthy home, he had erected a large main building behind the Old Hermitage, known today as the New Hermitage; construction lasted nine years, from 1840 to 1849. The czar called in the German Leo von Klenze, a specialist in museum architecture, who created for St. Petersburg his chef d'œuvre in this genre. Since the museum was to be a continuation of the neighboring imperial palace, nothing was spared to give it a regal appearance. One entered by walking up a huge, impressive staircase (¹) revetted with yellow marble, the first instance of these sweeping *escaliers de musée* that later became so commonplace. On the ground floor was the antiquarium with its polychromed marble revetment, the last example of the type of museum created by Simonetti in the eighteenth century for the Museo Pio-Clementino in the Vatican. On the second floor paintings covered the walls *en tapisserie,* forming part of the over-all decor; galleries and cabinets were embellished with gilt woodwork, coffered ceilings, vaults covered with arabesques, marquetry shelves, parqueted floors, ostentatious furniture, vases and fountain basins in malachite and precious stone from the Urals, and, above all, with a prodigious quantity of gilded bronze lighting fixtures: chandeliers, girandoles, sconces and "Victories" of all sizes, even some as large as life. Leo von Klenze designed everything himself; his delicate water colors, now in the drawings cabinet of the Hermitage, show that nothing has been changed in these rooms he laid out more than a century ago. By a curious paradox, the most socialist country in the world offers us today the best preserved example of a *palais-musée,* conceived for a sovereign's diversion. This ensemble creates a noble impression the personnel of the Hermitage has had the foresight not to change; to lighten the presentation, suiting it to the tastes of the last half century, would disrupt the harmony of the decor of the last beautiful palace interior to escape the decadence of Second Empire and Victorian tastes, already manifest in the degeneracy of the Louis-Philippe and Biedermeier styles. Doubtlessly, the light archaism of von Klenze's interior, which prolongs with a little flourish the beautiful cadences of neoclassicism, explains the persistence of a sense of proportion and harmony at a time when these qualities tended to disappear.

The museum built, the czar proceeded to a large-scale regrouping of the collections dispersed in the various royal palaces; there were even "surplus" sales conducted in

1853. The *vernissage* took place on February 5, 1852. The museum was completely integrated with the palace, being used for evening receptions and after-theatre suppers; furniture was disposed throughout the rooms; certain precious paintings, chosen to embellish the imperial apartments in the Winter Palace, were hung in the museum during the absence of the sovereigns. The czar permitted the public but on conditions recalling those of the *Ancien Régime*. One visited the emperor, not the museum; full dress was *de rigueur* and visitors were announced. These requirements lasted until 1866, after which it sufficed to present a decent appearance, a condition required in a bylaw of the British Museum as early as 1810. Until the October Revolution each painting bore a label in French and Russian. The Hermitage continued to grow through gifts and acquisitions under the reigns of Alexander II, Alexander III and Nicholas II.

Museums long looked like temples; the Old Hermitage was an early evocation of the palace format—a Roman palace on the ground floor, a neoclassical palace on the upper. For the picture gallery at Dresden, begun in 1848, the architect Gottfried Semper resolutely adopted the Renaissance *palazzo* style; moreover, he was obliged to adapt the new building to the baroque Zwinger structure, which he accomplished through rich exterior ornamentation. Semper's plan was an elaboration of Munich's Alte Pinakothek; a long gallery, this time accompanied by two rows of cabinets, was repeated on either side of a monumental staircase, an architectural tour de force that gave the visitor a taste of the riches awaiting him. Paintings were hung *en tapisserie* in the high-ceilinged rooms, conforming to the tastes of the time.

Semper had repeated the gallery on either side of a stairway. Carl Hasenauer followed a similar course for the new building of the Kunsthistorisches Museum in Vienna (1872-1891), repeating the gallery four times rather than twice to create a quadrilateral. His plan was shortly afterwards adopted for the Rijksmuseum in Amsterdam; it inspired Boston's first museum and, later, the new (1893) building for the Art Institute of Chicago.

From 1849 to around 1875 the Louvre underwent considerable changes. As early as 1850 the architect Jacques Felix Duban, in response to the new taste for luxury, embellished the Salon Carré with a large, gilt stucco dome; in imitation of the Tribuna in the Uffizi, there was an effort to turn the Salon Carré into a "Pantheon for master-pieces," where busts of great artists, with cartouches giving their names, underlined this intention. An affectation of richness characterized the exterior as well as the interior architecture of the Louvre under Napoleon III. Miraculously managing to complete "the bold design of the kings," a project abandoned by Louis XIV and resumed by Napoleon I, the emperor did not hesitate to complicate his task by razing a section he found insufficiently sumptuous. There was a political *raison d'être* for the showiness of the Louvre's exterior: to affirm to citizen and foreigner alike France's prosperity under the imperial regime.

The architects Louis-Tullius Visconti (son of the curator of antiquities during the First Empire) and Hector-Martin Lefuel built within a few years this palace that had been left unfinished for centuries. The result was a colossal structure joining the sovereign's palace, administrative and ministerial offices and a museum. With the *antiquarium* and the archeological collections in place, it was the Paintings Department which especially profited from this enlargement. It put at its disposition enormous rooms with overhead lighting and high walls that received large paintings, of which the Louvre has many, and several rows of superposed pictures. The monumental stairways were, of course, one of the embellishments of the museum, following a fashion that continued until the twentieth century. The most sumptuous of these staircases, on which polychromed marble was lavished, is the one in Vienna's Kunsthistorisches Museum.

During the reign of Louis-Philippe, the Louvre profited from acquisitions made by him, like the collection given by the Scotsman Standish, an admirer of the prince, and that astonishing Spanish cabinet which the king ordered bought on his behalf during the Carlist War on the Iberian peninsula. France was destined to lose both collections; respecting an offer that was made to the deposed king, the Second Republic gave them to him rather than repurchasing them. A buying policy was resumed under Napoleon III. The emperor procured for France most of the enormous collection of the self-styled Marchese Campana di Cavelli (Gian Pietro Campana) which was put up for sale in Rome by Pope Pius IX to cover the loans made by this gentleman, director of the *Mont-de-Piété*, who constantly acquired paintings and objects put up for security at the public pawnshop under his management. Russia, England and France were among the bidders and, although some of the best paintings were bought by the Hermitage and the British Museum, France succeeded in carrying off most of the lot in 1864. The Louvre was primarily enriched with Italian primitives and antique vases; entrusting the collection to the administration of the imperial museum met with difficulties. One segment of the population opposed having the Campana collection put into the Louvre on the grounds that it had been bought with funds voted by Parliament while, in theory at least, the museum's collections still belonged to the Crown; the public was, then, still aware that the museum adjoining the palace reverted to the sovereign, whose person supposedly represented the nation.

The creation of museums devoted to modern art is one of the most significant developments in museology. To show examples selected from contemporary production and no longer only works of the past became an essential goal of the administration of the Beaux Arts; harvesting for the future, the museum concentrated on the present. It is no surprise that France took the initiative in this field; thanks to the institution of the *Salon,* continued from the seventeenth century to the present, living art has always played an important role in French society. In 1818 King Louis XVIII had established by ordinance a museum in the old Palais du Luxembourg, scene of the first exhibition, in 1750, of paintings belonging to the Crown. The new museum opened on April fourteenth of the same year, with its principal attraction five large compositions by David, whom Louis XVIII had generously pardoned from regicide in view of his genius. During the Empire a rather embryonic museum of French painting—chiefly "civic" pictures, including *The Oath of the Horatii* and *The Lictors bringing to Brutus the Bodies of his Sons*—had been maintained in the Luxembourg. Throughout the century and until the transfer of the Impressionists, the Palais du Luxembourg functioned as a sort of novitiate for the Louvre, a situation that finally came to an end because the building was both structurally and environmentally wrong for exhibiting twentieth-century works. The turbulent artistic life of nineteenth-century Romantic Germany

110. **Portrait of a Young Woman, by Petrus Christus.** *This is one of the most beautiful works among the 677 pieces purchased in 1821 by Frederick William III of Prussia from the English dealer, Solly, and installed in Berlin.*

217

spurred the creation of museums of modern art. Thanks to the foresight of Louis I of Bavaria, truly one of the great "princes" of museology, Munich's museum of modern art opened its doors in 1853; Berlin had to wait until 1876; London, longer still; the National Gallery of British Art, now the Tate Gallery, was opened in 1897 in Millbank, London, in a building erected by Sir Henry Tate to house his gift of contemporary paintings.

In use in English since the beginning of the seventeenth century, the word *archeology* referred, at first, to both early and ancient history; its meaning was expanded later to include the study of antique monuments and, still later, to designate the scientific study of past human life and human activities. In the nineteenth century this broader concept of archeology was applied to the very origins of occidental civilization, suddenly plunged into the depths of time by the breakdown caused by the French Revolution which, in destroying the monarchical system, simultaneously broke the dynastic chain that had interlocked the different periods in history. This chain was never to be re-established, even outside France, despite the efforts of the Holy Alliance to strengthen the tottering edifice and re-knot the broken thread of history. It was normal for this rupture to be felt in France more keenly than elsewhere for here it had set off an epidemic of destruction which, in its turn, engendered a counterattack. While in the other countries of Europe the metamorphosis from the Old to the New World came about through a slow and progressive replacement of the structures of the past, according to a rhythm that did not exceed that of previous historical mutations, France approached the nineteenth century in an immense field of ruins. Châteaubriand could write of his *Génie du Christianisme*: "The book appeared [in 1802] amidst the debris of our temples. Everywhere one saw the remains of recently demolished churches and monasteries."

Nowhere more than in France was the impulse to save—out of which the museum grew—so closely connected with the act of destruction. All over France depots swelled with debris from destroyed monuments throughout the century. Some of these store-houses had been begun during the Revolution (e.g. the Couvent des Augustins in Toulouse); although picture galleries were soon opened to the public under the Revolution, it was only in 1817 and 1827 that it was decided to put on exhibition the admirable Romanesque and Gothic sculptures salvaged from the city's demolished monasteries. France's so-called "lapidary museums" date, in general, from the 1830's, that is, from the decade which saw the founding in 1834 of the *Société française d'archéologie* by a Norman, Arcisse de Caumont, and, the same year, the establishment of a *Commission des Monuments historiques* to safeguard and restore monuments. The repositories formed in secularized convents, often at the initiative of those local archeological societies then springing up all over France. As examples let us cite the Musée des Antiquités de la Seine Inférieure, opened in Rouen in 1831 by the society of the same name; the lapidary museum of Bourges, installed in 1834 in the Hôtel Cujas by the *Société des Antiquaires du Centre*; the beautiful museum set up in 1844 in the Unterlinden convent at Colmar by the *Société Schongauer* which boasts the famous *Isenheim Altar* by Grünewald; the archeological museum of Angers, founded in 1841 but not installed in the former Hôpital Saint Jean until 1874. In these museums works accumulated haphazardly, with no care given to presentation—reminiscent of the ossuaries of medieval cemeteries.

111. **The Salon Carré in 1865, by Joseph Castiglione.** *Louvre Museum, Paris. To transform it into a "Pantheon for Masterpieces" in imitation of the Tribuna of the Uffizi in Florence, the Salon Carré was given a ceiling sumptuously decorated with gilded stucco. The walls were completely covered with paintings disposed without any concern for chronology or style.*

112. Gothic Room in the chapel of the Germanisches Museum, Nuremberg. *When* objets d'art *from the Middle Ages and the Renaissance began to be assembled in the 19th century, the main concern was to find a suitable setting for their exhibition, and it was often the case that former monasteries were used for this purpose. For example, in Nuremberg a former Carthusian monastery was bought to house the collections of the* Germanisches Museum.

113. Gothic Room in the Bayerisches Museum, Munich, *founded in 1852. A far less happy solution was to erect a building in the eclectic style evoking the spirit of the Middle Ages and the Renaissance. This is what Gabriel von Seidl did for the Bavarian Museum, which was rebuilt between 1894 and 1900. Some of the rooms are very successful imitations.*

In Europe's large cities, afflicted by rapid growth during the second half of the century, special museums were set up to safeguard the remains of a municipal history being destroyed by progress. In Paris the founding of the Musée Carnavalet was the direct consequence of a city-wide remodeling project which razed old convents and townhouses by the hundreds. In fact, it was Baron Haussmann himself, author of the plan for urban re-design, who presented to Napoleon III in 1865 a report proposing for the city a "department of historical works" whose first task would be to found a municipal museum to receive the "flotsam from the wreck of old Paris." In November 1866 the Hôtel Carnavalet, once the residence of Madame de Sévigné, was acquired for this purpose.

These museums contained, in particular, remains of monuments. However, from the beginning of the century certain amateurs had been collecting medieval and Renaissance *objets*—all the more easily because they were considered worthless. As early as 1800 the city of Lyons had a school of history painting which concentrated on medieval themes but in Paris the interest was in antiquity. The most celebrated of these artists, Pierre Révoil, had brought together a collection of precious medieval objects: armature, chests, vases, tapestries, paintings, enamels, manuscripts; acquired by the Louvre in 1828-1830, it formed the basis of the future Département des Objets d'art. Thirty years later this department was enriched by a considerable gift from Charles Sauvageot (1781-1860). Formerly a customs official who retired in 1847, Sauvageot had been first violinist with the Paris Opera. There, in the company of his colleagues Norblin, a numismatist, and Lamy, a Sinologue, his taste for *antiquailles* developed. His motto was *"Dispersa coegi."* By the time he gave his collection to the French State in April 1856, these objects that had been bought for nothing already had a market value—an Englishman had offered 500,000 francs for them. The only conditions attached to his gift were that he be lodged near his collection in the Louvre and that he have exclusive rights to it during his lifetime. The public did not have

114. **Portrait of John Julius Angerstein and his Wife, by Sir Thomas Lawrence,** *1792. Louvre Museum, Paris. The purchase of the collection of John Julius Angerstein was the first important acquisition of London's National Gallery which opened at Number 52 Pall Mall on May 10, 1824.*

to wait long; Sauvageot died four years later.

At this time Paris already boasted a remarkable museum devoted to the Middle Ages and the Renaissance, installed in the former residence of the abbots of Cluny, a fifteenth-century *hôtel*. The city had keenly felt the loss of Lenoir's museum of French monuments, dissolved by ordinance on April 24, 1816, as much to restore the royal tombs to Saint Denis as to raze this homage to the "barbarous centuries" that the neoclassical aestheticians and artists, led by Quatremère de Quincy, deplored. In the old tradition of parliamentary "antiquarians," Alexandre du Sommerard, a counsellor at the Cour des Comptes, installed himself and all his collections in the Hôtel de Cluny in 1832. It was, he said, his idea to "store in a series of more or less obscure garret rooms and to exhibit for the veneration of the initiated the fruits of [my] harvest of *objets d'art* in the hope that these old things would evoke appreciation for all that our arts comport of science and poetry." The *hôtel* and its collections were bought by the city with the stipulation that the nephew of the seller serve as curator during his lifetime. The museum opened on March 16, 1844. Swelled by numerous purchases, the Musée de Cluny remained, until its recent renovation in the purist spirit of modern museology, a wonderful hodgepodge, transporting the imagination to the medieval and Renaissance worlds of the novels of Alexandre Dumas and Jules Michelet's *Histoire de France*.

Here and there in Europe museums of this genre began to appear; their creation was stimulated around 1850 by the new sense of nationalism manifest everywhere. One of the finest ensembles of this type that can still be seen today is Copenhagen's Rosenborg Museum. In this small château Frederick VII collected the most beautiful pieces from the royal *Kunstkammeret,* hitherto dispersed in the various residences, and in 1859 turned it into a museum consecrated to the keepsakes of the royal family. In 1854 King Maximilian II of Bavaria founded the Bayerisches Nationalmuseum which opened the following year. Devoted to Bavarian art, this "national" museum contained only medieval and Renaissance creations; baroque works, then scorned and judged decadent, did not enter the collection until the present generation. The Bavarian national museum still reflected the political disunion of Germany. A loftier ideal inspired the Germanisches National-Museum in Nuremberg. This museum was the result of a proposition made in August 1852 by the knight von und zu Aufsess during a meeting of a scholarly society convened at Dresden by Prince John of Saxony. Aufsess was named director of the museum, which was to treat all the sources of German art and literature in the most universal sense. Nuremberg, Dürer's birthplace, was chosen as the place which best embodied the spirit of Germanism; Hitler was to follow the same course when he made this city the center of Nazism.

The ideal place in which to install this type of museum was an old building suited to the character of the collection. In Paris the Hôtel de Cluny, although rather limited in space in spite of the nearby Roman baths which had been annexed to house the lapidary collection, was a perfect answer. Nuremberg chose a former convent, a type of structure ideal for the installation of a museum of this kind by virtue of the wide variety of rooms it offered; in 1857 the city bought for this purpose the old Carthusian convent dating from the fourteenth and fifteenth centuries, which was enlarged at different times and eventually annexed to the neighboring Augustinian monastery.

In Munich, where there was a mania for building, a special structure was erected but the Bayerisches National-Museum had to wait half a century to move into its new quarters. In 1892 the architect Gabriel von Seidl began construction on the Prinzregentenstrasse. In the Munich tradition of museum architecture, this building presents a heteroclite synthesis of Gothic and Renaissance styles; some rooms were rather successful pastiches; in others, the desired effect was achieved by incorporating architectural or decorative motifs from the same period as the objects, statues and furniture on exhibition.

All these museums were institutions of an historical rather than an artistic character; their purpose was to show the formation and development of the life of a people, of its different social classes, industries and handicrafts, through specimens of decorative art. We can hardly imagine what they were originally like since in our generation they have been purged to make them more like "art museums."

Archeological museums appeared all over northern Europe wherever there was a revival of interest in the arts of the Middle Ages. New buildings were constructed in the Romanesque or Gothic style. It was toward a more distant past that the archeological investigations of Russia were directed, the impulse having been given as early as the beginning of the eighteenth century by Peter the Great in his ukase ordering the collection of all unearthed artifacts; in 1739 the historian V. Tatichtchev published a handbook on excavations. In the second half of the eighteenth century Russia's annexation of the coastal land north of the Black Sea provided archeologists with new territory to explore in the area of Greek influence; in 1763 General Melgounov unearthed the first Scythian tumulus. The beginning of the nineteenth century saw the establishment of archeological museums to house the recovered antiquities—at Nikolayev (1806), Feodosiya (1811), Odessa (1825) and Kerch (1826).

For those who waged it as for those who rebelled against it, the French Revolution broke the continuity of time. Led by Napoleon from victory to victory across Europe,

115. **View of the "Salle des Croisades" at Versailles.** *This hall, one of several set aside for a history museum, was created at Versailles by the French King Louis Philippe and was realized in a Gothic, troubadour style with paintings about the Crusades.*

116. **View of the Waterloo Chamber at Windsor Castle.**
To commemorate the victories over Napoleon, the English king decided in 1830 to install at Windsor Castle a history cabinet which was called the Waterloo Chamber. The ceiling in the form of the top of a ship evokes the victory at Trafalgar. Here we see the table laid for the Battle of Waterloo anniversary banquet which is given here every year.

the Grande Armée, harbinger of a new era, tumbled a whole world into the abyss of the past and, despite efforts to bring it to life again, the irresistible course of the new history accelerated the flow of the old. Once the epic events had ceased to rage, romantic man became uneasily aware of the singularity of times past which brusquely appeared to him as unlike the time in which he lived; he became an historian in the hope of re-knotting the broken thread of continuity, of finding—somewhere beyond the zero point of the new era—the man he had once been but who now appeared as a stranger.

As institutions created by the new age to give man a fuller awareness of himself, museums opened wide their doors to an overwhelming history. Heads of state and governments availed themselves of this means to shape the public conscience; the museum of history came to be closely linked to politics throughout the nineteenth century.

Once peace was achieved after twenty-five years of war, Europe immediately sought to preserve the memory of this turbulent period when nations clashed. Napoleon's conquerors desired to commemorate a victory so dearly bought at the price of many defeats in order to assert their good right to the respect of the future. Vanquished France wanted a complete picture of her history in order to rediscover her grandeur. Paris already had a magnificent Musée Napoléon whose trophies were masterpieces of genius. Windsor, St. Petersburg and Vienna founded their Napoleonic museums to celebrate his defeat. The first was installed in the Winter Palace by Czar Alexander I. A long gallery, built in 1826 by the architect Rossi, was hung with three hundred thirty-two portraits of Russian generals who had fought against the French emperor; since the English were considered specialists in portraiture, Dawe was summoned who, for ten years, assisted by the Russians Poliakov and Goliki, painted these effigies with the help of whatever documents could be assembled; a few spaces were left blank for want of iconographical information on certain heroes; these lacunae were later filled by the Soviets with portraits of simple soldiers fallen during the October Revolution; thus was the continuity of Russian history affirmed in the Winter Palace. Among all these waist-length likeness of generals caracoles Czar Alexander the Victorious.

The English more than the Russians have a sense of the universal; the Waterloo Chamber at Windsor Castle, proposed by the king in 1830 and achieved by covering a court with a ceiling like that of a ship—an allusion to Trafalgar—did not celebrate Napoleon's defeat as a national victory but as the fruit of a European coalition against the "Ogre of Corsica." In fact, Sir Thomas Lawrence, John Hoppner, Sir David Wilkie, Sir William Beechey and other artists painted the portraits of sovereigns, chiefs of state and generals who had taken part in the struggle; even Pope Pius VII was included and some Frenchmen as well (Charles X and his son the Duke d'Angoulême). The *fleur-de-lis* appeared side by side with various heraldic emblems of Great Britain. Modern England begins with Waterloo; the memory of it is celebrated with fervor and every year on the eighteenth of June, the anniversary of the battle, a banquet is held in this museum at an immense table that can seat one hundred fifty guests.

Vienna was not to have her "anti-Napoleon" museum until later and then as a result of events that will be detailed later in this book.

The idea of installing an historical museum at Versailles originated with Napoleon. In his *Mémorial de Sainte Hélène* he revealed that he wanted to banish from the gardens "all these ornaments *à la Turcaret*" and "I would replace them with mosaic panoramas of all the capitals we had entered victorious, of all the celebrated battles where we had shown our strength. They would have been eternal monuments to our triumphs and our national glory." Versailles was to have a panorama to commemorate a battle of Napoleon but it was of Waterloo. The vogue for panoramas, "endless paintings" in a circular format whose forms were mathematically calculated to give an illusion of reality in dim light, began then and continued until the end of the century. The process had been invented by an Englishman in 1787 and from the time of Napoleon, war panoramas were the most popular. London boasted the *Naval Battle at Aboukir* and the *Battle of Trafalgar*; Paris, the *Army at Boulogne* and the *Encounter at Tilsit*. Pierre Prévost (1764-1823) and Thayer, creators of the *Tilsit* panorama, wanted to build eight rotundas along the Champs Elysées to commemorate great battles fought in the principal cities of the Empire from 1789 to 1815.

One wonders if Louis Philippe had been thinking of these panoramas (forerunners of the dioramas invented by Daguerre and C. M. Bouton) when he commissioned Horace Vernet to paint for Versailles the sixty-three-foot-wide canvases, like the *Capture of Abdu-l-Kadir*. In 1830, the year of the July Revolution, one could see a panorama of the *Battle of Navarino* by Jean-Charles Langlois (1789-1870); throughout the whole century the great battles of contemporary history were presented in dioramas to which the crowds flocked.

The idea of reconsecrating Versailles and transforming what had become the symbol of a dishonored despotic regime into a temple to "all the glories of France" was a personal vision of Louis Philippe. He wanted it to express the reconciliation of all Frenchmen whom he claimed as his subjects by creating a liberal and parliamentary monarchy. He was the ruler France was awaiting, the ruler whose "patriotism was both lively enough and profound enough to endear to him all the great things she [France] had created" (Alexandre Louis Joseph, Comte de Laborde). He offered his people a double claim to legitimacy, that of having been descended from Saint Louis and that of having been hoisted by the *citoyens* over the walls of the barricades. The historical museum at Versailles was a mammoth undertaking, realized with the felicitous rapidity that distinguished the museological creations of that period. The architectural alterations of the palace—which were considerable—and the completion of the first iconographical series took three years and cost twenty-four million francs, most of which the king paid out of his own pocket as he regarded the project a personal creation. He took with him to exile the immense graphic documentations which, in forty volumes bound in red Morocco leather, had been compiled by a team of historians; it included the likenesses of great personages and the iconology of important French historical events; it was in short, Roger de Gaignières' dream realized on a royal scale where one felt the influence of Paolo Giovio, certain of whose illustrious men figured in portrait galleries up until the present day. The backbone of the museum was the *Galérie des Batailles*, a hall almost four hundred feet long where thirty-three colossal paintings, executed by the most esteemed contemporary artists, celebrated the great victories of France—from Tolbiac to Austerlitz, Jena, Friedland and Wagram. Napoleon figured prominently here; what an answer to the Waterloo Chamber and to the Gallery of War Heroes in the Winter Palace! Other rooms, in particular the Coronation Hall, celebrated the Napoleonic era; the *Galérie des Batailles* led into the *Salle de 1830* with its pictures exalting the peasants who had constructed the barricades which had served as a pedestal for the throne of the "citizen king."

Each class of French society had its place in the museum. The old aristocracy was honored in the *Salle des Croisades* where, in a decor of battles in troubadour style (among them Delacroix's *Entry of the Crusaders into Constantinople*), were painted the coats of arms of the families that had taken part in the crusades. All the nobility wanted to be represented there and, since proof was necessary, a brisk trade, known as *Les faux des croisades,* sprang up. A former sheriff's clerk, a certain Courtois, turned out these forgeries for a five hundred franc gold piece. It was a matter of fabricating loan contracts made between crusaders and Italian merchants, of deeds lost in the Holy Land or pay receipts from knights or squires. Lacabax, director of the Ecole des Chartes in Paris, was summoned to the Salle des Croisades to authenticate the candidates' documents and even he was fooled! This museum to the glories of France, once opened, was continuously enriched with subjects drawn from contemporary history. From 1838 to 1845 the conquest of Algeria was retold in a series of immense canvases; the Second Empire commemorated the wars in the Crimea and in Italy; the most heroic deeds of the Franco-Prussian War (1870-1871) were illustrated and a large painting by Alfred Philippe Roll perpetuated the memory of the Centennial in his *States General Celebrated by President Carnot at Versailles*. One cannot underestimate the importance which this colossal tribute to the glories of France had for several generations at a time when military exploits constituted the substance of history. For some seventy-five years Versailles served as a lesson in patriotism for French children and young people, a lesson which bore fruit in 1914 when, in a single move, the entire nation rallied against the invader despite differences of political opinion, even despite strong pacifist tendencies. Was not the military academy of Saint-Cyr within easy reach of this museum to the glories of France? Since that time, films have mocked the virtue of this patriotic iconography and the notion of heroism now rests on other than military actions. Those who were once hailed with respect as "dead on the field of honor" are now regarded with contempt by many.

It was the revolutionary shock of 1848 which, in forcing Austria to retrench, sparked the creation at Vienna of a museum to commemorate national glories. After the first instance of revolt flared up in the working-class districts, rioting spread through the whole of Vienna and the government had to recover the city from the insurgents. This prelude to the Commune of Paris made a profound impression on the Hapsburg monarchy and Viennese society. To avoid a recurrence, the government conceived the idea of building on a high plateau to the southeast of the city a sort of citadel safe, if not from war, at least from an insurrection. The complex included barracks, ammunition depots, an arsenal with a gun factory, an officers' school and a museum containing armor, old weapons, historical paintings, flags and uniforms, some of which had come from an embryonic museum which had already existed in the old arsenal founded by Maria Theresa. Quarters for this arms museum (Heeresmuseum) were constructed from 1850 to 1856 from plans by Ludwig Förster, chief architect for the arsenal, and Theophil Hansen. Money was not spared; in the main hall, columns (each of which cost 100,000 florins) were interspersed with fifty-six statues of great Austrian men from various eras. The Salon of Honor was Moresque in style, as was the exterior architecture of the entrance—an allusion to the role played by Austria in defending the Occident against the Turks. When war-torn Austria was liberated from foreign occupation after World War II, this monument to past glory was the first museum rebuilt by the Austrians, even before the great museum of art; at that time it was renamed the Heeresgeschichtliches Museum. In its new installation it offers, besides the special galleries devoted to artillery, four sections pertaining to the Thirty Years' War, to the struggles with the Turks, to the conflicts of the eighteenth century and to the wars against Revolutionary and Napoleonic France. At the time of the re-opening of this museum, I was in Vienna with the Congress of the International Council of Museums; a reception was given in the museum restaurant for the delegates. I arrived late because it was the Fourteenth of July, the French holiday commemorating the storming of the Bastille, and I had been to pay my respects to the French ambassador. The congress gave me an ovation when I entered; all the delegates, including the Japanese, sang in unison every verse of the *Marseillaise*. And this transpired in galleries where historical paintings marked the imperialistic tyranny of Revolutionary and Napoleonic France, the terror of peaceful Austrian families who until then had enjoyed an idyllic life under the wise rule of the Dual Monarchy. What a message of liberty this anthem conveyed and what a profound solidarity it bespoke in a Europe made one even by the memory of struggles and conflicts.

Doubtlessly no monarch more than Napoleon III exploited museums for their propaganda value. He was one of the great benefactors of the Louvre, rebuilding it partially and providing it with funds that permitted important acquisitions, particularly in the field of painting. He also conceived new institutions of a personal character. Like Louis Philippe, Napoleon III, a monarch brought to the throne by a revolutionary movement, affirmed through visible works his intention to resume traditions, to follow in the mainstream of French history. The completion of the Louvre had no other objective. With the creation of the Musée des Souverains, established December 15, 1852, the intention became even clearer. It offered an apology for the monarchical regime, showing at once how the monarchical institution was able to, and sometimes had to, renew itself through a providential man who, lacking a hereditary claim, owed his right to rule to that which another dictator (who also came into power through a plebiscite) was to call the "profound legitimacy." In a series of rooms along the Louvre's Colonnade the public was invited to admire the relics of the different dynasties that had reigned in France from the Carolingians to the *Napoléonides*.

This form of the legitimacy of power conferred by genius was demonstrated in another museum which set forth the value of Caesarism as a justification of the Napoleonic dynasty. Napoleon III, who manifested a great taste for history, was an enthusiastic admirer of Julius Caesar, whom his uncle had wished to rival. He undertook excavations at the identifiable sites mentioned in Caesar's *Commentaries on the Gallic Wars* (Alesia, Gergovia), intending to write a monumental book. To receive the findings from these excavations the *Musée des Antiquités Nationales* was established by decree on March 8, 1862, in the château of Saint-Germain en Laye. Napoleon III did not have long to wait to see a success even greater than his expectations; this became the richest museum of prehistory and protohistory and, in the end, celebrated the conquered rather than Caesar.

The institution long known as the *Musée de Sculpture comparé,* but renamed the *Musée des Monuments français* after the old Lenoir museum, was not realized until the 1879 exposition; it had, however, been proposed under the Empire as the plan for it by the fervently neo-Gothic architect Viollet-le-Duc had been exhibited as early as 1855. The nationalistic intention of this museum was unmistakable; it sought to affirm, by means of casts, the superiority of French medieval and Renaissance sculpture by comparing it with foreign examples. Today, the casts after foreign works have been removed and the museum is devoted exclusively to reproductions of French paintings or sculptures. Viollet-le-Duc's conception brings to mind an earlier museum that had been created in Paris by the painter and world traveler Louis-François Cassas (1756-1827); in existence from 1806 to 1814, it contained models of "architectural masterpieces in different countries." In the Musée de Sculpture Comparé considerable sums were expended, not for works of art but for copies which assume great didactic value when brought together as a collection; this is an important stage in the evolution of the pedagogical function of the museum, an aspect developed more and more by the modern world.

Napoleon III's Musée des Souverains did not last beyond his reign. A decree of the provisional government dated May 8, 1872, ordered its dissolution—the very time when Austria chose to open her museum. The defeat at Sadowa and, still more, the elevation of William II, King of Prussia, to the title of Emperor of Germany were keenly felt by the Austrian nation, whose foundations the historian Franz Bock had established in a monumental work brought out in 1864 on the heraldic devices of the former empire of the House of Hapsburg. In 1871 the Austrian government decided to open to the public the Treasury of the Hofburg with its enormous collection of princely and imperial crowns and emblems; thus the Austrians could revel in the spectacle of their grandeur at a moment when it was on the wane.

117. **Ottonian Art. So-called Crown of Charlemagne** *in the Schatzkammer of the Hofburg, Vienna. Events during the wars of the Revolution resulted in the placement in Vienna of the regalia of the Holy Roman Empire and the Treasury of Burgundy. This crown, which was used for the coronation of German emperors, was kept at Nuremberg but was taken to Vienna in 1796 along with other pieces of the imperial treasury at Nuremberg in the retreat from French troops.*

228

117

About the same time Europe could admire another *Musée des Souverains*. In 1859 the Danish King Frederick VII was motivated by dynastic devotion to regroup in Copenhagen's small Château Rosenborg all the objects, mementoes and historical portraits of his family as well as the most sumptuous furnishings of the various royal residences, attributes of sovereignty ill-suited to a parliamentary monarchy. Filling rooms devoted to the different reigns, these treasures, which have remained the personal property of the Crown, constitute a fabulous whole; the museum contains the crown jewels, an extraordinary suite of furniture in solid silver made in Augsburg in the eighteenth century, a fine collection of porcelain and crystal and magnificent weapons and armor.

On the eve of its downfall, the monarchical regime delighted to contemplate its extravagances. The museum is an institution which feeds on the used forms of life; the Musée des Souverains of Napoleon III and Emperor Franz Joseph's Schatzkammer were created to justify monarchy at the very moment it was about to perish.

Toward the middle of the century England also decided to celebrate her national glories and in a particularly British way—through portraiture. In 1846 the historian Philip Dormer, fifth earl of Stanhope, proposed forming a national portrait gallery. In 1852 Parliament furnished funds for the project; after several temporary installations, this gallery to the glories of Empire, a last incarnation of Paolo Giovio's idea, found a permanent home in 1896 in a building erected at the expense of William Henry Alexander of Shipton.

Denmark did not have to wait so long for her museum of historical portraits. In 1812 Christian IV had created a veritable Danish pantheon in the royal château of Frederiksborg.

Nineteenth-century England, in the avant-garde of modern economy, was the first country where industry influenced the museum; this was manifested in a seemingly paradoxical way, through renewed interest in the *arts mobiliers*. In the nineteenth century the dividing line between art and technology fell between the major and the minor arts, an attitude derived from an old philosophical prejudice from Antiquity and the Middle Ages which classified the arts as liberal or servile, the first being of a purely intellectual nature; the second, essentially manual. The Renaissance freed the major arts, but not the minor, from this "mechanical" condition; and the nineteenth century ranked *objets d'art,* handmade creations, with industrial products at a time when the latter still only required moderate use of the machine.

The state of affairs among artisans vis-a-vis the arts preoccupied the British Parliament at an early date; in 1835 it appointed a Select Committee on Arts and Manufactures to explore means for propagating knowledge of the arts and of the principles of design, specifically among the working class. The Committee recommended opening public galleries with exhibitions of models of art objects from the past; collections of this type were to be annexed to regional schools under the aegis of the Government School of Design, which also had a gallery.

The 1851 Great Exhibition (or World's Fair) in London gave strong impetus to this project. It was the first exposition of its kind in which the modern world took stock of itself, re-evaluating the progress of industry and technology in an international competition marked by a certain retrospective element. It took place in the Crystal Palace

118. Eltenberg Reliquary. *Rhenish, 2nd half of the XIIth century. Enameled and gilded copper. Victoria and Albert Museum, London. Acquired in 1861, this is one of the most ancient pieces among all the magnificent Medieval objects of which this museum—at that time known as the South Kensington Museum—is so rich.*

119. **Studio of Alexandre du Sommerard at the Hôtel de Cluny, by L. V. Fouquet.** *Musée des arts décoratifs, Paris. Counsellor at the Cour des Comptes, Alexandre du Sommerard installed himself in the Hôtel de Cluny where he accumulated his Medieval and Renaissance collections.*

120. **The first Refreshment Room of the Victoria and Albert Museum, London,** *in 1865. From a water color by Anthony Stannur. Since the XIXth century, Anglo-Saxon museums have concerned themselves with the comfort of visitors.*

in Hyde Park, an audacious structure of iron and glass designed by Sir Joseph Paxton expressly for the fair. Prince Albert, whom Queen Victoria forbade any interference in politics, concentrated his energies on the arts; it was he who had made the exhibition a success despite violent criticism; certain opponents went so far as to pretend that England would lose her insularism and be invaded by the "light-fingered gentry of Europe." The Great Exhibition enjoyed such tremendous success, however, that it was decided to prolong it with a permanent institution. The following year, therefore, a Department of Practical Art (renamed the Department of Science and Art a year later) was founded. The profit of £186,000 realized by the Exhibition was used to purchase land in South Kensington while Parliament voted a loan of £5,000 for acquisitions. On September 6, 1852 the Museum of Manufacture opened in temporary quarters at Marlborough House, with objects from the Government School of Design and purchase from the exhibition on display. In order to be better understood by the artisans to whom they were directed, the collections were classed by materials: textiles, metals, ceramics, wood. The successive names of the museum attest to a certain confusion about its nature; it became the Art Museum, then the Museum of Ornamental Art and, finally, the South Kensington Museum in 1857, when it was relocated at its present site—an adroit way of avoiding too precise a designation. A large iron structure to house it was completed in 1867 but the museum grew so rapidly that thirty years later it needed more space. On May 17, 1899 Queen Victoria laid the cornerstone for a new building; the museum was opened on June 26, 1909 by Edward VI, taking for its permanent name the Victoria and Albert Museum; during the course of the ceremony, its director was knighted, by the flat of the sword, by the king himself, a medieval spectacle that only England would dare at the inauguration of a modern institution.

The National Museum of Science and Industry, founded in 1857, is housed in a twin building near the Victoria and Albert Museum. Both are administered by the Board of Education. As its founders had conceived it, art was to be admitted to the museum on technical criteria alone, as a means of furnishing artisans with useful examples. Thanks to the talents of its directors who had substantial funds at their disposal, this museum boasts the most beautiful decorative arts collection in the world. However, this aesthetic triumph has not submerged the original educational intentions. From the beginning the Victoria and Albert Museum was distinguished by this very Anglo-Saxon trait of being well organized from the pedagogical point of view; it circulated exhibitions, lent books and lecture materials to all the Commonwealth countries; in addition, public comfort was an early concern; the first museum restaurant was set up in the Victoria and Albert Museum in 1863 in an Anglo-Norman structure.

Interest in the decorative arts in France was also stimulated by a world's fair, the third of its kind, held in 1855. A comparative exhibition of old and new furniture underlined the inferiority of contemporary productions and revealed the tendency of artisans around mid-century to imitate earlier styles rather than to create their own. The reporter for the *Union des Arts et de l'Industrie* wrote in 1855, "To pastiche the past has become a rule blindly and indiscriminately applied in art. How does one explain that an entire society, catapulted into a dizzying world of innovations and novelties by its discoveries in chemistry and physics, rather than demanding bold, new things from the arts, rather than spurning whatever is old, copied or repeated, contents itself with the most servile imitation of century-old styles?" It is curious that in 1855, at the moment when railroads were just beginning, men felt nonplussed by the rapid changes; but Châteaubriand had also been troubled fifty years earlier by the prospect of steamship travel! A century of discoveries has made us, it seems, somewhat blasé to Sputniks! Whatever it was, the cure was worse than the evil; opening well-installed and well-catalogued museums for the decorative arts, putting before the eyes of artisans excellent examples of the mobiliary arts of the past only encouraged the very imitation it was meant to suppress. Everyone wanted an Henri II dining room, a Louis XV drawing room, a Louis XVI bedroom.

In 1863 a *Union Centrale des Beaux-Arts appliqués à l'Industrie* was founded in France; its objectives were to create, "in the heart of industrial Paris," a museum, a library and a professional school. Charles Blanc, in an article on the organization of this society for his *Gazette des Beaux-Arts* (the oldest arts magazine, it was founded in 1859 and is still being published) hailed it as a "great step toward the regeneration of drawing schools in France and the re-application of the fine arts to industry." He cites Britain as an example and states that "English industry, very unsophisticated from the standpoint of art, has made prodigious progress in the ten years since the exposition of 1851 and if it continues to develop at the same rate, we could soon be surpassed." The list of founders gives some indication of their intentions; one encounters: "an architect-decorator, a manufacturer of needlework patterns, a lace manufacturer, an upholstery manufacturer, a financier, a rug manufacturer, a builder-mechanic, a manufacturer of bronzeware, a manufacturer of fine furniture, a gilder and silverer, a piano maker, a manufacturer of wallpaper, a manufacturer of fine plate."

The *Union Centrale* merged in 1882 with the *Société du Musée des Arts décoratifs,* founded in 1880; the latter had installed a museum in the famous Galerie des Machines, left vacant after the World's Fair of 1879. This fusion produced the *Union Centrale des Arts décoratifs* which signed a contract with the State in 1897 to set up the museum, library and school in the Pavillon de Marsan, a wing of the new Louvre.

The organization of a decorative arts museum in Paris was a long, slow process. Lyons, on the other hand, began work on one almost immediately after the 1855 World's Fair; the museum was created by the Chamber of Commerce (in a resolution dated January 24, 1856) and installed in 1864 in the recently completed headquarters of this institution. The connection with industry is obvious here—the aim was to furnish artisans in the Lyons silkworks with a repertory of patterns. Therefore the museum concentrated especially on the acquisition of fabrics. Its textile section became so rich that in 1890, at the suggestion of the great collector Edouard Aynard, then president of the Chamber of Commerce of Lyons, it was established as a separate museum, the Musée historique des Tissus, the finest of its kind in the world.

Curiously, decorative arts museums in several European countries were born out of private initiative. Such was the case in Germany where as early as 1827 the two architects Beuth and Schinkel had founded the Deutsches Gewerbemuseum at Berlin, whose objective was the formation of an art school and museum; renamed the Kunstgewerbemuseum in 1879, henceforth the usual title for this genre of museum in Germany, it was installed in 1921 in the royal château on the Museuminsel, since destroyed. Vienna's Oesterreichisches Museum für Kunst und Industrie is older; it was installed in a building erected from 1868 to 1871.

The slow and progressive formation of museums through chance gifts and felicitous purchases offered visitors only incomplete collections. The idea was conceived of presenting the public with temporary exhibitions methodically put together and therefore pedagogically invaluable. In 1857 England set the example with a grandiose exhibition organized with the working classes in mind. Manchester was chosen as the site because it was an industrial city where works of art could serve local interests, in this case the textile designing business. The Prince Consort could not help being passionately interested in an exhibition so suited to his educational bent. It was a mammoth show, presenting a wide variety of paintings from all schools; works were on loan from private collectors, particularly from the Queen. Nor were sculpture and the decorative arts neglected. There was even a refreshment room with facilities to serve 100,000 meals daily and to cook 300 chickens in an hour. The Art Treasures of Manchester was a *succès fou*; all Europe flocked to see it and a number of articles in the foreign press hailed this dean of great art exhibitions. This was the first time the public could see the famous collection Sir Richard Wallace was to make into the most exquisite ensemble of French eighteenth-century art. It belonged at that time to Sir Richard's father, the Marquis of Hertford, an eccentric who practiced amateurism as though it were a sport; he relished triumphing in the salesroom at the expense of the Crown. But, once acquired, the works no longer interested him; he would leave them crated. In 1897 Lady Wallace left the celebrated collection to England; one can admire it today in London, in the former Hertford House, which was bought by the State. Frenchmen could see other treasures lent by the Marquis of Hertford to the large exhibition entitled *Musée Retrospectif* which was organized in Paris in imitation of the Manchester show and for the same reason, by the Union Centrale des Beaux-Arts Appliqués à l'Industrie; thus the society made its brilliant debut. The taste for exhibitions was launched; the following century it would end by denuding the museums.

Of all the domains invaded by museums in the contemporary period, the most recent, the most unexpected has been that of popular culture. While museums concentrated on masterpieces or the scientific and archeological remains of mature civilizations, the humblest creations of popular art were long considered valueless. But suddenly they became objects worth collecting and the study of their significance sparked feverish activity among teams of specialists; the simplest bowl was given as much care as a sculpture by Michelangelo. This re-evaluation of the products of popular culture was prepared for by the discovery of the prehistoric civilizations of the Nordic regions, mute civilizations whose traditions have been perpetuated by popular cultures. Actually the concept of archeocivilization assumes a common beginning for civilizations, primarily agricultural in character, which would fall in the period of humanity's first great technical discoveries, that is, in Neolithic times; variously mutated by the mythologies, literatures and arts of mature civilizations, this nascent culture would be preserved in its original state with remarkable constants in different regions of the world until the Industrial Revolution brought about a rapid change. The revelation of the importance of this common beginning—without the connection being apparent to its own investigators—was corroborated by Jung's discoveries in psychoanalysis revealing the existence in the human psyche of a collective unconscious, source of archetypes from which the reactions and attitudes of the individual flow.

This culture of the people was christened *folklore* by the English antiquary William John Thoms (1803-1885) in 1846; in France a more complex term—*arts et traditions populaires*—was used. Museums of folklore began to appear about 1875, a period when the thrust of the modern world, growing more imperious, began to substitute a new standard of life for the old beliefs and traditions, a consequence of industrialization. Man experienced nostalgia for all those traditions that formerly constituted the poetry of simple life and which, as variants on a common theme, gave a certain personality to the provincial soul while human life developed within a regional framework dominated by one or another craft or agricultural activity.

This form of museum found its most original expression in the Scandinavian countries. It is part of a wealth of regional investigations which manifested themselves with a great deal of precocity. The Swede, Johannes Rubens Burens (1568-1652) had tried to decipher at a very early date the ancient runic writings. On May 20, 1630 King Gustavus Adolphus of Sweden issued an edict ordering historians and antiquarians to study ancient monuments and runic inscriptions; these instructions were renewed in 1643 and regional inspectors were charged with compiling inventories; military successes did not keep Gustavus Adolphus from interesting himself in these investigations into the life of early Swedish people. A professor at the University of Uppsala, Ulof Rudbeck (1630-1702), first set forth the thesis, on which Germanists later based their *constructo bellicistes,* that the sources of European culture were to be sought in the north rather than along the Mediterranean or in the Orient as generally supposed. In the eighteenth century Linnaeus (Karl von Linné, 1707-1778) interwove in his researches geography, ethnography and botany. Romanticism in Sweden was firmly rooted in the exaltation of the protohistoric and popular culture of the nation; the

121. **Thirteenth century timber church, transported to the Bygdøy open-air museum, near Oslo.** *In the open-air museums belonging to the art and folk museums of Scandinavia various examples of rustic buildings have been assembled. Being constructed of wood, they can easily be dismantled. Here at Bygdøy can be seen one of these famous Norwegian timber churches (Stavkerk) which was transported from the province of Hallingdal, restored and reassembled in the heart of a wood.*

236

decade from 1850 to 1860 witnessed the founding of numerous scholarly societies across the country for the exploration and study of Scandinavian folklore. The most zealous champion of this movement was Dr. Artur Hazelius (1833-1901), an ardent supporter of pan-Scandinavianism who in 1873 organized in this spirit a comprehensive exhibition at Drottningatan and founded Stockholm's Nordiska Museet on the broad concept of a Nordic civilization reaching from the Alps to Lapland. To show the artifacts in a proper atmosphere, Dr. Hazelius created a new form of museum—the open-air museum. In 1891 he opened his new genre of museum in Skansen Park, where the public could visit many types of rural structures—an early wooden church, a Lapp village, farms, windmills and workshops—in the middle of a botanical and zoological park where the animals were uncaged. The interiors of the buildings were reconstructed; men and women in regional dress plied the old trades, because one of the museum's objectives was to continue the manufacture of traditional articles that were then sold to the public. Concerts and folk fests were held periodically; in winter a family of Laplanders came to live in one of the Lapp houses. Restaurants served regional dishes. This museum is, in the words of Georges-Henri Rivière, "a microcosm of Sweden."

The undertakings of Dr. Hazelius were motivated by an instinct to preserve, at a time when new agrarian laws and rapid industrialization were profoundly altering the rural population, forcing it from its old habitations. This type of open-air museum enjoyed enormous success in Sweden and in all the Nordic countries before spreading to central and eastern Europe. It was particularly successful in regions where rural timber construction permitted buildings to be moved easily. It was a question of blockhouse rather than framed timber construction, a point confused by Strzygowski. This type of construction made the house portable as it could be disassembled and moved long distances; one moved with one's house and all that remained of the former dwelling were two stones; the hearthstone and the doorstep. Tolstoi, when he inherited his family's immense wooden palace, hastened to sell it, keeping for his use only the portion built in stone.

Norway created her folklore museum, the Norsk Folkemuseum, in 1895, before she voted to end the union with Sweden; its foundation was a claim to independence. The Norse Folk Museum also had an open-air annex, the Folkemuseet on the Bygdøy Peninsula. Bernhard Olsen founded Copenhagen's Dansk Folkemuseet which opened to the public in 1885; the open-air Frilandsmuseet near Kongens Lynby is one of the most beautiful of its kind in Scandinavia and dates from 1901. Finland and the Baltic states, following the example of Sweden, Norway and Denmark, encouraged the creation of folklore and open-air museums. Scandinavia now has them by the hundreds.

The earliest open-air museum in western Europe was set up at Arnhem in the Netherlands in 1912. In this Openluchtmuseum are houses in the various regional styles of Dutch architecture, even including some stone structures; others were copied in brick, using the doorframes of the original houses. With the draining of the Zuider Zee a whole regional culture dependent on fishing disappeared; to perpetuate its memory a museum was installed at Enkhuizen, a port on the Ijsselmeer, in a former customs house; the open-air annex consists of various types of boats grouped in a canal at the end of the building. Thus museums feed on the death of a culture.

The British Isles also boast a few open-air museums, notably at St. Fagans, Wales, an annex of the Welsh Folk Museum.

Quite naturally this genre of museum enjoyed great success in socialist countries where, according to Marxist principles, a humble object used by the people has more value because it is a token of the collective life than a sculpture by Michelangelo, for example, which represents nothing more than one time and one individual. Let us also mention the village of Cloppenburg in Lower Saxony with its Museumsdorf, a reconstruction of some twenty houses, a church and a foundry, scantling or framed timber constructions brought in from the various outlying districts. Bucharest's *musée-village* takes up ten acres of a municipal park; with its hundred or so rustic dwellings and two churches, it is a microcosm of Rumania, illustrating ways of life in the different regions —in the mountain, plains, hill and marshland cultures.

The formula, as we shall see in the next chapter, spread to the United States. One of the last countries to show interest in folklore was France. There was, however, one quite typical museum of this genre, the Mouseon Arlaten, founded in Arles in 1899 by the Provençal poet, Frédéric Mistral (1830-1914). Study on a national scale of the vestiges of popular culture is closely connected with politics in France. The government of the Popular Front, backed by a majority comprised of communists, socialists and radical left-wingers, took an interest in folklore art and traditions. A bill passed in 1937 provided for the creation of open-air museums in the country's principal centers of provincial life; they were to be under the aegis of a central *Musée des Arts et Traditions populaires* at Paris where a synthesis of national folk treasures would be shown. A committee headed by Georges-Henri Rivière from the Musée de l'Homme encouraged the formation of several folklore museums throughout France and amassed at Paris hundreds of thousands of objects chosen from all over the nation. The central museum is presently under construction but the open-air museums will never be realized; their establishment is made quasi-impossible by the fact that through most of France rural construction is in brick, stone or sun-dried clay.

Folklore museums have close affinities with ethnographic museums. In France it has become a custom to refer to European popular cultures as *ethnologie* and to foreign popular cultures as *ethnographie*. (In English ethnography refers to the purely descriptive treatment of peoples and races while ethnology denotes their comparative study and analytical classification.) The many ethnographic museums in Europe were, for the most part, the by-products of colonial expansion, such as the beautiful museum of Congolese art in Tervuren, Belgium; this is not the case, however, with two of the finest museums of this kind, Hamburg's Museum für Völkerkunde und Vorgeschichte and the Musée de l'Homme in Paris, both born of purely scientific efforts and exploration rather than conquest.

In general, these museums of popular culture strive for an exact as possible reconstruction of the life of the past; period costumes adorn more or less lifelike mannequins. To this fashion that pleases the general public France, on the contrary, has preferred a more scientific and abstract presentation.

Chapter *11*

The New World

Even before their independence, the Thirteen Colonies experienced great intellectual activity, which manifested itself in the creation of libraries, scholarly societies, educational institutions and, eventually, in museums. An overwhelming drive for knowledge and culture was the heritage of an essentially Protestant and English beginning, a heritage, as we shall see, that would profoundly alter the concept of the Museum in the hands of the New World. Other factors—especially patterns of philanthropy and ingrained democratic traditions—would also share in making the American museum the unique institution it now is.

The first museological centers sprang up around learned societies, usually taking shape as curiosity cabinets where works of art were extremely rare. Specimens of natural history predominated, reflecting the passionate interest eighteenth-century Americans took in this science. Harvard University, following the distinguished precedents set by Oxford and Cambridge, began collecting "curiosities" as early as 1750. President Thomas Jefferson had a fossils cabinet in the newly constructed presidential "Palace," not yet called the White House. There were few cultivated Americans who were not naturalists of a sort. The Fine Arts were not entirely neglected, however. By 1743, Benjamin Franklin could write in his *Proposals for Promoting Useful Knowledge among the British Plantations in America:* "The first drudgery of settling new Colonies, which confines the attention of People to mere Necessaries, is now pretty well over; and there are many in every Province in Circumstances that set them at Ease, and afford Leisure to Cultivate the finer Arts..." Following a suggestion by Thomas Jefferson, the College of William and Mary at Williamsburg added the Fine Arts to its curriculum in 1779.

When the Charleston Library Society (founded 1743) of Charleston, South Carolina, voted in 1773 to annex a museum, this word appeared, it seems, for the first time in America. The Society's collection was a curious mixture of art and scientific exhibits. Philadelphia in the 1770's boasted two similar museums, one at the American Philosophical Society (founded in 1743 by Benjamin Franklin and others) and a second at the Library Company (founded 1731); the latter significantly expanded its art holdings in 1784, with the acquisition of paintings and drawings by Pierre Eugène du Simitière (1736-1784), whose works had been exhibited two years earlier at the American

122. **Number I, 1948, by Jackson Pollock.** *Collection the Museum of Modern Art, New York. A remarkably efficient cultural institution, the Museum of Modern Art in New York has a huge collection of modern works from American and European artists.*

241

123. **Peale's Museum in Philadelphia,** *from an old engraving. Charles Willson Peale (1741-1827), once a pupil of Benjamin West in London, served as a captain during the Revolutionary War and painted portraits of war heroes. In 1784 he founded, in Philadelphia, a museum which was both historical and scientific; portraits of heroes hung in rooms where one could also see natural history and ethnographic specimens and machine models.*

Museum in Arch Street. Furthermore, the Library Company holds the distinction of being the first institution to entrust important commissions to native painters.

A family of artists—the Peales—played an important role in the museological growth of the United States. In 1802 Charles Willson Peale (1741-1827), celebrated American portraitist who had served as a captain of volunteers during the Revolutionary War, opened his Peale's Museum in Philadelphia; it was housed in Independence Hall. Portraits by Peale of the great men of the Revolution hung above fossils and shells arranged in vitrines; ethnography was represented by wax figures of North American Indians, given their characteristic dress and weapons. There were also models of machines. The tendency to combine science, technology, and art began a museological tradition that would continue into the nineteenth and twentieth centuries: prime examples include the Brooklyn Museum, incorporated as the Brooklyn Institute of Arts and Sciences in 1891, and the Los Angeles County Museum, opened in 1913. The elder Peale instilled in four of his eleven children—Raphaelle, Titian, Rembrandt and Rubens—a museological interest. From 1814 to 1830 Rembrandt and Rubens ran a gallery and art museum in Baltimore which became a rendezvous for artists and amateurs; Rembrandt gave lectures there and performed scientific experiments, demonstrating, for example, the use of gas for lighting.

In 1825 the East India Marine Society (formed 1799), of Salem, Massachusetts, opened a museum whose heterogeneous and specialized collections perfectly mirrored the interests of its members. It contained portraits of Salem merchants, members and officers of the East India Marine Society, nautical instruments, ship models and figure-heads, the tools of the different marine industries, examples of maritime art and costumes, and a rich collection of ethnological material from the South Seas and the Far East. Its name was later changed to the Peabody Museum of Salem, after George Peabody of London who had enabled the Society to purchase the natural history collections of the Essex Institute.

A Boston society known as the Athenaeum (founded 1807) opened a museum in 1826 to house the works of art it had been buying at the annual exhibitions it sponsored; the gallery adjoined the Society's library. Leaning heavily to sculpture, the pride of the Athenaeum's collection was a copy of Hiram Powers' sculpture *Greek Slave*. In 1876 most of the Society's holdings went on permanent loan to Boston's newly established Museum of Fine Arts to form the nucleus of that collection.

Although there were already some more or less questionable dealers who pretended to sell "old works," by and large it was contemporary American painting which attracted patronage. The Pennsylvania Academy of the Fine Arts, founded in Philadelphia in 1805, took the initiative in building a first-rate collection of American painting and sculpture. It acquired important pictures by Benjamin West and Washington Allston. In addition, the Academy's annual exhibitions afforded unknown artists and architects an opportunity to show their work. Art schools were started which later grew into museums, like the American Academy of the Fine Arts in New York, founded in 1802 by Chancellor Livingston. Teaching art within the context of the museums seems to be an American development.

Private collectors became the benefactors of the public, devoting themselves to the establishment of institutions to further the cultural education of the masses. Daniel Wadsworth, amateur architect, offered land to the city of Hartford, Connecticut, for the construction of the Wadsworth Atheneum, the erection of which (1842-1844) was in part financed by him; the neo-Gothic building opened in 1844 with some eighty paintings, to which the collector added his own cabinet, rich in works by Trumbull and Thomas Cole, a close friend. The museum formed a cultural complex with the Connecticut Historical Society and the Hartford Young Men's Institute, later the Public Library. Innovator, pacesetter, the Wadsworth Atheneum is America's oldest museum in continuous operation. J. Pierpont Morgan financed new construction in 1910 and his son subsequently donated outstanding collections of porcelain and the decorative arts; a monetary gift from the latter made possible the purchase of the Wallace Nutting collection of early American furniture. Thus, from the beginning, the American museum depended primarily on private patronage. The Avery Memorial, completed in 1934, added exhibition space for modern art, studio facilities, and a fully equipped theater, which opened with the world *première* of Gertrude Stein's *Four Saints in Three Acts*. The Atheneum thus became the first museum in the United States and possibly in the world to list theatre among its regular activities. New York's Metropolitan Museum of Art has recently attempted a daring experiment: bringing drama into the gallery itself. At intervals throughout 1967 a non-profit theatrical group will

perform fragments of plays before appropriate period settings, Euripides among the Greek amphorae, Ionesco in front of Rauschenberg.

The concept of the university museum, a breed of institution virtually unknown in Europe outside England, took shape in the first decades of the nineteenth century. Yale set the precedent in 1832, building a gallery to house a large gift of paintings by the famous artist-patriot Colonel John Trumbull, aide-de-camp to General Washington. Yale took the pictures, giving Trumbull, in straitened circumstances, an annuity of a thousand dollars until his death. From that moment, art collecting became one of the University's active interests. A new gallery, in the Renaissance *Palazzo* style, was built in the 1870's to house the expanding collections and in 1953 Louis Kahn designed a glass-and-steel addition with facilities for the teaching of art history, architecture, and design.

In 1966, Paul Mellon, philanthropist, collector and a Yale alumnus, gave the University thirty-five million dollars' worth of British paintings, water colors, drawings, prints and illustrated books. The collection spans the period between Hogarth's birth in 1697 and Turner's death in 1851—the golden age of British painting. Mr. Mellon will also finance the construction of a four-story gallery and library to house the donation. The gift of art complements Yale's vast holdings in British literary and social research materials, which include the Walpole and Boswell papers; the University has thus become the most important center outside England for the study of the cultural life of eighteenth-century Britain.

The Honorable James Bowdoin III, an American minister to France and Spain, bequeathed his collection of paintings and drawings to Bowdoin College (Brunswick, Maine) in 1811. Among the drawings, valued at $7.50 the lot, figured a Bruegel landscape. It was not until 1857, however, that Bowdoin was to build a museum to house the art. Harvard likewise began collecting at an early date. Its Fogg Art Museum, founded in 1891, owns one of the finest collections of drawings in America, rivaled only by the Metropolitan Museum and the Morgan Library in New York. It also operates a conservation laboratory. These New England colleges—Bowdoin, Yale and Harvard—set a pattern that was subsequently followed all over the nation, making the university museum a unique feature on the American cultural scene.

As Walter Pach noted, the men who figured prominently in the early history of the museum were men who were serving the country well in other fields—Jefferson, Livingston, Bowdoin. "It is notable how, from the first, the men who represent the country at its best in every field are the ones who aid in the movement for art."

124. **Chinese Ceremonial Vase,** *Shang Dynasty. Freer Gallery of Art, Washington, D.C. The museums of the United States are much richer in collections of Far Eastern art than are those of Europe.*

The Corcoran Gallery in Washington was the first to combine a rich collection of contemporary foreign works with an array of American paintings. Corot, Millet, Théodore Rousseau, Diaz, Monticelli, Albert Thorvaldsen, Crawford, Canova and Antoine Barye intermixed with John Singleton Copley, Gilbert Stuart, Benjamin West, Thomas Sully, Thomas Cole, Charles Elliott and Hiram Powers. William Wilson Corcoran (1798-1888) was a banker who had made a fortune in the Mexican War. In 1859 he asked James Renwick, architect of the Smithsonian, to design a building to house his collection and show it to the public—"for the perpetual establishment and encouragement of Painting, Sculpture and the Fine Arts generally." With its Mansard roofs and square cupola, the building imitated seventeenth-century French archi-

tecture. The large, sky-lighted gallery on the second floor, with its neo-baroque decorations, recalled the Salon Carré of the Louvre. The collection, too, had a strongly Gallic flavor. For instance, Corcoran instructed a trustee of the Gallery, the collector William T. Walters of Baltimore, to order original replicas of every bronze the sculptor Barye had produced. Because of the Civil War, the museum was not incorporated until 1869; the collection was transferred to a new building in 1897. The original structure now houses the United States Court of Claims.

The World's Fair held in New York in 1853 made that great American city aware of its conspicuous lack of a museum; several years passed before one was proposed. The idea took shape during a dinner for certain American personalities, among them several diplomats, on Independence Day, July 4, 1866; the festivities were held at the Pré Catelan, an elegant restaurant of the Second Empire in the Bois de Boulogne, Paris. In 1869 a provisory committee of fifty prominent people was set up in New York, and a board of trustees was appointed the following year. Monetary donations were soon forthcoming. In 1871, the trustees bought at cost ($116,180.27) one hundred seventy-four paintings, principally Dutch and Flemish works (e.g. The *Malle Babbe* of Frans Hals). The pictures were stored in Cooper Union until the new museum could open in temporary quarters. Oysters and punch were served at the *vernissage* of the Metropolitan Museum of Art on February 20, 1872. Its earliest home was the Dodsworth Building on Fifth Avenue between Fifty-third and Fifty-fourth Streets, During the first three months there were six thousand visitors.

Following a contract with the City of New York, which granted the land and also agreed to assist in erecting and maintaining the building, construction began in 1874 on a site in Central Park. The chartering of the Metropolitan starts a new tradition—municipal aid to the art museum. City support has become the second largest source of museum income in the United States as a whole. In 1953, municipal governments provided $8,400,000 for operating expenses alone—about fifty percent of total operating costs. In addition to direct city aid, museums have benefited considerably from tax exemptions and gifts of land. The Philadelphia Museum of Art and The Detroit Institute of Arts depend almost entirely upon their respective cities for maintenance funds. A few institutions, like the St. Louis City Art Museum, receive money for acquisitions from city taxes.

The Metropolitan's new building was completed in 1880; it was enlarged in 1888 and again in 1902, when McKim, Mead and White, architects for the renovations to the White House, provided it with a classicizing, columned façade.

125. **The Mérode Altarpiece, by the Master of Flémalle.** *The Cloisters, Metropolitan Museum, New York. Acquired with great secrecy in 1957 from the d'Ursel family for the Metropolitan Museum, this is one of the most important works of art to be exported from Europe to the United States in recent years.*

The museum soon began a drive to increase its acquisitions fund. In 1903, Jacob S. Rogers, an obscure citizen of Paterson, New Jersey, who had amassed a fortune as a locomotive builder, bequeathed the institution $4,000,000.00 stipulating that the money be used for the "purchase of rare and desirable art objects and ... books for the library." In the decade that followed, the museum attracted a series of superb gifts. 1913 was an historic year for the New York art world: the Armory Show introduced the American public to contemporary European art and the treasures of J. P. Morgan, Benjamin Altman and William H. Riggs entered the Metropolitan. New York suddenly had an international museum, encyclopedic in its scope—the equal of any major museum in Europe.

126. Philadelphia Museum of Art, *Philadelphia, Pennsylvania. Under construction from 1919 to 1928, this museum (at that time known as the Pennsylvania Museum of Art) demonstrates the American predilection for the Greek revival style.*

The first director of the Metropolitan Museum was an uncommon man, General Luigi Palma di Cesnola (1832-1904). Of an old, noble Piedmontese family, he had chosen a military career; he fought beside Garibaldi for Italian unity and, afterwards, sought adventure in the United States which was then in the throes of the Civil War. Cesnola served on the side of the Union, organizing an officers' school which later became a military academy. In 1865 he was appointed by President Lincoln as consul to Cyprus; there he discovered a talent for archeology and, for nine years, carried out a series of excavations. His most important discoveries were sold in 1870 for $60,000.00 to the Metropolitan Museum; he was later appointed director of the museum, a post held until his death in 1904. A French dealer in antiquities, one Gaston Feuardent, questioned the authenticity of the collection, declaring that, in part, it was made up of forgeries. Shortly after the accusation was made, Palma di Cesnola published a brief and total denial of the charges; Feuardent retaliated by suing him for libel. The general won the case but never recovered from the affront. Some years later, however, other objects from his collection brought $1,200,000.00 in a public sale. Today in a palace in a small town in the Piedmont, the last descendant of the Palma di Cesnola family guards the remains of this celebrated collection. Part of the collection at the Metropolitan Museum—the Babylonian cylinders, the Egyptian mummies and cases—is considered unrivaled in the world.

MAIN FLOOR (2nd)

127. **Plan of the Museum of Fine Arts,** *Boston, Massachusetts. Main Floor (2nd story). The façade of this museum was inspired by the Propylaea of Athens (which was also the architectural source for the British Museum). The central axis is formed around a monumental staircase with a vestibule and rotunda; the building was completed in 1909.*

From the beginning the Metropolitan Museum aroused a lively curiosity. It was then open only on weekdays; a proposition to open it on Sundays to permit workers an opportunity to attend met with violent opposition on the part of society. The Sunday openings were later made possible through funds raised by a committee of thirty thousand citizens. And just recently, plans were made to keep the galleries open late one evening a week. A great period of prosperity began for this museum with the election in 1905 of John Pierpont Morgan as president. Simultaneously with the acquisition of art works, the Metropolitan Museum undertook active research in the sphere of archeology, holding its own beside the British Museum and the Louvre; like the latter, it endeavors to present the art of all civilizations. Today the Metropolitan is the most visited museum in the world; the yearly attendance is now over 6,000,000 and on one Sunday afternoon in 1965 some 56,000 visitors were counted.

Boston, Philadelphia and New York all founded major museums within the same six years. This sudden proliferation of art museums in the early 1870's coincided with a deep concern among the educated over the quality of American cultural life. The Civil War had just ended. Reconstruction and immigration problems faced the nation. The founding of settlement houses, educational institutions and museums was viewed as a kind of constructive charity: a means to improve the welfare, taste and standards of the American public. Now, almost a century later, we can say that museums have become significant arbiters of contemporary taste, influencing standards in industrial design, architecture, advertising and even in the home.

Collections of European Old Masters began to penetrate the United States toward the end of the nineteenth century. In 1871 James Jackson Jarves sold to Yale University for $22,000.00 a fine cabinet of Italian *trecento* and *quattrocento* paintings which had been offered first to his native Boston for the nucleus of a museum there but had been refused. Italian Renaissance art in the United States was assured a lasting success by Bernard Berenson through his writings and, more directly, through his acquisitions for Isabella Stewart Gardner. Already a strong patron of the opera and an ardent collector of rare books and manuscripts, she, encouraged by Whistler and John Singer Sargent, became interested in painting in the 1880's. She became the patron of young Berenson, an 1887 graduate of Harvard University: she helped finance his study trips to Europe and entrusted him with assembling for her a collection of early Renaissance paintings. By 1896 this collection had become important enough for "Mrs. Jack" to think of having a building constructed to house it, which she wanted to look like a Venetian palazzo. Fenway Court in Boston, a strange edifice filled with marbles, ironwork and *objets d'art* imported from Italy, was completed in 1903. At her death in 1924 it was left to the city of Boston as a public museum which could not be changed from its original form. The place evokes the heady world of Ruskin and Walter Pater, the quintessentially Anglo-Saxon ambience in which Berenson first made his mark. Together Mrs. Gardner and Berenson created the prototype of the "period museum" which was to become so successful in the United States.

In 1873 the city of Philadelphia received as a gift the William P. Wilstach collection which contained some important European paintings. It was put on view in Memorial Hall, a grandiose neo-baroque windowed edifice that had been built originally to house the Centennial Exposition of 1876.

In this crucial moment of their development, American museums looked to Europe for inspiration. Techniques of layout and exhibition were freely borrowed, but the basic concept of the Museum—how it should function and whom and how it should serve—was modified by "American patterns of philanthropy, education and government." (1) In the gift she made to the city of Philadelphia, Mrs. Wilstach specified that the proposed gallery be laid out like the one Carl Hasenauer had designed for Vienna's new Kunsthistorisches Museum, a very practical plan subsequently copied by Amsterdam. Boston's Museum of Fine Arts followed the same formula for its new building designed by Guy Lowell and completed in 1909. The principle behind having two lateral wings is to balance two quadrilaterals about a central axis comprising a large hall, a monumental staircase and a rotunda; the courts enclosed within the two quadrilaterals, which are dismal corners in European museums, are here transformed into gardens for the relaxation of the visitor, whose comfort preoccupied American museologists from the start. The construction of the Boston Museum of Fine arts sparked in the United States theoretical and technical studies on museology, particularly on problems concerning the lighting of works. Boston was the first museum to create a series of small galleries devoted to specific schools. The expatriate artist John Singer Sargent decorated the upper hall and rotunda with allegorical frescoes in 1921-25. Boston's is truly an encyclopedic museum. Its Asiatic collections are considered the finest in the western world. Rich in Old Kingdom sculpture, its holdings rank second only to Cairo's. Since 1905 the museum has sponsored excavations in Egypt. It boasts an outstanding cabinet of Greek and Roman engraved gems, comparable to those of Vienna and pre-war Dresden. The paintings collection is wide-ranging: choice examples of Flemish art, seventeenth-century French and Spanish works, first-rate Manet and Degas. Winslow Homer and John Singer Sargent hang side by side in one gallery—an interesting juxtaposition that shows the two strains in late nineteenth-century American art, the native and the expatriate. This building, however, where all the services of a great museum

128. **Madame Charpentier and her Children, by Renoir.** *Detail. Metropolitan Museum, New York. Acquired by the Metropolitan Museum in 1907 for the sum of $17,800, this painting aroused such controversy that it cost the curator of paintings his position.*

have been rationally analyzed and disposed and which was the first art museum to divide works into galleries for masterpieces and galleries for study, hides its functional organization behind a neo-Greek façade. This style was frequently adopted for museum architecture in America, possibly because it seemed to suit the dignity of an institution consecrated to the arts and possibly because of its autochthonous associations with the Colonial and Federal aesthetic. No building of this type was more ambitious than Philadelphia's colossal Pennsylvania Museum of Art, erected from 1919 to 1928. (Its present name, the Philadelphia Museum of Art was adopted in 1938.) Its sculpted and painted pediments were the fruit of years of painstaking research to determine the exact polychromy of the monuments of antique Greece. "Philadelphia's new art museum… will be for several centuries, perhaps, the most interesting of these neo-Greek edifices," wrote Horace H. F. Jayne, shortly after its completion. So much money was lavished on this architectural display that hardly any funds remained for the disposition of the interior; although conceived according to Hasenauer's principle of the double museum, it is functionally not too satisfying.

The Cleveland Museum of Art, completed in 1916, adopted the general plan of Boston for its layout. All the galleries are on one floor, grouped about two large courts and a rotunda. The superfluous grand staircase was thus omitted. Offices occupy a lower level. Cleveland is one of the country's most important privately supported museums. Detroit's Institute of Arts, designed in 1927 by Paul Philippe Cret, is an elongated version of the Cleveland plan. Exhibition galleries occupy one level, offices and working areas, another; a large interior garden leads to the auditorium at the end of the long central axis. But once again, a neo-Greek façade hides a functional, carefully planned interior. Fittingly, New York's Museum of Modern Art (completed 1939) became the first major art museum to employ a contemporary style of building throughout; movable walls and better artificial lighting were introduced.

The Worcester Art Museum (Worcester, Massachusetts), one of the finest small museums in America, was founded in 1896 by the industrialist Stephen Salisbury III. An endowment fund comprised of gifts and bequests provides money for maintenance and acquisitions; the only additional income derives from annual membership contributions. The custom of selling memberships, a universal practice in the United States, is almost unknown in Europe. Worcester was the first museum to arrange its collection chronologically in twenty galleries around a central court. One gallery is a reconstructed Chapter House from a twelfth-century Benedictine Priory near Poitiers. The museum has played an active role in the American art world, mounting important exhibitions and hosting conferences on various aspects of the arts.

129. **Annunciation, by Jan van Eyck.** *National Gallery of Art, Washington, D.C. This is one of the 31 paintings from the Hermitage which were purchased from the Soviet government in 1930 and 1931 for $ 7,000,000.00 by the Secretary of the Treasury Andrew W. Mellon who later gave his entire collection to form the basis of the National Gallery.*

In contrast to their European colleagues the curators of American museums attach great importance to exhibiting objects in period rooms, acquired at great expense in Europe or in the United States. Another means of creating a total ambience is to install a collection in antique frames. To understand this American taste for reconstitution, even more prevalent in science museums, one must remember that the European museum goer, surrounded by history since birth, has less need of this evocation of atmosphere than the American visitor whose sense of the past has been less keenly developed by his environment. The opening of the American Wing of the Metropolitan Museum of Art in 1924 generated interest in this system of installation, actually first used in Europe toward the end of the nineteenth century in the Swiss National Museum

252

130. **Room from the Wentworth House, Portsmouth, New Hampshire** *(1671; wood paneling from about 1710), Metropolitan Museum, New York. An exhibition devoted to Colonial America at the Metropolitan Museum was instrumental in fashioning the vogue for Period Rooms in museums. As a result of the exhibition the American Wing, one of the most popular departments in the Metropolitan Museum, was opened in 1924.*

at Zurich. A gift to the museum from Mr. and Mrs. Robert W. de Forest, the three floors of the American Wing comprise an evocation of the Colonial, Revolutionary and Republican periods; reconstructed rooms containing period furnishings alternate with exhibition galleries for metalwork, glass and silverware. An exhibition of American painting and decorative arts, 1625-1825, held at the Metropolitan in 1909 in conjunction with the Hudson-Fulton Celebration, and the subsequent gift to the museum of the H. Eugene Bolles collection of Americana sparked its creation. The Philadelphia Museum of Art has made the most systematic effort in this respect with its American and European period rooms; the major styles of the Occident are recreated in settings imported from France, England, Germany or Holland and from all over the United States. The museum also has a sixteenth-century hypostyle from a temple at Madura and the reception hall from an early nineteenth-century Chinese palace. Fiske Kimball, a former director of the museum whose scholarly writings have made a great contribution to our knowledge of the French rococo style, devoted a great deal of effort to this project.

Even Paris has an ensemble of period rooms—the eighteenth-century rooms bequeathed to the Musée des Beaux-Arts de la Ville de Paris, commonly known as the Musée du Petit-Palais, by the American Edward Tuck (1842-1938). This mode of presentation has been severely criticized on both sides of the Atlantic; it presents, in effect, numerous inconveniences; it renders the museum inflexible, making future alterations difficult and costly. In keeping with the atmosphere of the period the lighting, whether natural or artificial, is usually insufficient, which does an injustice to the paintings on exhibition, frequently too far from the viewer in any case. Precious objects cannot be protected under glass because this would destroy the ambience; a clear labeling of works is almost impossible and the circulation of the public difficult because of the narrowness of the passageways; moreover, dividing the museum into a succession of small rooms complicates surveillance. Despite all these disadvantages, American museologists have not abandoned this manner of presentation. Quite recently, in 1951, an entire museum organized on this principle opened at Winterthur, Delaware: the Henry Francis du Pont Winterthur Museum, which has 125 period rooms.

The re-location of ancient settings can even be applied to architecture. A case in point is The Cloisters, a branch of the Metropolitan Museum. This magnificent ensemble, which is, along with Washington's National Gallery of Art, the crowning achievement of American museology, owes its origins to a collection of architectural elements, chiefly large sections from four cloisters, acquired in France and Spain by the American sculptor George Grey Barnard. In 1914 Barnard put his collection on display in a special building he had constructed on Fort Washington Avenue; somewhat Romantic in style, the composite structure recalled Lenoir's pastiches for his defunct Musée des Monuments Français. In 1925 John D. Rockefeller Jr., one of the great benefactors in American art, bought the collection for the Metropolitan Museum, supplementing the gift a year later with medieval pieces of his own. Barnard's building soon seemed an unsuitable setting for this exemplary collection and plans were drawn up for a new one. In 1930 Mr. Rockefeller gave to the city a 62-acre tract of land, Fort Tryon Park; the site chosen for The Cloisters was a wooded promontory at the end of the park. To preserve the beauty of the view from the area, the patron also bought property along the Palisades in New Jersey, on the opposite shore of the Hudson River. Construction began in 1934; the four cloisters were dismantled and re-assembled inside the new building, a colored granite, tile-roofed edifice vaguely reminiscent of a Rhenish burg. The whole is dominated by a high tower inspired by the twelfth-century one of the Benedictine abbey of Saint Michel de Cuxa, whose admirable Romanesque cloister has been reconstructed within (on a somewhat smaller scale than the original since one gallery remained in France). The rooms radiating off the cloisters and chapels are filled with some of the most beautiful objects from the medieval department of the museum. Nothing has been overlooked in this evocation of life in the Middle Ages; near the cloister of Bonnefont-en-Comminges (thirteenth and fourteenth centuries) lies a monastic herb garden; another garden is planted with flowers found in the *Unicorn Tapestry*. The museum continues to grow; the last monument imported from Europe was the Romanesque apse salvaged from the ruins of the Church of San Martín at Fuentidueña in central Spain; the Metropolitan Museum sent six medieval Spanish frescoes to the Prado in exchange for it in 1958.

The atmosphere of The Cloisters is singularly suited for exhibiting the extraordinary *Mérode Altarpiece* by the Master of Flémalle, bought in Belgium in 1957. This museum is very popular among New Yorkers for Sunday excursions but is less appealing to European visitors, especially the French who, having seen several of their cloisters carried off to a new home on the Hudson, are wont to accuse Americans of "Elginism"; but the French have only themselves to blame since they had allowed these chefs d'œuvre of their national architecture to fall into ruin. And while they so audibly lament the loss of the least stone from their soil, for half a century they have remained indifferent to the exodus of major works by Renoir, Seurat and Gauguin—a loss much more harmful to their national patrimony. In the last analysis, how can one remain unmoved by so pious a tribute to one of the highest forms of western civilization? For my part, I have often succumbed to the quiet charm of the place on a weekday. I have seen The Cloisters in winter under a blanket of snow, in autumn when the surrounding beeches wear a mantle of purple and gold and I felt as sharp a delight on my last visit as on my first.

When Barnard's cloisters were dismantled to be rebuilt in the new museum, it was discovered that Saint Michel de Cuxa contained a certain number of spurious elements the dealers had had fabricated to complete the structure because they had been unable to procure it *in toto;* the Philadelphia Museum of Art was happy to acquire this surplus, with which it formed a small cloister. Other American museums joined the quest in Europe for doors, windows, chimneys, even whole cloisters (e.g. the Cloister of Saint Pons de Thomières in the Toledo [Ohio] Museum of Art) which could be added to their medieval galleries to impart "atmosphere."

A period reconstruction might also be a street, a section of a city or even an entire town. Aware that their past in constantly threatened by the rapid growth of modern society, Americans have undertaken important measures to safeguard their historic houses and monuments, an enterprise vigorously supported by private organizations similar to England's National Trust. The most ambitious project along these lines was the reconstruction of an entire town in the colonial style, the idyllic early (from 1699 to 1780) capital of Virginia. Rustic yet urban Williamsburg, settled in 1633, figured as prominently as Boston or New York in the life of the Thirteen Colonies. Thomas Jefferson was graduated from its College of William and Mary, the second oldest college in the nation. The First Continental Congress was called from here by the House of Burgesses in 1774; during the Second Continental Congress the Virginia delegates demanded independence for the colonies on May 15, 1776. At that time the British flag was lowered from the mast atop the Capitol and a continental flag took its place. The houses lining the principal avenue—the broad, tree-shaded Duke of Gloucester Street—have been restored or reconstructed to look as they were in pre-Revolutionary Williamsburg. The reconstruction project, a dream of the Reverend W. A. R. Goodwin of Bruton Parish Church, benefited from a generous gift of $35,000,000.00 from John D. Rockefeller Jr. in 1926. (More than $76,000,000.00 in addition have been spent to date.) Hundreds of reproductions of the old buildings have been erected, three hundred reconstructed and eighty-three restored. Reconstruction of the Governor's Palace and its delicious gardens began in 1930, made possible by the discovery of a floor plan drawn by Thomas Jefferson, an even earlier engraving found in the Bodleian Library at Oxford and a so-called Frenchman's Map which was also a chief source of material for reconstructing other buildings. Today's visitor to Colonial Williamsburg enters an enchanted world where all is as it was two centuries ago; at Raleigh Tavern, once a favorite meeting place for Thomas Jefferson, Patrick Henry and other Revolutionary patriots, liveried servants wait on the tables and the guests wear bibs knotted around their necks just as their ancestors did; concerts of early music and costume balls are held at the Governor's Palace; craftsmen in eighteenth-century costumes practice the old traces of printer, silversmith, apothecary, wigmaker and blacksmith; saddlers make harnesses, winnowers weave baskets, pork is smoked in reconstructed ovens and in the street pass wagons and carriages.

Nowhere more than in Colonial Williamsburg does one sense how much modern man, caught in a whirl of constant change, seeks a refuge in searching out a past which is at once so near and yet so far away. Twenty or thirty years ago one thought the automobile would replace the horse and yet, in France today, a revival of the sport of equitation even at the working-class level has created such a demand for saddle horses that now they have to be imported. Automobiles are banned from the streets of Williamsburg which echo, instead, the clip-clop of horses' hoofs.

In 1907 Bernard Berenson, already acclaimed for his scholarly works and for the brilliant collection he had assembled for Mrs. Gardner in Boston, formed an association with the English dealer Joseph Duveen; their collaboration ended when Berenson refused to authenticate as a Giorgione a painting the dealer had sold as such to Samuel Kress, considering it an early Titian (*The Allendale Nativity* in the National Gallery of Art in Washington). After that time Berenson played the intellectual game of attributions for Italian Renaissance works, a brand of speculation that would foster another kind—financial speculation. Without exaggerating Duveen's role, one can say in all fairness that he, more than any other dealer in the first half of the twentieth century, helped to create the snob appeal of the expensive painting, going to the extreme of paying a price higher than that which had been asked, relishing a dizzying rise in prices, from which he ultimately profited. A lingering of the Anglo-Saxon taste for the Pre-Raphaelites assured the success of Italian primitives in the United States. Berenson periodically published his famous lists, a mention in which meant a price increase of thousands of dollars. As early as the end of the nineteenth century interest was being shown in all the early European schools as well as in the French Impressionists who were not yet accepted in their own country. Thanks to important donations of money, the Metropolitan Museum was able to undertake a methodical policy of buying which would give it the richest painting collection in the United States before the opening of the National Gallery of Art in Washington. Since the American public was not yet very knowledgeable in matters of art, certain purchases were strongly criticized; an *Adoration of the Shepherds* by El Greco, bought for $37,000.00, was described as a "disorderly lot of badly drawn figures not worth $50.00." Despite the taste certain avant-garde collectors showed for the Impressionists, they were not yet generally understood and the acquisition of Renoir's *Madame Charpentier and her Children* in 1907 was a daring move on the part of the Metropolitan's trustees; Roger Fry, curator of paintings for a brief time, recommended the purchase and Bryson Burroughs, his assitant curator, enthusiastically supported him. Three substantial gifts made to the Metropolitan in 1913 by J. Pierpont Morgan, Benjamin Altman and William H. Riggs launched that philanthropic tradition which within half a century would enable American museums to rival the established European institutions. These donations, made in the form of cash or in works of art, were encouraged by a law which permitted an appreciable tax deduction for a gift to a non-profit institution. (In France the amount allowed is only .8%.) For a number of years a donor could make an official gift of works of art, keeping the treasures in his possession until death while still taking advantage of tax exemptions but this is no longer true. The system is held responsible by many for the inflation in prices of works of art. Dealers, collectors and curators are to a certain extent responsible for the constant rise in prices because the assessment of the value of a gift has such bearing on a donor's decision to present it. When a Rembrandt jumps from $100,000.00 —a fairly normal price for paintings by this master—to $2,300,000.00 (in 1961 for *Aristotle Contemplating the Bust of Homer*), all American collectors owning his works suddenly found themselves in a position to realize considerable tax relief by either selling or giving their art away.

Awed by talent, some American collectors seem to buy only at high prices. A painting priced at less than $100,000.00 is little more than a trifle and difficult to sell. Thus is re-established in the democratic twentieth century the old princely system of patronage. Now few except great corporation magnates can afford the art that fifty years ago men of moderate means but sure taste could acquire. As a compensation, these princes who surround themselves with such luxury, the spoils of fallen kings and emperors, dukes and cardinals, often let the general public enjoy their treasures after their death or even before. Further, they have sparked emulation at a more modest level. The vogue for buying nineteenth-century furniture and appointments—a taste current on both sides of the Atlantic—was precipitated not only by a dissatisfaction with modern creations but also by the attitude that an antique interior imparts prestige.

Most American museums are private, self-supporting organizations (gifts and special appropriations from corporations and foundations constitute their capital) run by a Board of Trustees whose members really control the establishment more than the directors and curators whom they choose to appoint. The directors are charged with running their museums efficiently and the curators with the constant improvement of their collections. The only similarly organized European museum is Copenhagen's Carlsberg Glyptotek; its founder, Karl Jacobsen, the great beer brewer, had a passion for archeology; he concentrated his business profits on the formation of a museum, proposed in 1888 and built soon after; to assure its continued existence, he established the Ny Carlsberg Fondet in 1902, which is maintained by profits from the brewery.

James Smithson (1765?-1829), a brilliant English chemist and mineralogist, grew embittered because his illegitimate birth had prevented him from his place in society and from inheriting his father's title; spurning his native England, he turned to the United States and bequeathed his fortune to a country "where no such contemptible royal mortgage" hindered advancement. For ten years the Congress of the United States deliberated over whether or not to accept the bequest but finally, in 1846, the funds were used to set up the Smithsonian Institution, so named to respect a wish of its founder. Subsequently enriched by many gifts and government subsidies, this organization now plays a global role in the advancement of learning and the diffusion of culture. In the century since its creation the Smithsonian Institution has founded and developed two of the finest science museums in existence but its art museum, the formation of

258

which was stipulated in a by-law of the society, is not particularly successful. One of its newest branches, founded in 1962, is the National Portrait Gallery for the exhibition and study of paintings and statues of those who have made significant contributions to the history, development and culture of the United States. Lack of popular interest in the arts in the United States is easily explained; science is immediately accessible to the mind of a new country whereas the arts need to be cultivated; no doubt America owes its technological superiority over Europe to its early proclivity for scientific positivism. Charles Lang Freer (1856-1918), Detroit manufacturer, fastidious connoisseur and friend of the artist Whistler, bequeathed his admirable collection of Far Eastern art, on exhibit in a museum annexed to his house, to the Smithsonian in 1904. For a long while the Capitol had only one museum devoted to western art—the Corcoran Gallery. In an effort to remedy the situation, the Smithsonian Institution named a commission in 1923 to study the creation of a national gallery and accumulated $10,000.00 for this purpose through public subscription. This procedure was destined to fail; it was hardly in keeping with the American tendency to put cultural institutions in the domain of private initiative. A *deus ex machina* was not long in appearing in the person of Andrew W. Mellon, a Pittsburgh financier who had been Secretary of the Treasury from 1921 to 1931, then ambassador to the Court of St. James. Accused of tax evasion by the government which claimed he owed several million dollars in additional taxes and penalties for the year 1931, Mellon became the object of a famous Federal investigation in 1935. He was eventually exonerated in 1937, four months after his death. For several years he had been building up a collection of rare paintings with the intention of creating a national gallery. In 1936 Mellon handed over to the Smithsonian's trustees not only his masterpieces but also sufficient funds for the construction of a large building to house them, stipulating that the new institution be named the "National Gallery of Art." By an act of Congress on March 24, 1937, Mellon's offer was accepted and the A. W. Mellon Educational and Charitable Trust was authorized to undertake construction of the gallery. From that time, everything proceeded very rapidly. Four years later, on March 17, 1941, the National Gallery of Art, located on the Mall, opened. Nothing had been spared to make the building beautiful; its architect John Russell Pope and his associates had designed it in the classical style traditional for Washington, giving it an elegant yet unpretentious appearance. "The architects," wrote J. B. Eggen, "aspired to follow the precepts of Washington and Jefferson, both of whom believed that the architectural style to adopt for the Capitol ought not deviate from the broad fundamental base of classicism." The results were remarkable; whether one considers the exterior masses or the interior spaces, the National Gallery of Art is of a correctness and elegance of proportion that makes it a worthy twin of Munich's Glyptothek. The exterior refinements were carefully done; thirty-five thousand blocks of marble were specially cut from quarries in Tennessee, re-opened expressly for the task, and were hauled to Washington in 800 wagons. As in the Altes Museum in Berlin, built by Leo von Klenze more than a century earlier, the center of the structure is a vast rotunda, inspired by the Pantheon in Rome, supported by twenty-four Ionic columns more than thirty feet high, with shafts made of green Italian marble cut from quarries near Lucca. Giovanni da Bologna's *Mercury* stands in the center of the rotunda. Mr. Mellon's hope was realized: a beautiful museum attracts gifts. When the gallery opened, it contained not only his collection but also that of Samuel H. Kress of New York, who established funds for the purchase of paintings for the National Gallery and also for many other American museums; in 1942 Joseph E. Widener presented his famous collection of paintings, sculpture and decorative arts. One of the Gallery's greatest benefactors was Chester A. Dale who made numerous gifts during his lifetime and bequeathed his enormous collection. The finest paintings acquired by America between the two World Wars converged on the nation's capital. Among these number thirty-one canvases from the Hermitage, sold by the Soviets for the lump sum of $7,000,000.00; included in this lot were Raphael's *Alba Madonna* and *Saint Michael,* Botticelli's *Adoration of the Magi,* Jan van Eyck's *Annunciation* and Titian's *Venus with a Mirror.*

Museums are living institutions in this progressive country. As I write these lines, there are more than four thousand of them scattered throughout the country, a total which increases by one every 3.3 days. The least keepsake of a great historical personage is reverently preserved; the Kentucky log cabin in which Abraham Lincoln was born has been enshrined in a museum the way former ages enshrined the Porziuncola at Assisi, the Santa Casa at Loreto or the house of Peter the Great at Leningrad. Shortly before his death President Franklin D. Roosevelt was drafting plans for converting his country estate into a museum, indicating where he wanted his dressing gown put, where his armchair should be placed.

America has tapped the artistic resources of the entire world in the last half century. In order to understand the museological phenomenon in America, one must realize that in the political life of the country the State does not have that authority—shaped by Roman jurisprudence, monarchical absolutism, revolutionary nationalism, Hegelian metaphysics, Prussian militarism, Machiavellian cynicism and Marxist dialectic—which is unquestioned in old European countries. This "state-empire" will eventually suffocate what it hordes and paralyze the life of European nations in the modern world. As set forth in its Constitution, the American State owes its life to the general consent of the people and is, therefore, nothing more than the representative of the nation.

Federal aid to museums has steadily increased since the 1930's. A recent survey showed that specific contacts between museums and the federal government are varied and complex, "involving at least fifteen bureaus, offices or departments of nine of the twelve cabinet departments and five independent federal agencies." [2] Funds have been provided for additional personnel, education programs and exhibitions. There is some federal aid to museums for construction and renovation purposes, but in the period 1957-1965, this accounted for only a small fraction of the total capital outlay on building. On the other hand, the federal government is lavishing its support on research programs. Aid is channeled through a bureau or agency whose interests appear to coincide with those of the museum in question. For instance, the U.S. Bureau of Public Roads gave financial support to a state museum exploring methods of highway salvage archeology. The Urban Renewal Administration gave aid to a city historical commission to prepare a report on the historical value of an area scheduled for redevelopment. The Vocational Rehabilitation Administration of the U.S. Department of Health, Education and Welfare has provided assistance to a state art museum designing exhibits for the blind.

Perhaps the most significant contribution America has made to the concept of the museum is in the field of education. It is common practice for a museum to offer lectures and concerts, show films, circulate exhibitions, publish important works on art. The museum has metamorphosed into a university for the general public—an institution of learning and enjoyment for all men. The concept has come full circle. The museum of the future will more and more resemble the academy of learning that *museion* connoted for the Greeks.

Major museums opened in Los Angeles and New York in the last two years. The Los Angeles County Museum of Art moved to new quarters in the Spring of 1965. It now occupies a seven-acre site between downtown Los Angeles and Beverly Hills. The land, valued at more than eight million dollars, was donated by Los Angeles County, which will also provide annual funds for operation, maintenance and staffing. Money to build the $11,500,000.00 museum was raised privately. The largest museum west of the Mississippi, it is part of a newly emerging cultural establishment in Southern California. The new building, designed by William L. Pereira and Associates, comprises three separate pavilions around a central plaza; they are interconnected by a system of open terraces and covered walkways—a variant of the *Museumsinsel* theme. A shallow reflecting pool or moat surrounds the entire complex. The Ahmanson Gallery, conceived as a four-story atrium with galleries radiating off it, houses the permanent collection. The Lytton Gallery, with its movable walls, was designed for temporary exhibitions. The third structure, the Leo S. Bing Center, contains a 602-seat theatre and facilities for lectures, films, concerts and other educational programs.

The new Whitney Museum of American Art in New York opened in October 1966. The five-story structure, designed by Marcel Breuer and Associates, looks like an inverted pyramid with overhanging galleries, "meant to receive people before they are actually in the building," as Breuer commented. A concrete bridge, spanning a sunken sculpture garden, leads from the street to the lobby. The museum makes bold use of few materials—large masses of unpolished stone, raw concrete, slate, bronze and teak. The seven oddly-shaped windows were conceived as sculptural contrasts to the strong, unbroken contours of the building. Inside looking out, they frame a portion of street or house and offer it for contemplation, "transforming the vitality of the street into the sincerity and profundity of art," as Breuer desired. Museum offices occupy the fifth floor; a restoration laboratory, the fourth; an adaptable area on the second floor can be transformed into a 110-seat auditorium. Many technical innovations distinguish the building: floodlights with diffusion lenses that spread light evenly on objects; flagstone flooring that cushions walking; floor-to-ceiling portable gallery walls and lights that can be plugged into every six inches of ceiling; sliding storage racks; and facilities for drive-in art delivery. Severe yet handsome, a building with dignity and presence, the new Whitney has advanced the art of the museum, both technically and architecturally.

Fifty years ago America had so despaired of ever being able to compete with Europe in the field of museums that an amateur architect, Franklin Webster Smith, [3] proposed building in the District of Columbia a walled "city" made up of pastiches of the great buildings of the world, filled with copies after renowned masterpieces; the Parthenon was to be reproduced but half again as large as the original. The responsibility for social service is firmly rooted in the souls of the citizens of this puritan and positivist country where human advancement is by education. The magnificent flowering of museums in the United States in less than half a century is the spontaneous creation of the American public whose richest citizens have thus acquitted their debt to the less fortunate.

Chapter 12

Present and Future

By the beginning of the twentieth century, certain age-old museums were about to suffocate to death; paintings climbed the walls, *objets* crowded the vitrines or sprawled over the floors blocking passersby. These alarming conditions preoccupied curators, critics, aestheticians. Built in the last century, the great museums could not meet the many demands imposed upon them: to offer to the general public a wide range of masterpieces, to the amateur a more extensive choice, to the scholar complete series, to all visitors services facilitating the pedagogical exploitation of the collections.

In the course of the nineteenth century, many critics and museologists proposed creating two collections: one for the public, one for connoisseurs. The English essayist and critic John Ruskin dreamed of seeing paintings in London's National Gallery hung in a single line, a desire its director Charles Eastlake also shared; toward the end of his trusteeship and shortly before his appointment as director, Eastlake had published an article in the *London Times* in 1853, in which he discussed the concept of the bipartite museum, twenty years before the noted Swiss-American naturalist and museologist Louis Agassiz would make the same proposal. Both had an illustrious predecessor in Goethe who launched the idea in an article in *Kunst und Altertum* as early as 1821. The English were the first to adopt this system of installation; when the Natural History Museum was moved from Bloomsbury to its own quarters in South Kensington (1881-1886), its vast collections were rearranged according to the bipartite concept. In 1907 the principle was applied to the installation of two art museums, the Bayerisches National Museum in Munich and the Museum of Fine Arts in Boston. In Germany, Dr. Wilhelm von Bode had discussed its merits as early as 1903 (in an article in the weekly *Die Woche*), but he did not follow it in the arrangement he made for Berlin's Kaiser-Friedrich-Museum. In France, in an article for the *Revue Archéologique* in 1909, Salomon Reinach, curator of Antiquities at the Louvre, suggested creating subterranean storerooms under the museum; nearly sixty years later, his idea is becoming a reality.

Endeavoring to create more space, several American museums went to the extreme of selling less popular works—an adventurous practice, because a revolution in taste might very well restore to fashion works formerly considered démodé. It is quite

131. **View of the Museum of Jerusalem.** *The most recent of the world's museums (opened in 1965) presents a plan of a series of buildings forming independent cells, which permits easy future development. It has two rows of buildings devoted to services (This museum was damaged during the war of June 1967.)*

263

conceivable that the Barbizon painters, many of whose works the Metropolitan Museum sold as "surplus" a few years ago, might return to vogue one day.

Meanwhile, museums still remained overcrowded. The Louvre made only half-hearted attempts to disencumber its galleries. The concept of the museum was partly to blame: "The dead corrupt the living," declared the French writer Maurice Barrès and the curator Salomon Reinach referred to museums as morgues, cemeteries, hypogea. The attitude of avant-garde artists, willfully determined to upend traditional aesthetic values in any case, was even more extreme: certain of the more rebellious ones proposed razing all museums. Mere braggadocio, for these artists continued to seek inspiration in museums; Matisse, in the mainstream of French tradition, trained his eye by copying the Old Masters in the Louvre, while Derain pondered over Gothic paintings; as for Picasso, his *œuvre* is the history of art recast in the Cubist idiom.

Wars rudely accelerate the course of history by creating a rupture between the Past and the Present, by provoking a sudden awareness of new times. What had seemed irritating before war became intolerable after it. The great museums, many of which were partially evacuated from 1914 to 1918, would soon undergo a face lifting; sparseness and rationality would govern the presentation of collections; museums would leave a portion of their treasures in reserve and concentrate on showing only their choicest pieces. Lavish pre-war interiors suddenly seemed outmoded; when construction on the National Museum of Wales at Cardiff was resumed, after having been interrupted by the war in 1914, the previously proposed heavy decor was eliminated. The museum must no longer be a palace but, as I termed it at the time of my first course in museology at the Louvre in 1941: a clinic. A clinic for masterpieces, a functional edifice where everything is designed to maintain the best possible conditions for the conservation of objects and to assure the public's comfort. Proud of their climate-control systems, curators hurry distinguished visitors through exhibition galleries, impatient to whisk them off to cellars to admire motors, filters and valves. In this clinical spirit two beautiful museums were conceived in Europe, Rotterdam's Museum Boymans (1935) and Basel's Kunstmuseum (1932-36) and one in the United States, New York's Museum of Modern Art, which was opened in 1939.

The state of affairs in museums is further aggravated by fluctuations in taste. In the last half century, the public aesthetic has been profoundly modified. Statues must be isolated in space, paintings hung far apart, a glittering jewel placed against a field of black velvet and spotlighted; in principle, only one object at a time should appear in the field of vision. Iconographic meaning, overall harmony, aspects that attracted the nineteenth-century amateur, no longer interest the contemporary museum goer, who is obsessed with form and workmanship; the eye must be able to scan slowly the entire surface of a painting. The act of looking becomes a sort of trance uniting spectator and masterpiece.

Partiality to a hedonistic aesthetic has fostered disdain for minor masters among a public blasé to everything except the most impressive masterpieces. Works that once filled galleries to overflowing are now inundating the storerooms, with every curator inventing some ingenious system to make optimum use of limited space.

Museology was still a matter of habit rather than a science, but it was soon to have its theories and dogmata. In January 1926, Henri Focillon, professor of art history at

132. **The Rubens Room at the Kunsthistorisches Museum in Vienna before 1914.**

133. **The Rubens Room at the Kunsthistorisches Museum in Vienna after 1914.**
The metamorphosis undergone by this room is indicative of the profound changes after the war of 1914. All museums partially stripped their galleries and placed many works in reserve.

the Sorbonne and one of the most perceptive critics his generation produced, delivered a report to a special committee of the recently established League of Nations proposing the formation of an international organization to assure lasting cooperation among all museums in the member countries—the International Office of Museums; the society would continue on a vaster scale the work already begun by divers national museum associations: the British Isles' Museums Association (founded 1889), the United States' American Association of Museums (founded 1906), Germany's Deutscher Museumsbund (founded 1917). In publications and at congresses and conclaves of experts, the national societies in cooperation with the International Office of Museums explored in depth matters of organization, administration, conservation and presentation. Technical questions led to scientific investigation. Hereafter, every large museum, following the examples set by Munich and the Louvre, would have its study laboratory.

The International Office of Museums did not survive the League of Nations; but following World War II, the American director of the Buffalo Museum of Science took the initiative in founding a new international society of museologists, the International Council of Museums (ICOM), which convened for the first time in 1947 in Paris. Thanks to the efficacious support of UNESCO, a considerable rapport has developed among museum men the world over; direct contact has fostered a wonderful esprit de corps, a veritable professional solidarity reminiscent of the spirit that animated many of the medieval guilds. Opinions on controversial topics are freely traded. For instance, there are two schools of thought on restoration, especially regarding the restoration of paintings; the English deplore the prudent practices of continental Europeans, who in turn accuse Americans and Englishmen of too radical an approach that risks altering the quality of an artist's brushwork, a criticism Baldinucci had already leveled at restorers in the seventeenth century.

Museums suddenly proliferated; even the smallest cities boasted them. Public service became the *raison d'être* of the museological institution; this was particularly the case in America, where the pedagogical habit inherited from England metamorphosed into a veritable obsession. "The term *collection* fairly well defines a European museum," wrote Laurence Vail Coleman, American museologist and former director of the American Association of Museums. "One could define the American museum," he continues, "as an institution which uses its collections for a specific end: to raise the general public's level of culture and knowledge; it does not serve the interests of a particular class or group." Almost every American museum offers educational services for adults, but the instruction of children is also a chief concern. Many museums have their "junior wings" and there are even some institutions reserved exclusively for young people, like the venerable Brooklyn Children's Museum, founded 1899. In the previous century, the German architect and aesthetician Semper had already remarked "Museums are excellent educators"; by the early 1900's several congresses and associations were exploring means for transforming German museums into pedagogical instruments. Museums had to "speak"; if limited to original works, they risked being incomplete and consequently less valuable as educational tools; therefore, models, photographs and and written commentary were introduced; progress from room to

134. Exhibition of modern painting at the Guggenheim Museum, New York, in 1954. *A typical example of the "clinical" museum where works of art are exhibited in an entirely neutral setting—no picture wires, no frames, and plain white walls.*

room would then convey a sense of development or evolution. Munich's Deutsches Museum (Deutsches Museum von Meisterwerken der Natürwissenschaft und Technik) is an unparalleled example of this genre of museum; founded in 1903 by the engineer Oskar von Miller (1855-1934), it has grown into the largest and most important institution of its kind, offering limitless opporunities for surveying developments in science, engineering and industry; in addition to machines of historical importance, there are working models and extensive exhibits; it also boasts an immense library devoted to science and technology. The museum became such an integral part of everyday life that totalitarian regimes saw it as a powerful means for conditioning citizens, as an instrument of collective brainwashing. The Soviets suddenly found themselves heirs to a prodigious patrimony the Revolution had spared, thanks to Lenin's intervention; it constituted the palaces and art treasures of the czars as well as private collections that had been confiscated. The Soviet government set about creating museums—five hundred forty-two were founded between 1921 and 1936. Their purpose was not to delight but to re-teach Russian and world history according to Marxist doctrines: "Beauty is but the manifestation of the ideas, aspirations, or biases of one or another class," a prominent Soviet museologist wrote in 1930. The most prestigious masterpieces were scorned. Beset by financial worries, the Soviets did not hesitate to sell some of the finest works in the Hermitage to foreigners.

Germany also exploited museums for their propaganda value. To this end, a new breed of institution was created—the *Heimatmuseum*; over two thousand were founded between the world wars. It was a matter of restoring national pride to vanquished Germany and of awakening it to its strength—prelude to agression. The new museums were small and specialized, concentrating on the riches of a particular province, on the genius of one man, on the development of a single industry, on early popular traditions, in short, on whatever had shaped the German soul. "Patriotism is a matter of personal morality equally inspired by the land and its people, and the task of the national museum is to give the visitor a picture of his ambience, to foster a deeper understanding of the country, its people, and its economy." Born of an exhibition organized in 1925 to commemorate the thousandth anniversary of the annexation of the Rhineland to the German Empire, the Haus der Rheinischen Heimat exemplifies the didactic, nationalistic museum. Italy imitated the German example, but only at the level of exhibitions. Held in Rome in 1937-38 to celebrate the bimillenary of Augustus' birth, the Mostra Augustea della Romanità honored what Rome had given the world; it constituted a deliberate attempt to awaken Italian imperialism. Freed of all political overtones, the exhibition metamorphosed into a museum after World War II. Milan's 1939 Mostra di Leonardo da Vinci was similarly intended; considered the precursor of modern technology, Leonardo was thrust before the world as evidence of the superiority of Italian genius; the exhibition ended portentously with an immense photographic reproduction of a Leonardo drawing of a gun factory.

World War II interrupted this vigorous life. In the belligerent countries museums were closed and collections evacuated to rural areas; Spain had set the example earlier, when the Republican Government, fleeing the victorious Franco, sent the Prado's treasures to Geneva. Leningrad's collections traveled the farthest—to a hiding place

135. **Las Meninas (after Velázquez), by Picasso.** *Detail. Even the most audacious modern artists have not brought an end to the prestige of museums which throughout the XXth century have remained inexhaustible reservoirs of styles and inspiration.*

136. **View of a gigantic inscription saying "Musée du Louvre."** *During the last world war special civil defense measures were taken to protect museums in all the belligerent nations of Europe, particularly in England and France. Works of art were evacuated to mansions and castles deep in the country where arrangements were made to receive them. In 1944 the author of this book, who was director of the depository for works of art at Sourches, designed an enormous notice made of planks, painted white and placed on the green lawns of the castle, as a protective measure against air raids, indicating the presence of the depository.*

beyond the Urals. France cached her art in provincial châteaux all over the country. A member of the Resistance, the Directeur des Musées de France, kept the Allies informed of the various depots, who in turn acknowledged the receipt of messages over the B.B.C.: "La Gioconda smiles." "Reynolds salutes Fragonard." At the suggestion of Count Metternich, the German army set up a Commission to safeguard works of art in the occupied countries; the organization helped French museums protect themselves against the perils of combat, the depredations of German troops and the requisitions of Nazi leaders. Thus, in the heat of war, France was able to defend her national patrimony through the cooperation of Germans and Allies. The most vulnerable countries were Germany and Italy: confident of an easy victory, their governments had never even considered the possibility of invasion and were forced to take hasty measures at the last moment. Evacuated under fire, Dresden's Gemäldegalerie lost 704 paintings; the havoc wrought in Berlin was unbelievable; in addition to the treasures that were pillaged, 1,353 paintings were burned or lost, of which 427 were anterior in date to the nineteenth century; a nearby explosion destroyed some of the most beautiful pieces in the Kaiser-Friedrich-Museum.

War-torn Europe heralded the re-opening of her museums as a sign of deliverance, as a kind of phoenix. After four years of darkness, Paris rediscovered with joy the light of the Impressionists, installed in 1947 in the Jeu de Paume, the first museum to open in the Capital. The intoxication of peace sparked intense cultural activity, from which

270

137. **Fragment of the Tomb of the Empress Marguerite of Luxembourg, by Giovanni Pisano.** *Palazzo Bianco, Genoa. In reaction against the too heavy presentations of the past, Italian museologists are often tempted to exhibit art objects in a futuristic fashion with the result that the modern materials and styles for the exhibition accessories contrast violently with the works.*

museums especially profited. Those in the provinces stirred from the lethargy into which they had fallen after their golden age in the nineteenth century; the evacuations effected during the war at the insistence of the State had awakened municipalities to the value of their art treasures; museums sprang up in small towns, in boroughs; regional institutions similar to the German *Heimatmuseen* flourished: the Musée du Tabac at Bergerac (1950), the Musée du Vin de Bourgogne at Beaune (1947), the Musée de la Chasse à Tir et de la Fauconnerie at Gien (1952).

All of Italy had sustained heavy damage, but within twenty years she completed a vast reconstruction program that would change the museological face of the peninsula; new museums were created, old ones renovated. Some institutions attempted boldly modern installations reflecting period tastes fully as much as the heavy decor of the nineteenth century (Palazzo Bianco, Genoa; Castello Sforzesco, Milan; Galleria Nazionale della Sicilia, Palermo). Others remained more traditional. Through the indefatigable efforts of its director, Professor Fernanda Wittgens, the Pinacoteca di Brera in Milan, almost completely destroyed by bombs in August 1943, seemingly rose from its own ashes within a few years; the elegant yet restrained pre-war decor in precious marbles was kept. The Palazzo Reale di Capodimonte in Naples, likewise burned, underwent reconstruction from 1952 to 1957; its director, Professor Bruno Molajoli, installed the picture gallery and history museum in a neoclassical setting that makes beautiful use of the polychromed marble revetment for which Italy is distinguished; this palace hides a veritable factory—a generator that can supply ten days' worth of electrical power, an exhaust system for cleaning display cases, automatic devices for regulating the amount of light in the exhibition galleries. Italy can boast of having built the world's technically most modern museum.

The clinical interior went out of vogue after the war and there was a return to the well-appointed gallery; this taste is reflected in the presentation I

271

designed for French nineteenth-century paintings at the Louvre; I installed the smaller works in a series of remodeled garrets opening onto the Cour Carré; the decor is simple, restrained, suggesting rather than recreating a nineteenth-century ambience. At the same time, contemporary museum architecture is rejecting the classical palace format in order to explore the bold effects modern technology permits. An expanse of glass wall gives an illusion of diaphanous space to the interior of the ultramodern Musée du Havre, designed by Lagneau and Andigier. The Israeli Museum in Jerusalem gives a modern interpretation to the old principle of the *Museumsinsel*; long galleries interconnect the divers buildings. Frank Lloyd Wright designed New York's Guggenheim Museum as a spiral unwinding skyward—symbol of the space-time continuum that distinguishes the modern effort. But new buildings are the exception; European museologists prefer an old structure on two accounts: it brings to the public's attention a monument worth preserving and affords an opportunity of installing works of art in an authentic period setting. Examples of such *musées-monuments* include Ca' Rezzonico in Venice, a splendid eighteenth-century *palazzo* containing paintings, sculpture and furniture of the epoch; the Palazzo Davanzati in Florence, a magnificent example of a *trecento* mansion; the Barock Museum in Vienna; the imperial museum at Petropolis, Brazil. The American public has a taste for historic houses, another type of museum-monument; the restored homes of former presidents, such as Wakefield, Washington's birthplace, and Mount Vernon, his home in later life, Jefferson's Monticello, Theodore Roosevelt's delightful summer place at Sagamore Hill, are particularly well-visited.

An astringent mode of presentation tends to be reserved for museums of modern art or for archeological collections. The public's preference for museums with atmosphere marks a shift in taste. The purely formal approach, the object of so much speculation on the part of critics, philosophers and aestheticians in the last half century, is being abandoned in favor of the older attitude that sees the work of art as a product of its times, the expression of a particular temperament. Current literature on art reflects this reorientation. Museums tend to concentrate on evoking the style of a period rather than on showing off their masterpieces. Europe has assimilated the American taste for period rooms. Versailles is making every possible effort to retrieve the furnishings that graced the château under the *Ancien Régime*. Enormous sums are being expended to recapture some of its former splendor; copies will replace lost originals; the work of reconstruction has been pure hypothesis in many instances, since no old models existed to serve as guides. A vigorous taste for the authentic, born of a painstaking analysis of the work of art, is on the wane; a larger public, that lives by sensation more than by knowledge, contents itself with appearances. The same public is more sensitive to the quality of an installation than to the quality of the art it presents; it wants interior decorators for curators. An adroit museologist can elicit admiration for a mediocre collection through recourse to draperies, laces, tassels, brocades, festoons and astragals; because soigné interiors are particularly admired, curators have begun to borrow "ideas" from decorators. Abandoned by artists who have plunged into the abstract, the informal, into pop and op art, the museum is no longer a course in art but a course in decorative art. Museums of modern art seem to have evolved into a sort of laboratory where the public is confronted by the aesthetic experiments of the moment.

138. **Guggenheim Museum,** *New York. Designed for the display of modern paintings, this museum is the last—and the most original—work by the architect Frank Lloyd Wright. The exhibition areas are along the rounded walls of a spiraling ramp.*

The great museums like the Louvre, the Metropolitan Museum, the National Gallery in London have not been able to overcome an anchylosis the shock of war accelerated. Only Washington's National Gallery has a future before it, thanks to the wisdom of its founder who provided ample space for new acquisitions and even set aside land for future construction. The city of New York refused the Metropolitan Museum permission to expand at the expense of Central Park; the National Gallery in London has not yet re-opened all the galleries closed on account of war damage. As for the Louvre, its majestic façades mask fierce departmental competition for everything—a room, a corridor or even an armoire; the Louvre houses not only the largest museum in the world but also all the administrative offices of the Direction des Musées de France and a special school, the Ecole du Louvre; the complex occupies the entire palace including the Pavillon de Flore, its original home eighty years ago. After the last war, the attics were refurbished as galleries; subterranean reserves were created. The crisis at the Louvre is common to all great twentieth-century museums that must adapt themselves to buildings conceived at a time when the museological institution was not yet beset by technical and administrative problems. At the Louvre as at the Metropolitan Museum, it is a contest between collections and services. An ever-increasing public is making enormous demands on the museum; it must provide space for a whole battery of craftsmen including weavers, carpenters, upholsterers, framers, locksmiths, binders; for a conservation center; for a climate-control system; for shipping facilities; divers kinds of storerooms; parking facilities for museum personnel and visitors; conference rooms for trustees, department heads and union representatives; cloakrooms; cantines and rest areas for the general staff; all the technical services including electricians, lighting specialists, photographers; custodial services, temporary exhibition areas; a public relations department; a publications office; health facilities; a bookshop; quarters for visiting museum officials; an education department; a "Junior Wing"; an art reference library; photographic services; a fully-equipped auditorium; archives; rest areas for the public; a cafeteria—the Metropolitan offers the choice of an elegant or simpler one. The Israeli Museum in Jerusalem, opened in 1965, houses eighty offices, twice the number the entire staff of the Direction des Musées de France occupies in the Louvre! Offices fill two thirds of the building; the collection, one third. The present situation is by and large the reverse of that in the nineteenth century; little by little, administrative offices have encroached upon exhibition space, forcing curators to store more and more of their collections; storerooms have become so overcrowded as to render any systematic arrangement impossible and consultation, therefore, increasingly more difficult.

Another contemporary phenomenon is contributing to the dismantling of museums: the vogue for exhibitions. Everyone launches them—scholars for study purposes, public officials for political reasons, curators to show off their talents; and the general public clamors for more. Formerly, a good curator was one who built up a collection; today, it is one who has a flair for dramatic exhibitions. In 1965, two European capitals witnessed this paradoxal situation: at the Louvre, part of the paintings collection was put in storage in order to make space for two temporary exhibitions; in Brussels, the Musées Royaux des Beaux-Arts emptied all its galleries in order to install the exhibition *Rubens and His Time*. The state of affairs in Brussels is typical

139. **Prehistoric painting of an ox and horses in Lascaux** *(France). The caves at Lascaux, which contain the most beautiful prehistoric paintings, are symbolic of the deterioration of works of art because of their usage by human beings. Intact until their discovery, the paintings have had to be withheld from the public in order to avoid hygrometric variations and microbiologic formations which threaten to destroy them.*

274

—although the city has, in contrast to Paris, a very functional exhibition hall, it is not under the same administration as the Musées Royaux, to whose curator it was, therefore, unavailable. The Musée Jacquemart-André in Paris is currently enjoying a renaissance, thanks to the brilliant temporary exhibitions it has organized; but this success marks in reality the failure of the museum, since it was obliged to store its permanent collections in order to attract a public. As early as 1930, the American museologist Ralph Clifton Smith declared, "The most beautiful sculpture in the world makes a greater impact when workmen wheel it through the galleries on a little chassis than when it is finally set up as part of a carefully planned, well-lighted installation." Tortured by a desire for realism that has assumed neurotic proportions, contemporary man—*homo televidens,* the successor of *homo sapiens*— will soon no longer evince interest in a work of art unless it is somehow associated with aspects of daily life. The eternal will have to masquerade as the temporal in order to entice him. The original purpose of a great museum, to fortify the cultural reserves of the mind, has lost all reality except for a handful of amateurs. Collections are constantly rotated and the museums themseves are perpetually in repair; one begins to long for the old installations of the nineteenth century, when works were never moved. With its well-stocked galleries—unchanged for the last century, its rationally organized storerooms that facilitate consultation, its up-to-date catalogs, the Hermitage is an amateur's paradise.

As for exhibitions, amateurs and scholars alike resent the phenomenon of mass attendance, hating being obliged to wait in long lines before each work; they clamor to be admitted to exhibitions when they are closed to the general public, which poses administrative and custodial problems. The attendance at certain museums is likewise staggering; it is impossible to enjoy a quiet moment no matter what the time of year in Michelangelo's Medici Chapel in San Lorenzo, Florence. Galleries resound with the voices of guides chattering away in every imaginable language; few museums and exhibitions have acoustiguides for rent. And if the visitor wants to know something more about the collections? Catalogs are a rarity; the amount of scholarly preparation that must go into such a work makes publication a long ordeal; moreover, curators disdain this kind of work which once was their *raison d'être*. There is no catalog to the Louvre (excepting guides to specific areas of the paintings collection) and yet its team of curators has found time to produce scores of exhibition catalogs over the last thirty years. The situation in American museums is worse; their fabulous treasures are known. In addition, the general public shows little interest in detailed catalogs; in France, fewer than ten percent buy exhibition catalogs; in England, the percentage is somewhat higher (25%). Quite often, guides to American collections are merely perfunctory, illustrated lists.

Museums are frequented by a widely diversified public—collectors, connoisseurs and art historians intermingle with educated laymen, children, the man in the street. Of all these visitors, the connoisseur is the one who is shortchanged—he feels the masses have purloined an institution he helped to found. The contemporary museum is, paradoxically, least geared to the individual most likely to understand it. But does the general public at least profit from it? From the roster of exhibitions offered by the large cities, in addition to the many other "must" activities that furnish cocktail conversation among "in" people, a restless public absorbs only a predigested dose of culture, the

140. **A too curious visitor commenting on a picture at an exhibition.** *This expressive example of the daily dangers encountered by works of art shows how a too eager admirer runs the risk of scratching a painting with her lorgnette.*

141. **Queue of visitors at the Picasso exhibition** *at the Grand Palais in Paris in 1966. Mass culture poses a very grave problem for museums and increases the impending danger of making works of art inaccessible to the very public for whom they are so widely offered.*

educational value of which is dubious. A visit to an exhibition or museum has considerably less impact than it did in the past, when one frequented them again and again, notebook in hand; going to the movies, going to the museum, they leave the same impression. This public rejects knowledge and the attendant responsibility for a hedonistic aesthetic. But what does it matter? All the efforts are worth it for the few who do care. As for the rest, as long as they are distracted, that is, able to forget themselves for a while, that suffices.

So many thousands lined up to see the *Mona Lisa* when it was exhibited in New York that each visitor was allotted only a few seconds to view it. And still everyone felt hallowed by the experience, just as a medieval pilgrim did when, after having waited for hours in the narthex of a church, his turn finally came to approach the crypt and behold the golden light emitted by the reliquary containing the holy remains. Humanity's new idols: movie stars, athletes, works of art. The contemporary world treats the masterpiece as though it were goods meant for consumption. Curators are constrained to hold colloquia to discuss the surest methods for prolonging the life of the precious things in their care; they are subject to countless dangers—sudden changes in climate, vibrations sustained in transport, air pollution, vandalism, theft, carelessness, even the fluctuations in humidity caused by respiration. Will access to works of art have to be restricted or even forbidden some day? Monstrous but possible. Were not the Lascaux caves, whose paintings remained intact for thousands of years, closed to the public after a short time, because exposure to the atmosphere was causing their disintegration? The museum devours the work of art.

Museums are hypersensitive to the forces at work in the contemporary world, in particular to the effects being wrought by the population explosion and the rapid advances in technology. Prefabricated housing can always be put up to shelter the surplus of humanity, but it is quite another matter to try to establish a museum or a university in an urban area in constant flux. The trend is toward small museums in suburban settings that are a pleasure rather than an ordeal to visit. One wonders if the great museums might not metamorphose into organisms analogous to centralized libraries—vast reference collections of authentic pieces, consulted or read about but not casually visited. The study of art would continue in "cultural complexes," flexible institutions coordinating the various disciplines—art, letters, science, the theatre; France and the United States already boast centers of this kind.

The museum in its present state reflects the contemporary inclination toward universality; it is a hybrid born of science, philosophy, ethics, politics; it has its U.N., its technical commissions, its laboratories and research centers, its body of laws. Its form seems perfected and yet it enters a difficult period. Must one agree with the historical philosopher Mumford that an institution realizes its perfect form at the moment when it is about to perish? Only the American museums seem to be escaping this institutional vertigo. They seem better equipped to face the modern crisis because they have been spared the sclerosis of state control. The following example is a case in point: the curatorial and technical staff supervising all the museums and monuments in Italy is two hundred strong, the same number which serves the Metropolitan Museum alone! Endeavoring to wrest its artistic patrimony from political hands, Italy seeks to entrust its care to an autonomous administration, as many States have done for certain essential public services. American museums are not created by laws and decrees but are the spontaneous product of American life. Continually befriended by amateurs, they have managed to retain something of the original museological spirit. Private organisms managed like corporations, their flexibility enables them to meet more readily the challenge of change in this age that is the Museum Age.

NOTES

Chapter I

(¹) The only original seen by Pausanias which would have been rediscovered *in situ* would be the Hermes of Praxiteles at Olympia but the present tendency of experts is to see it as a copy of great quality.

Chapter V

(¹) In 1676 this cabinet contained forty portraits of women; since then, some have been replaced by portraits of men.

(²) Cf. Lada Nikolenko, *The Beauties Galleries,* in *Gazette des Beaux-Arts,* January 1966, pages 19-13.

Chapter VI

(¹) Bachaumont is in error here. Louis Antoine Crozat, nephew of Pierre Crozat the collector, was the Baron, not the Count, of Thiers.

Chapter VII

(¹) Work was finished in 1719. Confiscated during the Revolution, four of the paintings were sent to the Louvre while the other two went to cities which were at that time, but are no longer, a part of the French empire. In 1870-1876 when the Bank of France, as owner of the gallery, sought to restore it, the Louvre refused to return its paintings and they were replaced by copies.

(²) F. Arisi, *Gian Paolo Pannini,* No. 208 and 209.

(³) *The Duke of Choiseul Visiting St. Peter's in Rome* (Arisi, No. 248) is in the Museum of Fine Arts, Boston (Athenaeum Collection).

(⁴) *The Duke of Choiseul in the Square before St. Peter's* (Arisi, No. 247) is in the National Gallery, Edinburgh (Collection, Lord Ellesmere).

(⁵) *The Duke of Choiseul in the Gallery of Antique Rome* (Arisi, No. 245) is in the National Gallery, Edinburgh (Collection, Lord Ellesmere). *The Duke of Choiseul in the Gallery of Modern Rome* (Arisi, No. 246) is in the Museum of Fine Arts, Boston (Athenaeum Collection).

(⁶) Arisi, *op. cit.,* No. 249 and No. 250.

(⁷) Arisi, *op. cit.,* No. 252 and No. 253.

Chapter IX

(¹) In 1797 the term *muséum,* in French, adjudged archaic, was replaced by *musée*; it was retained, however, in the Muséum d'Histoire Naturelle.

Chapter X

(¹) This staircase has not been used since the Soviets annexed the Winter Palace to the Hermitage; entrance to the museum is from the Neva side of the palace.

Chapter XI

(¹) Daniel Fox, *Engines of Culture; Philanthropy and Art Museums* (Madison, Wisconsin: State Historical Society of Wisconsin), 1963, p. 2.

(²) Elena Van Meter, "A Continuing Look at Federal Aid to Museums," *Museums News,* June 1967, p. 38.

(³) In a book entitled *National Galleries of History and Art... The Aggrandizement of Washington,* 1900.

Index

293

188, 193, 195, 198, 199, 201, 202, 204, 205, 207, 215, 216, 218, 221, 227, 249, 263, 265, 270, 273; Apollo Gallery - 103, 130; Assyrian Museum - 207, 209; Cabinet of Medals - 116, 153; Colonnade - 156, 209, 228; Cour du Carrousel - 198; Département des Objets d'Art - 220; Direction des Musées de France - 274; Ecole du Louvre - 129, 274; Egyptian collections - 205, 207; Grande Galerie - 130, 154, 156, 171, 172, 174, 180; Musée Américain (Musée Mexicain) - 210; Musée Carnavalet - 220; Musée Charles X - 198, 199; Musée des Souverains - 228; Natural History Cabinet - 153; Paintings Department - 215; Pavillon de Flore - 274; Pavillon de Marsan - 234; Royal Library - 153; Salle Clarac - 199; Salon Carré - 107, 155, 171, 172, 180, 215, 247 (Cour Carré - 272); *Salon Carré,* Castiglione - 218

Parma - 163, 186; Convent of Saint Sixtus - 114; Museum of Antiquities - 144

Parnassus (Mengs) - 167

Parthenon - cf Athens

Parthenon, copy near Regensburg - 199

Parthenon marbles - 201, 202

Passion, The (Rembrandt) - 120

Pater, Jean Baptiste François - 121

Pater, Walter - 250

Patinir, Joachim - 80

Paul II, Pope (Pietro Barbo) - 44, 46

Paul III, Pope (Alessandro Farnese) - 51, 73, 163

Paul I of Russia - 126

Pausanias - 12, 14, 15, 16, 44

Pausias - 20

Pavilion under the Trees (Ts'ao Chih-po) - 22

Paxton, Sir Joseph - 232

Pazzi family - 44

Peabody, George - 243

Peabody Museum of Salem - 243

Peale, Charles Willson - 242

Peale family (Raphaelle, Rembrandt, Rubens, Titian) - 242

Peale's Museum - 242

Peintre Gravure (Bartsch) - 110

Peiresc, Nicolas Claude Fabri de - 87, 104, 116

Peking - 23

Pembroke, Earl of - 166

Percier, Charles - 176, 198, 199

Pereira, William L. - 261

Pergamum, Pergameniens - 6, 14, 15, 16; Altar of - 196; *Canon* of - 15; library of - 15; sanctuary of Athena - 14

period rooms and reconstructions - 250, 252, 254, 255, 256, 257

Persia, Shah of - 76

Perugino - 57, 92

Pesaro - 141

Peter the Great of Russia - 112, 125, 222

Peterhof, palace at - 104, 135

Petrarch - 41, 51

Petronius - 20

Petropolis (Brazil) - 272

Petrus Christus: *Portrait of a Young Woman* - 216; (?) *St. Jerome* - 44

Phidias - 12, 15, 23, 201; *Horse drawing the Chariot of Selene* - 201

Phigalia, Temple of Apollo Epicurius - 202

Philadelphia (Pennsylvania): American Museum - 241, 242; American Philosophical Society - 241; Library Company - 241, 242; Peale's Museum - 242; Pennsylvania Academy of Fine Arts - 243; Philadelphia Museum of Art (formerly Pennsylvania Museum of Art) - 247, 248, 249, 250, 252, 254, 256 (Wilstach collection - 250)

Philip II of Spain - 79, 80

Philip IV of Spain - 86, 98, 101, 163

Philip V of Spain - 163

Philip, Duke of Bourbon - 144

Philip, Duke of Parma - 114, 144, 186

Philoctetes - 41

Philosopher, The (Rembrandt) - 154

Philostratus - 44

Pibrac, château of - 104, 133, 135

Picasso, Pablo - 265; *Las Meninas* (after Velázquez) - 269; exhibition at the Grand Palais - 277

Picault - 117

Piccinino - 73

Piccolomini family - 46

Pichon, Baron - 37

Piero della Francesca: *Madonna da Montefeltro* - 181

Piero di Cosimo - 58

Pietà (Bellini) - 181

Pietrasanti, Jacopo di - 167

Pietro da Cortona - 86, 103, 131

Pietro della Vecchia - 86

Pigafetta, Filippo - 58

pinakothekai, definition of - 14

Pinakotheke, Alte - cf Munich

Pio, Cardinal Carlo - 167

Piraeus - 17, 201

Pisa - 187; Duomo - 41, 42

Pisanello - 37, 43

Pisano, Giovanni - 41; *The Cardinal Virtues: Temperance* - 42; *Tomb of the Empress Marguerite* (fragment) - 271

Pisano, Niccolò - 41, 42

Pitti Palace - cf Florence

Pius II, Pope (Enea Silvio de Piccolomini) - 46

Pius VI, Pope (Giovanni Braschi) - 166, 167

Pius VII, Pope - 225

Pius IX, Pope - 216

Place, Victor - 209

Plaisance, Convent of Saint Sixtus - 118

Plato - 5

Pliny - 16, 19, 44, 62

Plotinus - 6

Poccetti, Bernardino - 61

Poggio - 49, 130

Poitiers - cf Diane de Poitiers

Poitou - 92

Poliakov (architect) - 224

Polignac, Princess de - 133

Pollio, Gaius Asinius - 20

Pollock, Jackson: *Number I* - 241

Polybius - 6

Polygnotos - 14, 15, 20

Polyhymnia, the Muse - 142, 147

Pommersfelden, castle of - 133

Pompadour, Madame de - 176

Pompeii - 117, 163, 185; House of the Cryptoporticus - 20

Pompey - 18; Portico of - 20

Pondre, Paulin - 116

Pontormo - 58

Pope, John Russell - 259

porcelain collections - 137

porcelain manufacture - 60, 121

Portici - cf Herculaneum

portraits, portraiture - 39, 67, 103, 104, 105, 139, 230

Portrait of a Man (Titian) - 151

Portrait of a Young Woman (Petrus Christus) - 216

Portrait of Leo X (Raphael) - 58

Pourbus the Younger, Frans - 104; *Portrait of Marie de' Medici* - 103

295

LIST OF ILLUSTRATIONS

Watch. *Rijksmuseum, Amsterdam.* 94. LOUIS TITZ, Arrival in Antwerp of paintings returned by France. From the original work by Ferdinand de Brackeleer, *in the Bibliothèque Royale de Belgique.* 95. DIEGO VELAZQUEZ, The Water Carrier of Seville. *Wellington Museum London.* 96. FRENCH ART. ANTOINE GANDREAU, Marquetry Commode. *Wallace Collection, Hertford House, London.* 97. Diagrammatic plan of the "Museum Island" in Berlin. 98. PHIDIAS, Horse drawing the Chariot of Selene. *British Museum, London.* 99. BENJAMIN ROBERT HAYDON, Drawing of the Horse of Selene. *British Museum, London.* 100. Attic mixing bowl from the last quarter of the 5th century. *Louvre Museum, Paris.* 101. EGYPTIAN ART. IV DYNASTY, *Louvre Museum, Paris.* 102. The Michaux Stone or Sumerian Kudurru. *Cabinet of Medallions, Bibliothèque Nationale, Paris.* 103. Mexican Mask in Turquoise Mosaic. *British Museum, London.* 104. Anonymous engraving. Arrival of a Winged Bull from Khorsabad at the Louvre. *Bibliothèque Nationale, Paris.* 105. CLAUDE GELÉE, LE LORRAIN, The Reconciliation of Cephalus and Procris. *National Gallery, London.* 106. Interior view of the National Gallery, London. *Private collection.* 107. The Rembrandt Room in the Hermitage Museum, Leningrad. *From an old engraving.* 108. LEO VON KLENZE, Hall of XVIth- and XVIIth-Century Italian works. *Drawings Cabinet, Hermitage, Leningrad.* 109. LEO VON KLENZE, The Dutch Gallery at the Hermitage. *Drawings Cabinet, Hermitage, Leningrad* 110. PETRUS CHRISTUS, Portrait of a Young Woman. *Staatliche Museen, Berlin.* 111. JOSEPH CASTIGLIONE, The Salon Carré in 1865. 112. Gothic Room in the chapel of the Germanisches Museum, *Nuremberg, Germany.* 113. Gothic Room in the Bayerisches Museum, *Munich.* 114. SIR THOMAS LAWRENCE, Portrait of John Julius Angerstein and his wife. *Musée du Louvre, Paris.* 115. View of the "Salle des Croisades" at Versailles. 116. View of the Waterloo Chamber at Windsor Castle. 117. OTTONIAN ART. So-called Crown of Charlemagne. *Schatzkammer of the Hofburg,* Vienna. 118. RHENISH, 2ND HALF OF THE XIITH CENTURY. Eltenberg Reliquary. *Victoria and Albert Museum, London.* 119. L. V. FOUQUET, Studio of Alexandre du Sommerard at the Hôtel de Cluny. *Musée des arts décoratifs, Paris.* 120. ANTONY STANNUR, The first Refreshment Room of the Victoria and Albert Museum. *London.* 121. Thirteenth century timber church, transported to the Bygdøy open-air museum, *near Oslo.* 122. JACKSON POLLOCH. Number I, 1948. *"Collection"* the Museum of Modern Art, New York. 123. Peale's Museum in Philadelphia, *from an old engraving.* 124. SHANG DYNASTY. Chinese Ceremonial Vase. *Freer Gallery of Art, Washington.* 125. ROBERT CAMPIN, The Campin Altarpiece (MASTER OF FLEMALLE, The Mérode Altarpiece). *The Metropolitan Museum of Art, The Cloisters. Purchase collection.* 126. The Philadelphia Museum of Art, *Philadelphia, Pennsylvania.* 127. Plan of the Museum of Fine Arts, *Boston, Massachusetts.* 128. RENOIR, Madame Charpentier and her Children. *The Metropolitan Museum of Art, New York.* 129. JAN VAN EYCK, Annunciation. *National Gallery of Art, Andrew Mellon Collection, Washington, D. C.* 130. Gallery View - American Wing. Room from the Samuel Wentworth house in Portsmouth, N. H. *The Metropolitan Museum of Art, New York.* 131. View of the Museum of Jerusalem. 132. The Rubens Room at the Kunsthistorisches Museum in Vienna before 1914. 133. The Rubens Room at the Kunsthistorisches Museum in Vienna after 1914. 134. Exhibition of modern painting at the Guggenheim Museum, *New York,* in 1954. 135. PICASSO, Las Meninas. *Private collection.* 136. View of a gigantic inscription saying Musée du Louvre. *Sourches, France.* 137. Fragment of the Tomb of the Empress Marguerite of Luxembourg. *Palazzo Bianco, Genova.* 138. The Guggenheim Museum, *New York.* 139. Prehistoric painting of an ox and horses in the Lascaux Caves, *France.* 140. A too curious visitor commenting on a picture at an exhibition. 141. Queue of visitors at the Picasso Exhibition. *Paris.*

FHOTOGRAPHY CREDITS

Contents

THIS VOLUME WAS PREPARED UNDER THE DIRECTION OF MARC VOKAER. THE ENGLISH-LANGUAGE EDITION WAS PREPARED BY ELIZABETH EARL, WITH THE ASSISTANCE OF JANE VAN NUIS CAHILL. THE COVER DESIGN IS BASED ON A DRAWING BY PIERRE PASTEELS. THE LAYOUT WAS PREPARED BY MARINA PONJAERT; DOCUMENTALIST: MYRIAM SICOURI-ROOS; COLOR AND BLACK-AND-WHITE ILLUSTRATIONS WERE ENGRAVED BY THE ETABLISSEMENTS DE REPRODUCTIE COMPAGNIE, ROTTERDAM. THE BOOK WAS PRINTED AND BOUND BY THE IMPRIMERIE DESOER, LIÈGE.